The Future
of Inter-Bloc Relations
in Europe

edited by
Louis J. Mensonides
James A. Kuhlman

The Praeger Special Studies program—
utilizing the most modern and efficient book
production techniques and a selective
worldwide distribution network—makes
available to the academic, government, and
business communities significant, timely
research in U.S. and international economic, social, and political development.

The Future of Inter-Bloc Relations in Europe

PRAEGER SPECIAL STUDIES IN INTERNATIONAL POLITICS AND GOVERNMENT

Praeger Publishers   New York   Washington   London

Library of Congress Cataloging in Publication Data

Main entry under title:

The Future of inter-bloc relations in Europe.

  (Praeger special studies in international politics
and government)
  Includes bibliographical references.
  1. Europe—Politics—1945-   —Addresses, essays,
lectures. 2. World politics—1945-   —Addresses,
essays, lectures. I. Mensonides, Louis J., ed.
II. Kuhlman, James A., ed.
D1058.F87   327'.11'094   73-15191
ISBN 0-275-28795-5

PRAEGER PUBLISHERS
111 Fourth Avenue, New York, N.Y. 10003, U.S.A.
5, Cromwell Place, London SW7 2JL, England

Published in the United States of America in 1974
by Praeger Publishers, Inc.

Printed in the United States of America

No one is now counting the chickens before the eggs have been hatched in the three baskets (institutionalization of political relations; economic interaction; and free flow of peoples, ideas, and information) of the Conference on Security and Cooperation in Europe (CSCE) in Geneva, though some observers were quick to do so at the beginning of Secretary of State Henry Kissinger's "Year of Europe." Not only are the problems of bloc relations still confronting pan-European cooperation but the very attempt at security and cooperation between Eastern and Western Europe has heightened tensions within each regional grouping. The post-Pompidou disarray in Western Europe seems to have prompted an equal amount of uncertainty in the East. The larger East-West dialogue has forfeited much of its credibility, paling in the light of Soviet-American détente.

With the passing of each day, hopes for concrete results from the CSCE diminish and reliance upon the more traditional bloc structures in Europe develops strength. Perhaps it is even more important now than at the beginning of the Geneva meetings to focus attention upon the nature of political, economic, and military issues conditioning bloc relations. The essays in this volume present the results of debate and dialogue at a Workshop Conference on Inter-Bloc Relations at Virginia Polytechnic Institute and State University, Blacksburg, Virginia, in December 1972. Developments in Europe since those deliberations have only reinforced the significance of the points raised by the contributors. While none of the presentations make claim to prophesy, the editors more than ever stress the perspective and potential of these essays to provide insight into the future of inter-bloc relations in Europe.

In Chapter 1, Charles Kegley empirically examines system change in Europe and concludes that there is little reason to expect an era of transition from bloc structures to a genuine pan-European framework. His analysis stresses the need to conceptualize and measure change in concrete terms before allowing the euphoria of political rhetoric to smooth over realpolitik in the international system. While continuing this theme of empirical investigation with an aggregate statistical comparison of the two blocs in Chapter 2, Charles Lewis Taylor and Jack Salmon assert that such data are open to reinterpretation by new decision-making elites and that traditional bloc policies might well be revised. In particular, the authors question the present character of the North Atlantic Treaty Organization in relation to the Warsaw Pact forces in the East and the Western insistence on maintaining or even increasing present force levels. The objective examination of change in Europe presented in Part I

v

becomes even more necessary in face of the frustrations encountered by the Romanians and Yugoslavs in the East and by the United States vis à vis her Atlantic allies in the West.

The recent Vienna Mutual Balanced Force Reduction talks have again raised the West European fears of an American-Soviet arrangement at European expense. In Part II on military issues, Richard Staar examines the military obstacles to East-West cooperation and security. His emphasis on the principles of the American commitment in Europe and Atlantic cooperation as fundamental to the balance of power in Europe support the notion of a bloc arrangement for the European future. Robert Donaldson scrutinizes the Warsaw Pact approach to European security in Chapter 4 and carefully outlines the inherent conflicts within the Eastern bloc. For anyone to maintain that the Soviet bloc presents a solid front to the fragmented Western alliance at the negotiation table, his analysis pinpoints areas within which the risks taken by the Soviet Union are as considerable as those faced by the Western powers. While military issues hardly lead one to an overly optimistic view of a Europe with peace and security, taken into consideration with economic and political issues the era of pan-European talks at the very least opens new possibilities for defusing traditional conflicts.

The overall concern of security and cooperation in Europe is most certainly a multidimensional issue. The many dimensions of the problem serve not only to heighten awareness of the magnitude of the issue but also of its complexity. Perhaps the most perplexing trends may be found in the economic issues discussed in Part III. William Welsh generally concludes that political forces increase integrative trends in the socialist community, but at the same time, in his content-analysis case studies on Bulgaria and Hungary, he notes that economic issues indicate disintegrative tendencies. The economic environment and its capacity to alter traditional political configurations is further explored by Dennis Pirages in Chapter 6. His speculations about the impact of resource and energy problems upon the domestic and foreign policies of Eastern and Western nations critically reevaluates many of the assumptions about political probabilities in Europe.

Part IV, on political issues, focuses upon concerns likely to remain in the forefront of European minds for some time to come. The volume editors look at the problem of the two Germanys and their respective policies toward the West and East. In Chapter 7, James Kuhlman stresses the significance of system bias at the regional level and the quest for legitimacy at the national level in looking at the policy of the German Democratic Republic and the maintenance of two German states in the European future. The continuing existence of the German problem is seen as a feature of European bloc politics with which both sides must work realistically and unemotionally for security and cooperation. In Chapter 8, Louis

Mensonides examines Chancellor Willy Brandt's Ostpolitik, concluding that the Federal Republic will continue to have significant influence in the East but that, in both the East and the West, the idea of convergence of systems is neither realistic nor desirable. While the trends toward disintegration in the West are counterbalanced by political tightening in the East, there seems to be a somewhat paradoxical result of increased flexibility in European relations as a whole. Although in Chapter 9 Gordon Tullock's pessimism about the Western position in Europe pictures the socialist community with a distinct advantage in an inter-bloc Europe, Walter Barrows' final chapter sees the playing down of balance-of-power values as an advantage to Europe as a whole. The CSCE has injected a spirit, if not yet fact, of a more flexible relationship among European nations. That the immediate future of Europe is seen in inter-bloc relations is an assumption thought necessary by many scholars and decision-makers, but it is no longer obvious that such a Europe is the universally sought objective.

As in any collective effort, all share in the positive results; the editors would like to give due credit to the contributors for their breadth of opinions and depth of analyses, while assuming full responsibility for any negative aspects that may arise in retrospect. A note of thanks is due also to our respective universities for their continued support of our efforts at an East-West dialogue. Finally, we should like to thank the following Conference rapporteurs for their consistence efforts and insights: Ann C. Agnew, Daniel W. Heister, Clayton E. Riley, John D. Tressler, and Everett E. White.

CONTENTS

                                                                    Page

PREFACE   v

LIST OF TABLES   xi

LIST OF FIGURES   xiii

PART I: ANALYSIS

Chapter

1   THE TRANSFORMATION OF INTER-BLOC RELATIONS:
    APPROACHES TO ANALYSIS AND MEASUREMENT
    Charles W. Kegley, Jr.   3

    Conceptualizing the European Region as a Single Subsystem   5
    Research Orientation   7
    Measuring Change in Inter-Bloc Conflict   10
    Measuring Change in the Structure of Inter-Bloc Behavior   14
    Summary and Conclusions   21
    Notes   23

2   A COMPARISON OF THE BLOCS
    Charles Lewis Taylor and Jack D. Salmon   28

    Power Profiles   28
    Qualifications on the Use of Aggregate Data   31
    Notes   44

PART II: MILITARY ISSUES

3   MILITARY CONSTRAINTS IN EAST-WEST RELATIONS
    Richard F. Staar   49

    Strategic Deterrence and Central Balances   50
    A European Defense System?   52
    Mutual and Balanced Force Reduction   54
    Attempts at Model Building   58
    Conclusions   61
    Notes   63

Chapter		Page

4   AN ANALYSIS OF THE WARSAW PACT CONFERENCE
     PROPOSAL
     Robert H. Donaldson   66

     Evolution of the Proposal   67
     Analysis of the Issues   81
     Objectives of the Conference   89
     Notes   97

                PART III: ECONOMIC ISSUES

5   ECONOMIC CHANGE AND EAST EUROPEAN
     REGIONAL INTEGRATION
     William A. Welsh   105

     Patterns of Change   107
     Content Analysis   113
     Predicting Integrative and Counterintegrative
          Orientations   117
     Notes   119

6   GLOBAL RESOURCES AND THE FUTURE OF EUROPE
     Dennis C. Pirages   121

     The Changing Resource Balance   124
     European Resources   129
     Resources and Politics   133
     Notes   139

                PART IV: POLITICAL ISSUES

7   EUROPEAN REALPOLITIC I: EAST BERLIN'S
     WESTPOLITIK
     James A. Kuhlman   145

     The German Problem and the Problem of Levels   146
     National and Regional Integration   152
     Notes   160

8   EUROPEAN REALPOLITIC II: BONN'S OSTPOLITIK
     Louis J. Mensonides   162

     The Postwar Era   163
     Developments in 1969   168
     The Ostpolitik: 1969-72   170
     Conclusions   175
     Unresolved Issues and Questions   177
     Notes   178

Chapter   Page

9   A NEOCLASSICAL VIEW OF POSTWAR EUROPE
       Gordon Tullock   181

       Postwar Developments   181
       The Humean Approach   183
       Notes   190

10   SPECULATIONS ON A MULTIPOLAR 1984
       Walter L. Barrows   191

       Dimensions of Power   192
       Prospects for Stability   194
       Behavior of Major Actors   203
       Prospects for Europe   205
       Notes   212

ABOUT THE EDITORS AND CONTRIBUTORS   215

LIST OF TABLES

Table		Page
1.1	Conceptual Parameters of a Systems Approach to Change in Inter-Bloc Relations	9
1.2	Factor Analytic Derived Typologies of Inter-Bloc Foreign Policy Behavior, Based on Two Time Spans	16
1.3	Data for Inter-Bloc Conflict, January 1966-August 1969	18
2.1	World Ranks and Bloc Standing for Defense Expenditures	34
2.2	GNP and Per Capita GNP for the More Wealthy European States, 1970	35
2.3	Defense Expenditures as a Percentage of Gross National Product in NATO and Warsaw Pact, 1970	36
2.4	Regular Armed Forces in NATO and Warsaw Pact, 1970	37
2.5	Regular Armed Forces as a Percentage of All Men of Military Age in NATO and Warsaw Pact, 1970	38
2.6	Military Manpower in Selected NATO and Warsaw Pact Countries, 1971	39
3.1	Ground Formations, NATO and Warsaw Pact	52
3.2	East European Defense Costs, 1971	56
5.1	Factor Analysis of Socioeconomic Data on Bulgaria	108
5.2	Factor Analysis of Socioeconomic Data on Hungary	109
5.3	Functional Distances Between Curves for Bulgaria and Hungary	111
5.4	Mean References to Selected Themes: Wages, Prices, and Standard of Living	114
5.5	Mean References to Relations with CMEA and with Non-Communist Countries as Proportion of Total References to Problems in Foreign Economic Relations	115
5.6	Correlations for Living Standard and Foreign Economic Relations with Political and Ideological Themes	116

Table   Page

5.7 Useful Predictors of Integrative and Counterintegrative
        Perspectives   118

5.8 Means for Integrative/Counterintegrative References   118

6.1 Key Minerals: Projected Year of Depletion   127

6.2 Energy Balance for Major European Nations   130

6.3 Mineral Demands of Major European Powers   132

6.4 Dimensions of Growth in Europe, 1963-70   137

6.5 Comparative Growth in Europe, 1963-69   138

10.1 GNP and Defense Expenditures, 1970   193

10.2 "Generous" Estimates of GNP and Defense Expenditures,
         1984   193

10.3 Soviet and American Preferences Among Alternative
         Models of the West European Future   209

LIST OF FIGURES

Figure   Page

1.1   Longitudinal Comparison of the Total Military
      Expenditures of the Blocs, 1949-68   11

1.2   Longitudinal Comparison of the Conflict Behavior
      Disposition Between the Blocs, January 1966-
      August 1969   13

2.1   World Defense Expenditures   29

2.2   World Armed Forces   29

2.3   World Gross National Product   30

2.4   Contributions to World Scientific Authorship   30

2.5   Relative Defense Efforts of NATO and Warsaw Pact
      Countries in Terms of Defense Expenditures   32

2.6   Relative Defense Efforts of NATO and Warsaw Pact
      Countries in Terms of Military Manpower   33

5.1   Curves with Highest Functional Distances for Bulgaria
      and Hungary, 1956-69   112

7.1   An Approach to the Question: What Impact Will a
      Changing International System Have Upon the Two
      Germanys?   149

7.2   An Approach to the Question: Will European Unity Be
      Achieved in Spite of or Because of a Reunified
      Germany?   149

7.3   An Approach to the Question: Will the Two Germanys Be
      Allowed to Reunite by Their Respective Alliance
      Systems?   151

7.4   An Approach to the Question: Will the Two Germanys
      Want to Reunite?   151

7.5   An Approach to the Question: Do Germans Identify with
      Their Respective States or with Their Common
      Nationality?   153

7.6   A Second Approach to the Question: Do Germans Identify
      with Their Respective States or with Their Common
      Nationality?   153

Figure   Page

7.7   An Approach to the Policy Process   156

7.8   An Approach to Policy Outcome   159

1

THE TRANSFORMATION
OF INTER-BLOC RELATIONS:
APPROACHES TO ANALYSIS
AND MEASUREMENT
Charles W. Kegley, Jr.

It has become commonplace among students of European inter-state behavior to note that the contemporary period is an era of transition.[1] Observations abound that European diplomacy is entering a new epoch and the contemporary pattern of European statecraft constitutes a new "system," differing markedly from its predecessor. These characterizations are presumably grounded on perceptions of fluctuation in the kind and quantity of behavior flowing across national boundaries in the European region,[2] as well as on evidence for the continued economic and political integration of the European states[3] and the reduction of tensions between the Eastern and Western blocs.[4] To be sure, change is undoubtedly endemic to international relations and in that respect the present European system is not unique. However, the current tendency to characterize the contemporary period as one of transformation in Europe is symptomatic of a consensus opinion that the European system is in the process of undergoing a fundamental change. The attitude of most observers is that substantial alterations are occurring and that these alterations are of such vast proportions that they are likely to precipitate the emergence of a new system clearly distinguishable from the past.

To posit that the present European state system is in the process of transformation is to postulate a probable restructuring of the system to emergent new forms. This is a proposition that deserves careful scrutiny. If it can be qualified and specified, that is, stated in a rigorous fashion--change for whom, with respect to what, and under what conditions--then it can be made amenable to empirical

The author wishes to thank Richard A. Skinner for his computational assistance and the Institute of International Studies at the University of South Carolina for its generous support for the preparation of this chapter.

examination. That is to say, the hypothesis that a new system of relations between states in the European region is evolving can be subjected, with proper operational procedures, to empirical verification. It is thus possible in principle to estimate its plausibility.

It is the purpose of this study to explore research strategies for systematically analyzing the problem of European subsystem transformation. In order to probe the veracity of prevailing notions about the nature and direction of change in the relations of European states, it is necessary to identify the principal conceptual boundaries of that analytic problem and to construct a theoretical framework for examining it. Consequently, this chapter will examine investigative strategies for ascertaining the existence of, and measuring the extent of, change in the structure of European foreign policy interaction.

This is a rather ambitious task. To render the objective more manageable, attention will be focused, for heuristic purposes, on only one aspect of European systemic transition, namely, the identification and measurement of change in inter-bloc relations. While this is only one component of European relations, it is assumed that the analytic principles and procedures governing its treatment will also govern treatment of the more general problem, and that therefore the lessons derived from exploring this narrower dimension will be instructive for further research efforts into other aspects of change in the European community.

Given this objective, cognizance should be taken before proceeding of some of the author's convictions which motivate this inquiry. The first is the belief that the objective identification of a pattern and trend to the evolving nature of inter-bloc relations requires replacing impression and conjecture with evidence and empirical inquiry. It will not suffice to merely assert, on the basis of intuition, that a new structure of inter-bloc relations is emerging; these subjective beliefs must be tested with evidence.[5] Supporting declarations to the effect that the present period constitutes a "completely new" European security system necessitate showing that the pattern of inter-bloc conduct has significantly shifted. When speculation and impressionistic judgment are substituted for systematic measurement, the empirical basis for the delineation of temporal boundaries around international subsystems is precluded and the determination of when one system ends and another begins sinks to the level of armchair conjecture whose plausibility cannot be estimated. Consequently, it is submitted that confirmation of hypotheses about a transformed inter-bloc system is contingent upon empirical analysis.

Second, it is contended that the place to begin an analysis of the future inter-bloc system is with the present and the past. We cannot hope to anticipate future developments until we are able to delineate and model the process of change through examination of past behavior and perceived experience. Methodologically this position suggests that description must precede explanation and prediction, as well as prescription. Until we can describe variations in what has happened, we cannot explain them (discover their causes) or prognosticate (forecast) what is likely to happen in the future.[6] Thus this study will seek only to describe the nature of change in inter-bloc relations, in order to facilitate the construction of explanatory and predictive statements about those transformations.

CONCEPTUALIZING THE EUROPEAN REGION
AS A SINGLE SUBSYSTEM

Analysis of the structure and future of inter-bloc relations is feasible from a plethora of potential research paradigms. Since there are many paths to knowledge, it would be inappropriate and premature to suggest that there is a right or wrong way to investigate this problem. All that can reasonably be asked is that the analyst make his assumptions and analytic framework explicit. All analysis requires conceptualization, and conceptualization invariably necessitates some simplification and distortion in order to make investigation manageable and orderly.[7] If we recognize that all research is invariably subjective in the sense that the concepts and methodology we choose to employ structure our observations and influence our findings, then it is obvious that rigor requires acknowledgment of the choices we make and their implications for our work.

For analytical purposes, we will submit that one reasonable approach (of many) to the study of inter-bloc relations is through the adoption of a systems theory framework.[8] That is, Eastern and Western Europe may be treated as one regional subsystem of the global interstate system.[9] Until recently, few scholars have recognized the advantages of systems theory as an investigative tool at the regional level,[10] and most have been hesitant to think of Eastern and Western Europe as comprising a single regional subsystem.[11] This reluctance stems more from tradition and intellectual habit than from articulated objections to the amenability of the problem from a systems theory perspective. Although subsystems can be defined in a variety of ways,[12] and empirically delineated according to a number of criteria,[13] in the most general sense regional subsystems refer to "a pattern of relations among basic units in world politics which exhibits a particular degree of regularity and intensity."[14]

Thus, if we accept the premise that the behavior flowing between the two blocs manifests a discernible pattern, and acknowledge the tendency of all interaction processes to exhibit systemic properties,[15] then it follows that treatment of inter-bloc conduct as a subsystem is warranted. Interactive behavior between the blocs appears to be of sufficient volume and stability to render it subjectable to systems analysis. Moreover, there are substantive as well as conceptual grounds to consider Europe a subordinate state system. As Raymond Aron has summarized it, Europe may be thought of as a whole subsystem for three reasons: The Eastern and Western coalitions tend to manifest a mutual equilibrium; they are conscious of joint membership in a common civilization and political culture; and Europe constitutes an autonomous diplomatic field.[16]

Precision requires not only that the analyst identify the theoretical paradigm through which he is working but also that the concepts of that paradigm be operationally defined in terms of empirical referents. To speak of inter-bloc relations as a regional subsystem requires that the units comprising it be specified so as to delineate the subsystem's boundaries. For convenience, the parameters of the European subsystem will be defined in terms of alliance structures; for a state to be included in the system, it must satisfy the following criteria: (1) all units must be national, sovereign political entities, independent since 1966; (2) they must have reached a population in excess of 10,000 persons by 1965; and (3) each must be a formal member of either the North Atlantic Treaty Organization (NATO) or the Warsaw Pact. These criteria enable the objective identification of the population of states constituting the European inter-bloc subsystem and serving as cases for analysis. Following these criteria defines the European subsystem as comprised of the following national members:[17]

Western Members	Eastern Members
Belgium	Bulgaria
Canada	Czechoslovakia
Denmark	East Germany
France	Hungary
West Germany	Poland
Greece	Romania
Iceland	Soviet Union
Italy	
Luxembourg	
Netherlands	
Norway	
Portugal	
Turkey	
United Kingdom	
United States	

Thus the European subsystem is defined as including a population of 22 states that are members of one of the two blocs. Although others may rightly regard other definitions of the European system as more deserving of study, it is submitted that the above definition is useful for investigating inter-bloc relations.

RESEARCH ORIENTATION

Given this selected orientation to the problem of researching the future of inter-bloc relations, the analyst is confronted with a number of other methodological choices. The list that follows summarizes and classifies some of the salient methodological questions and choices the analyst must address.

A Typology of Some Major Inter-Bloc Analytic Problems

Dimensionality. What aspects of inter-bloc relations, subject to change and fluctuation, do we care to investigate? Seeing inter-bloc relations as a system of foreign policy interaction, what features do we deem most worthy of description and explanation? The researcher must choose to focus his attention on one or more of the following dimensions of inter-bloc relationships: Europe as an evolving (1) political, (2) military-strategic, (3) normative-legal, or (4) economic system. These dimensions are logically and empirically distinct, and discussion of change in an inter-bloc system must differentiate between dimensions selected for analysis. Making this choice explicit enables the researcher to make clear in what respect European bloc relations are undergoing transformation.

Unit of Analysis.[18] The behavior of what unit (collectivity) is the object of investigation? Here the question involves choosing the appropriate definition of actor for analysis. That is, we may base investigation on the performance of individual statesmen (elites), subnational associational groups, nation-states, or groups of states such as blocs. The choice involves deciding which size collectivity is most meaningful for the research topic under consideration, and the extent to which actors should be aggregated into larger collectivities. The choice of units (what constitutes cases) is crucial.

Unit of Observation. What is it about the chosen unit of analysis that should be observed, recorded, and measured? What is being observed must be explicitly specified, along with the instruments used to systematically record these features in a reliable and valid manner. The scholar must indicate whether his conclusions about the units are based on observations of the units' attributes, attitudes, or overt behavior, and these sources of data should be conceptually distinguished.

Scope of Action. Given the choice as to what features of the case are to be observed, the researcher must define the conceptual boundaries of his observations. This is an intrinsic component of the task of operationalizing concepts. For the foreign policy researcher, the choice is among three basic ways of treating (recording) the external behavior of nations: (1) a monadic concept (what actor X says or does to all other actors in the system, recorded in an aggregate fashion); (2) a directed dyadic conception[19] (the behavior nation X directs to a particular external target Y); or (3) in a summed (or interactive) dyadic fashion (aggregating the kind and quantity of action flowing from unit X to unit Y with the type and volume of activity flowing from unit Y to unit X). The decision made with respect to this issue structures the data collection rules and consequently influences the nature of the conclusions.

Miscellaneous Questions. The essential choices to be made with regard to research design may be described in myriad ways, such as macro versus micro designs,[20] level of measurement[21] for dependent variables (in this case, the transformation of some dimension of the inter-bloc system), and universe of discourse.[22]

While nonexhaustive, the above checklist suggests that the empirical analysis of inter-bloc relations involves a number of conscious research decisions. There is a large combination of alternatives available to investigate this problem, and the choice should be made in terms of the researcher's major purpose. However, it is imperative that the researcher be aware that he is making these choices, and cognizant that they will influence the validity and generality of his findings. In short, while there is no one correct way to investigate the future of inter-bloc relations, the mode of analysis selected should be precisely identified and stated.

To illustrate the above points, the remainder of this chapter will be devoted to demonstrating one possible way of addressing the problem of change in the inter-bloc system. It is hoped that this example will suggest, in a heuristic fashion, how one's choice of analytic procedure influences the scope of findings, as well as the analytic problems involved in adequately dealing with the concept of system transformation.

In order to explore the extent to which the inter-bloc system has been transformed, the analytic boundaries shown in Table 1.1 will be employed.

While selections of alternate units and dimensions might have produced an equally attractive and feasible strategy for dealing with systemic transformation of inter-bloc conduct, let us now examine the potency of the present design for generating insights into the nature and structure of inter-bloc relationships.

TABLE 1.1

Conceptual Parameters of a Systems Approach to Change in Inter-Bloc Relations

Research Problem	Chosen Alternative
Generic problem area	Has the European inter-bloc system undergone transformation?
Dimensionality	Has the pattern of "affect" (friendship and hostility) between the blocs changed?[23]
Unit of analysis	Nation-states comprising the two blocs.
Unit of observation	Overt foreign policy output behavior operationally defined in terms of events data.[a]
Scope of action	Directed dyad (behavior initiated by national actor X_n to all members of adversary bloc Y).[b]
Temporal boundaries	Observations of behavior based on period from January 1966 through August 1969.
Miscellaneous	Macro study of interaction between blocs; dependent variable (change of affective relationships in inter-bloc system) measured on interval scale.

[a]Concise and useful reviews of the characteristics of events data can be found in Philip M. Burgess and Raymond W. Lawton, "Indicators of International Behavior: An Assessment of Events Data Research," Professional Papers in International Studies, Vol. I (Beverly Hills, Calif.: Sage Publications, 1972), and in Edward E. Azar and Joseph Ben-Dak, eds., International Interactions: Theory and Practice of Events Analysis (New York: Gordon and Breach, forthcoming 1973). The events data utilized in this study are from the World Event Interaction Survey (WEIS), collected under the direction of Charles A. McClelland at the University of Southern California; this data collection is described in Burgess and Lawton, pp. 28-31.

[b]That is, behavior is recorded in terms of type and quantity sent by each of the 22 actors in our population toward the bloc of which it is not a member (for example, from the United States, Canada or Great Britain toward all Warsaw bloc countries, or from Poland or the USSR toward all NATO bloc members).

MEASURING CHANGE IN INTER-BLOC CONFLICT

Seen as a system of interaction, inter-bloc relations may be classified dichotomously as either stable (persistent) or transforming (changing). To empirically categorize this affective system in these terms requires determining the amount of variation in inter-block relations, over time, from the normal range. While present commentary suggests that the nature and structure of inter-bloc relations have undergone sufficient variation to warrant classification of the system as a transformed one, it would be instructive to ground this classification on some evidence. One simple indicator of the amount of change in inter-bloc relations may be obtained, for suggestive purposes, by examining fluctuations in the degree of threat the two blocs have perceived as emanating from one another.

If it is posited that military preparedness and expenditure constitute a measure of threat perceptions, under the assumption that the two blocs commit resources to armaments out of mutual fear, then a longitudinal comparison of their relative military expenditures allows us to infer the extent to which these fears have varied over time. Figure 1.1 summarizes the fluctuation of threat perception between the blocs over time.

Examination of these trend lines suggests that while Western expenditures and threat perceptions have remained consistently higher than those of the Eastern alliance, there appears to be considerable stability in the ratio of armament spending of the two blocs. That is, the proportion of NATO militarization to total inter-bloc militarization has remained constantly high over time. This suggests two possible hypotheses regarding inter-bloc relationships:

H_1: The potential and propensity for inter-bloc altercation is not subject to wide variation over time.

H_2: There is a tendency for symmetry and reciprocity in inter-bloc relations; the kind of behavior manifested in one bloc tends to covary with the kind of behavior in the other bloc, so that the behavioral propensities of the blocs are correlated and tend to resemble one another.

However, while this evidence may enable us to generate some hypotheses regarding the nature and fluctuation of inter-bloc relations, it would be fallacious to infer foreign policy intentions from capabilities.[24] A more meaningful index of variation of conflict between the blocs can be derived from direct observation of behavior flowing between the blocs. For this purpose events data (the WEIS collection) may be employed to chart fluctuations over time in the

FIGURE 1.1

Longitudinal Comparison of the Total Military Expenditures
of the Blocs, 1949-68*

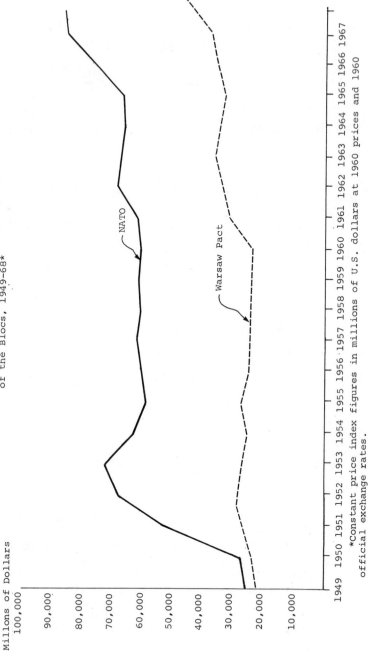

*Constant price index figures in millions of U.S. dollars at 1960 prices and 1960
official exchange rates.

Source: Sipri Yearbook of World Armaments and Disarmament, Scandinavian International
Peace Research Institute (Oslo: 1968-69), pp. 200-201.

level of conflict between blocs. Philip M. Burgess and his colleagues
have suggested a useful conflict disposition index that

> is obtained by summing the proportion of positive events
> (+%) and negative events (-%.) and dividing by 100. Thus,
> for example, if the A→B dyad has 100 events with 75 posi-
> tive and 25 negative, then the disposition score for A is
> calculated as follows:

$$D_{A \to B} = \frac{.75 - .25}{100} = +.5$$

> If no events are initiated or if the positive and negative
> events are balanced (i.e., +.50 and -.50) the disposition
> measure for the dyad is zero. A disposition score of
> zero is interpreted as "indifference" or "ambivalence."[25]

The WEIS data provide information about the foreign policy interactions flowing between the blocs,[26] and is amenable to treatment
with this index to construct a measure of inter-bloc conflict over
time. When we conceptualize the NATO and Warsaw Pact as unitary
foreign policy actors, we obtain two directed dyads ($D_{NATO \to WP}$ and
$D_{WP \to NATO}$) whose conflict behavior may be summarized in the form
of Figure 1.2. Since events data are here employed to measure the
overt official foreign policy actions states initiate toward their
adversarial blocs, we thus derive an indicator of behavior separate
and distinct from military preparedness. Perusal of these trend
lines suggests some additional propositions about the nature of inter-
bloc interaction:

> H_3: Inter-bloc foreign policy conflict behavior tends to
>   be subject to moderate fluctuation over time.
>   3.1: Warsaw bloc members manifest consistently
>   greater conflict toward the NATO bloc than
>   the NATO bloc members initiate toward it.
>   3.2: Whereas the conflict behavior of the NATO bloc
>   is subject to variation over time, the disposi-
>   tion of the Warsaw Pact to engage in conflictual
>   behavior is relatively stable over time.
> H_4: While there is a general tendency for foreign policy
>   conflict dispositions between the blocs to be sym-
>   metrical, marked deviations from symmetry in
>   relations occur in particular time spans, suggesting
>   that exogenous national and systemic circumstances
>   (e.g., the Czechoslovakian crisis) may disturb the
>   "normal" flow of behavior between the two com-
>   peting alliances.

FIGURE 1.2

Longitudinal Comparison of the Conflict Behavior Disposition
Between the Blocs, January 1966-August 1969

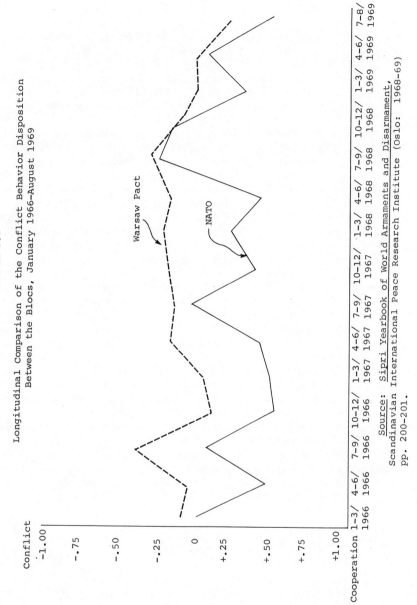

Source: Sipri Yearbook of World Armaments and Disarmament,
Scandinavian International Peace Research Institute (Oslo: 1968-69)
pp. 200-201.

13

H_5: In general, based on the evidence for the 44-month temporal span under investigation, the behavior between the blocs appears sufficiently patterned to warrant the conclusion that with respect to dyadic conflict the present inter-bloc interaction system is likely to persist and maintain itself in the near future.

These inductively derived descriptive statements thus suggest, in a very tentative way, that the conflictual behavior in the European inter-bloc subsystem exhibits tendencies toward regularity and repetitiveness. Substantively, this finding indicates that, contrary to contemporary impression, the previous European system seems to be a fairly enduring one, and that speculations that the inter-bloc system is in the process of undergoing a fundamental transformation are unsupported. If the recent past is a reliable guide to the future, then it would appear that inter-bloc conflictual relations are sufficiently stable to render dubious the expectation that a new system of relations is likely to emerge.

However, such a conclusion may be premature and reckless on the basis of this rather scanty evidence. Consequently, to more thoroughly address the problem, it is useful to probe the same interaction data from another perspective in order to ascertain whether there is empirical support for the hypothesis that the structure of the inter-bloc interaction system is in the process of transformation. That is, rather than inquiring whether the conflict flowing between the blocs has manifested sufficient variation to indicate that a new affective system is in the process of formation, it might be more worthwhile to examine the extent to which the kind of behavior in the system is subject to variation over time. If the structural dimensions of behavior demonstrate wide variation, then this would indicate that a new system of diplomatic exchange between the blocs is emerging, differing in type from previous behavioral configurations. To empirically probe this related question, we turn to a different research technique.

MEASURING CHANGE IN THE STRUCTURE OF INTER-BLOC BEHAVIOR

The determination of the temporal boundaries of the inter-bloc system ultimately requires making estimates of the extent of systemic variation over time; that is, it necessitates consideration of the degree to which the configuration of inter-state relationships in Europe is patterned, ordered, repetitive, and relatively enduring. To speak of systemic change is to imply that a previously ongoing pattern of state interaction has been altered in some fundamental way. Hence, if we are to assess systemic change we must discover the extent to which the inter-bloc system manifests transience and permanence in its performance, and determine what consistent regularities and discontinuities in inter-bloc behavior have empirically existed over time.

Events data provide a useful tool for the construction of indicators of change in the structure of foreign policy activity between the blocs. One exemplary aspect of the inter-bloc system that is subject to variation over time and might be tapped by events data is a measure of the system's overall nature and degree of order for a discrete time period. The structure of inter-bloc relations might be described with events data in terms of the type of foreign policy actions undertaken among members of the system, so as to compare the extent to which systems resemble each other in the kind of behavior initiated. The most direct means of doing this is by factor analyzing events data treated in blocks of time, so that the nature of interaction can be defined for each time period and the structure can be compared for similarities and differences.

This procedure recommends itself because factor analysis is a means for delineating order and regularity in phenomena. It facilitates the needed task of "pattern recognition"[27] by allowing us to probe the interrelationships among event types for the discovery of distinct patterns of shared variation in the data. By extracting a number of separate factors or dimensions, factor analysis can untangle the pattern of interrelationship among events, sort the event types into distinct (statistically independent) classes, and determine the extent to which each kind of foreign policy activity is related to these different sources of variation. Factor analysis thus economically summarizes the patterns of covariation to determine which kinds of foreign policy events share a common source of variation with which other events. An index of behavioral structure may thereby be indirectly constructed for a system of interaction with this technique.

This is an invaluable piece of information about the inter-bloc political system for a particular time span. It enables us to develop a typology of the behavior existing in the system in a specific time frame,[28] which can be compared with typologies from other time spans to determine the extent to which the time blocks are similarly structured.

To employ this procedure, the "principal components" method of factor analysis was applied to the WEIS foreign policy categories to construct typologies of inter-bloc behavior for two time frames: (T_1), the 22-month period from January 1966 through November 1967, and (T_2), the 22-month period from December 1967 through August 1969. Maximum off-diagonal elements of the correlation matrix of the variables were inserted in the principal diagonal of the correlation matrix before extraction, and an eigenvalue one

TABLE 1.2

Factor Analytic Derived Typologies of Inter-Bloc Foreign
Policy Behavior, Based on Two Time Spans

Foreign Policy Action Variables	Factors for T_1			Factors for T_2		
	Factor 1	Factor 2	h^{2a}	Factor 1	Factor 2	h^{2a}
1. Yield	17	92	88	27	83	76
2. Comment	73	64	94	72	68	98
3. Consult	89	40	95	84	51	95
4. Approve	53	76	86	71	64	91
5. Promise	22	90	85	48	82	91
6. Grant	48	83	92	70	70	98
7. Reward	75	34	67	57	75	89
8. Agree	82	54	96	72	67	97
9. Request	41	84	87	08	88	77
10. Propose	37	82	81	47	88	99
11. Reject	89	44	99	49	85	97
12. Accuse	97	13	97	94	33	99
13. Protest	74	65	97	69	67	93
14. Deny	23	85	77	04	91	83
15. Demand	82	32	77	99	06	98
16. Warn	80	56	96	87	46	96
17. Threaten	71	63	91	93	14	88
18. Demonstrate	60	45	57	54	75	85
19. Reduce relationship	48	79	85	12	68	48
20. Expel	85	31	82	71	35	63
21. Seize	60	62	75	95	11	91
22. Force	77	16	61	80	37	78
Percent of total variance[b]	75.4	10.8	86.2	75.3	13.5	88.8
Percent of common variance[c]	88.1	11.9	--	85.3	14.7	--
Eigenvalues[d]	16.4	2.2	--	16.5	2.8	--

Note: Both factor solutions are varimax (orthogonal) rotations, computed with the factor program of the Statistical Package for the Social Sciences (New York: McGraw Hill, 1970), pp. 208-44. Coefficients have been rounded to two places and multiplied by 100 to remove decomal points.

[a]h^2 = communality of each variable, that is, sum of square factor loadings for each variable.

[b]Total variance = sum of squares of each factor divided by number of variables.

[c]Common variance = sum of squares of each factor divided by sum of column of h^2 values.

[d]Eigenvalues = sum of column of squared loadings for each factor.

criterion[29] was utilized to determine the number of factors to be extracted. The scope of action for analysis, as discussed above, is the directed dyad. The results of these analyses are displayed in Table 1.2, based on the raw data shown in Table 1.3.

In interpreting these solutions, note that the variables refer to the 22 discrete types of acts that the WEIS category system postulates states are capable of initiating. By factor analyzing the intercorrelation of these variables for the two temporal spans, we observe that in each period two basic dimensions of foreign policy activity were emergent. The most important clue as to what these factors are describing is the substance of the variables loading highly and nearly zero on each factor.[30] In these terms, Factor 1 in both solutions (the most important factor with respect to the amount of variance it accounts for) seems to delineate a conflict behavior dimension of European diplomacy, whereas Factor 2 in both solutions appears to describe a diplomatic participation dimension to inter-bloc behavior. If this reading of the results is reasonable, then the factor analysis suggests that in the time periods under investigation interbloc behavior is most accurately characterized as conflictual in nature,[31] an unsurprising but informative substantive finding.[32] It supports those who classify inter-bloc relations as essentially hostile.

Hence, the factor solutions suggest that the behavior in these two periods may be considered invariant in the sense that they are classifiable in terms of the same descriptive dimensions. Moreover, the congruence of the factor loadings further suggests a fairly high degree of factorial similarity (and hence systemic structural similarity) for the solutions of these time periods. That is, by comparing the agreement of the solutions by visual inspection to determine whether events with high loadings on the first factor in one solution tend to have high loadings on the same factor in the second, we derive an estimate of the degree to which the structure of inter-bloc behavior is subject to variation over time. Comparison by this rather imprecise method suggests that the typological factor solutions tend to be invariant and consistent over time. Although the magnitudes of the loadings do differ somewhat, the event variables tend to load on the same factors in each temporal frame, indicating a close approximation to a congruent taxonomy of foreign policy behavior over time.

A more precise method of ascertaining the degree of correspondence of the typological solutions is to correlate the variable loadings between the time samples. This provides a systematic mode of comparison, a numerical measure of the pattern similarity of the factor structures. Calculating product-moment coefficients confirms our eyeball interpretation of the structural similarity of inter-bloc

behavior over time: The variable loadings on the conflict behavior dimension are strongly correlated ($r = 0.71$, significant at the 0.001 level) and positively correlated as well on the diplomatic participation dimension ($r = 0.56$, significant at the 0.004 level). These correlations inform us that there does exist a high level of behavioral similarity in inter-bloc relations across time; the structure of foreign policy interaction between the blocs is stable and reliable over time. The convergence upon a reliable structure of behavior suggests substantively that in the relatively short run the pattern of interstate behavior is not subject to drastic fluctuation.

Additional support for this finding is obtained by noting that the eigenvalues for the two solutions are similar as well, which informs us that the dimensions are extracting consistent proportions of the variance across solutions. This may be interpreted to mean that the strength of the two separate factors describing the dimensions of inter-bloc behavior is reliable over time.

An important related measure of change in the inter-bloc system is the extent to which particular time frames manifest variability in the extent to which behavior in the system is patterned. Do historical epochs vary in the extent to which the interrelationships among types of foreign policy acts flowing in the system demonstrate regularity? This question may be examined by again turning to the factor analysis of event frequencies for different time spans, but this time observing the communality (h^2) scores of the factor solutions. Referring to Table 1.2, we note that in both periods the two patterns (factors) that emerged were able together to account for a very high proportion of the total possible variation--the percentage of total variance explained by the two factors ranges from 86.2 to 88.8. This high percentage of variation among all the event variables suggests a high degree of uniformity or patterning in the two time periods. Substantively, this tells us that the foreign policy behavior emanating between blocs is highly structured behavior, and that the types of acts states direct toward their competing bloc demonstrate a high level of resemblance. It indicates that certain combinations of acts tend to co-occur more frequently than certain others. It thus informs us that there is a great deal of interrelationship among event types and that these behavioral patterns do not fluctuate over time. The structure of the inter-bloc system is both highly ordered and relatively enduring. Consequently, these convergent findings invite the conclusion that while an underlying pattern or structure of inter-bloc behavior is extant, this structural order does not vary over time in its basic dimensions.

SUMMARY AND CONCLUSIONS

This research effort has sought to confront prevailing theories about the emergence of a new system of inter-bloc relations with empirical evidence in order to estimate their cogency. Data were accumulated on the extent of change over time in (1) the relative levels of military preparedness, (2) inter-bloc conflict dispositions, and (3) the structure of foreign policy interaction between the blocs. Data analysis of the inter-bloc system in those terms did not sub- stantiate the hypothesis that a new system of relations is evolving between states in the European region. The evidence provided here clearly suggests that inter-bloc relations in Europe are governed by regularity and are not subject to significant fluctuation. If variability is a valid indicator of systemic transformation, as some have con- tended,[33] then the incremental nature of change in the inter-bloc system would seem symptomatic of a highly stable system mani- festing tendencies toward systemic maintenance. Substantial alter- ations in the patterns of European statecraft do not appear to be occurring, and the system's basic behavioral profile exhibits such invariance as to render extremely improbable the emergence of a new inter-bloc system clearly distinguishable from the past. Although we should guard against generalizing from this short-term stability to different or wider spans of history, this evidence does suggest that the structure of the inter-bloc political system does not demon- strate as much variability and change as some have presumed. It would obviously be improper to conclude from this finding that the long-run structure of the inter-bloc system will remain invariant over time, for better or for worse (from a normative standpoint), but the evidence investigated here suggests that we are not witnessing an era of transition in inter-bloc relations. Hopes for and predictions of a new epoch in inter-bloc behavior appear premature.

However, while the evidence examined here supports this inter- pretation, it would be reckless to accept it as conclusive. Caution dictates that research findings, even if empirically grounded, be regarded as tentative until verified through additional investigation. As previously noted, the question under scrutiny is fraught with analytic problems, and the research strategy chosen may influence the nature of the findings. Therefore we should be hesitant about accepting as definitive the findings of this or any research effort. Indeed, we would do well to ask the extent to which the research orientation one adopts determines what is discovered. Posing the analytic question in these terms prompts us to ask if perhaps the conclusions might have been different if different data sources had been consulted, if a paradigm other than systems theory had been employed, if we had chosen to measure systemic transformation of a different dimension of inter-bloc relations, or if the unit of analysis had been defined in another manner. Alternately, we might inquire if our findings might be an artifact of the statistical techniques we chose to employ. To be sure, making explicit the plethora of analytic avenues open to the investigator of social problems forces one to acknowledge the essential subjectivity of most research. Taking cognizance of this should not lead us to the conclusion that the acquisition of objective knowledge is precluded,[34] but it should encourage us to place greater emphasis on the need to regard research findings as suggestive until they can be validated.[35]

The implication of this observation for the analysis of the future of inter-bloc relations in Europe is rather obvious. It prescribes that the assessment of change in the inter-bloc system be approached from a multidimensional perspective with a diversity of analytic frameworks, and that data regarding these dimensions be gathered from a variety of sources. Before the problem of systemic transformation can be properly addressed, we need to know the extent to which the inter-bloc system has manifested fluctuations in the conduct of its members; periodization necessitates monitoring the level of change in the activities of European states in order to determine if the structure of the system has undergone sufficient alteration over time to warrant conclusions about the termination of one system and the advent of another. Only careful inquiry into the range of variation in the system's structure will enable us to address these problems empirically, and it is only after evidence of significant change in inter-bloc interaction has been provided that we can address the boundary and transformation problems.

Moreover, if the ultimate goal of inquiry is to obtain the capability to more accurately anticipate and predict the future course of inter-bloc relations, then it is clear that success is contingent upon our ability to accurately describe and model the process of change through the analysis of past behavior. The empirical analyst has no choice but to refer to the past as a guide to the future. Consequently, in order to address the problem of systemic transformation, the inter-bloc system must be parameterized in order to establish statistical descriptions about the range of variation of particular systemic conditions and to establish, on the basis of these characterizations, the critical range within which these conditions may vary for the system to be considered stable and continuous. Through observation of the past behavioral performance of the system, thresholds representing significant departures from past patterns can be established empirically, allowing indicators of systemic change to be derived.[36]

Hence, by parameterizing the system's structure, it is possible to determine whether there are statistically significant differences in the structure of the system over time that permit the identification of system transformation. In principle, if sufficient variation is present, then limits of variation can be specified to operationally define continuation of "systems;" when variation exceeds the expected range, then systemic change may be said to have occurred. But the system's "limits of variation" must be determined empirically rather than arbitrarily and impressionistically, and that requires that we first measure the extent of variation in the system's major dimensions and properties.[37] All scientific forecasting is predicated on this principle, and the solution to the problem of identifying, measuring, and predicting transformation in the inter-bloc system necessitates prior completion of the multidimensional description of past change in the system's major components. This is a difficult analytic requirement, but the importance of the problem of the future of inter-bloc relations renders worthwhile our efforts to meet it. The chapters that follow take a step in that direction by analytically treating various dimensions of inter-bloc relations from a variety of research perspectives.

NOTES

1. For example, Johan Galtung, Cooperation in Europe (New York: Humanities Press, 1970); Marshall D. Shulman, "Future Directions for United States Policy Toward the Soviet Union and Eastern Europe," in Robert W. Gregg and Charles W. Kegley, eds., After Vietnam: The Future of American Foreign Policy (New York: Doubleday-Anchor, 1971), pp. 130-44.

2. Johan Galtung, "East-West Interaction Patterns," Journal of Peace Research, Vol. 2 (1966), pp. 146-77.

3. Johan Galtung, The European Community: A Superpower in the Making (forthcoming); Barry B. Hughes and John E. Schwarz, "Dimensions of Political Integration and the Experience of the European Community," International Studies Quarterly 16, no. 3 (September 1972), pp. 263-94; Leon Lindberg and S.A. Scheingold, Europe's Would-Be Policy (Englewood Cliffs, N.J.: Prentice-Hall, 1970).

4. Pierre Hassner, "The New Europe: From Cold War to Hot Peace," International Journal 27, no. 1 (Winter 1971-72), pp. 1-17; Karl E. Birnbaum, "Pan-European Perspectives After the Berlin Agreement," International Journal 27, no. 1 (Winter 1971-72), p. 37 ff.

5. For elaboration on this point, see J. David Singer, "Modern International War: From Conjecture to Explanation," in Albert Lepawsky, et al., eds., Essays in Honor of Quincy Wright (New York: Appleton-Century-Croft, 1971), pp. 47-71.

6. For a brief but cogent discussion of the notion that it is easier to describe and predict phenomena than to explain them, see J. David Singer, "The Level-of-Analysis Problem in International

Relations," in James N. Rosenau, ed., International Politics and Foreign Policy (New York: Free Press, 1969), pp. 20-29.

7. James N. Rosenau, The Scientific Study of Foreign Policy (New York: Free Press, 1971), pp. 10-12 et passim.

8. For a general introduction to systems theory, see David Easton, A Framework for Political Analysis (Englewood Cliffs, N.J.: Prentice-Hall, 1965). For a discussion of systems theory at the international level, see Charles A. McClelland, Theory and the International System (New York: Macmillan, 1966). An excellent treatment of systems at the international region level can be found in Louis J. Cantori and Steven L. Spiegel, The International Politics of Regions: A Comparative Approach (Englewood Cliffs, N.J.: Prentice-Hall, 1970).

9. For a discussion of the distinction between systems and subsystems, see J. David Singer, "The Global System and Its Subsystem: A Developmental View," in James N. Rosenau, ed., Linkage Politics (New York: Free Press, 1969), pp. 21-43.

10. For a recent conspicuous exception, see Michael Banks, "Systems Analysis and the Study of Regions," International Studies Quarterly 13, no. 4 (December 1969), pp. 335-60. The entire issue of that particular journal is devoted to the problem of international subsystems.

11. For examples of recent—and welcome—studies that avoid this tendency by conceiving of Eastern and Western Europe as an identifiable unit, see Andre P. Donneur, "The Pan-European System: An Attempt to Define Its Variables" and Jean Siotis, "Western and Eastern Europe as a Single Subsystem," papers presented at the annual meeting of the International Studies Association, Dallas, March 14-18, 1972.

12. As Banks (op. cit., p. 338) puts it, "Regions are what politicians and peoples want them to be."

13. For a discussion of the problem of empirically delineating regions and how one might construct indicators of regional subsystems according to a number of dimensions, see Bruce M. Russett, "Delineating International Regions," in J. David Singer, ed., Quantitive International Politics: Insights and Evidence (New York: Free Press, 1968), pp. 317-52; International Regions and the International System: A Study in Political Ecology (Chicago: Rand McNally, 1967).

14. Karl Kaiser, "The Interaction of Regional Subsystems," World Politics 21, no. 1 (October 1968), p. 86. There seems to be a marginal consensus that a system connotes "a set of objects together with relationships between the objects and between their attributes." See A.D. Hall and Richard E. Fagen, "Definition of System," General Systems Yearbook, Vol. I (Ann Arbor, Mich.: Society for General Systems Research, 1956), p. 18. Ludwig von Bertalanffy's classic definition reads "a set of elements standing in interaction." (See his "General Systems Theory," General Systems Yearbook, Vol. I, 1956.)

15. H.L. Lennard and A. Bernstein, Patterns in Human Interaction (San Francisco: Josey-Bass, 1969); R.F. Bales, Interaction Process Analysis (Cambridge, Mass.: Addison-Wesley, 1950).

16. Raymond Aron, Peace and War: A Theory of International Relations (New York: Doubleday, 1966), pp. 389-95.

17. See Bruce M. Russett, J. David Singer, and Melvin Small, "National Political Units in the Twentieth Century: A Standardized List," American Political Science Review 62, no. 3 (September 1968), pp. 932-51; U.S. Department of State, Treaties in Force (Washington, D.C.: U.S. Government Printing Office, 1972).

18. See Patrick J. McGowan, "The Unit-of-Analysis Problem in the Comparative Study of Foreign Policy," paper presented at the Events Data Measurement Conference, Michigan State University, East Lansing, April 15-16, 1970. See also Singer, "The Level-of-Analysis Problem in International Relations," op. cit.

19. See Richard A. Skinner and Charles W. Kegley, Jr., "The Use of the Directed Dyad in the Analysis of Interstate Behavior: Conceptual and Methodological Issues," paper presented at the annual meeting of the Southern Division of the Peace Science Society, Lexington, Kentucky, April 18-21, 1973.

20. Philip M. Burgess, Raymond W. Lawton, and T.P. Kridler, "Indicators of International Behavior: An Overview and Reexamination of Micro-Macro Designs," paper presented at the annual meeting of the International Studies Association, March 14-18, 1972, Dallas.

21. "On the Theory of Scales of Measurement," Science 103, no. 2684 (June 7, 1947), pp. 677-80.

22. Fred N. Kerlinger, Foundations of Behavioral Research (New York: Holt, 1964), pp. 76-77.

23. Cooperation and conflict has by convention been regarded as one of the most salient dimensions for the description of interstate relationships, and there is substantial evidence that concentration on this dimension is empirically warranted. For a discussion of this point, see Charles W. Kegley, Jr., "A General Empirical Typology of Foreign Policy Behavior," Professional Papers in International Studies, Vol. II (Beverly Hills: Sage Publications, 1973).

24. William D. Coplin and Charles W. Kegley, Jr., eds., A Multi-Method Introduction to International Politics (Chicago: Markham, 1971), pp. 105-9.

25. Burgess, Lawton, and Kridler, op. cit., p. 38.

26. Like most international events data collections, the WEIS system employs an explicit conceptual definition of foreign policy event, which can be described as "the acts initiated by national governments on behalf of their societies, and pursued beyond their national boundaries, to effect changes in the behavior of other nation-states and international actors in the international system."

(See Charles W. Kegley, Jr., "Applying Events Data to the Measurement of Systemic Transformation: Problems and Prospects," paper presented at the International Studies Association South Meeting of the Southern Political Science Association, November 2-4, 1972, Atlanta, p. 7.) Thus an event is considered operationally to refer to foreign policy behavior. For the purposes here, the acts of NATO countries have been aggregated to summarize the behavior directed to the Warsaw Pact, and vice versa, to form two directed dyads.

27. For a clear and useful description of factor analytic procedures, including a discussion of the use of factor analysis for the purposes we are suggesting, see Rudolph J. Rummell, Applied Factor Analysis (Evanston, Ill.: Northwestern University Press, 1970).

28. Ibid.; Kegley, Jr., "Applying Events Data," op. cit.

29. Rummell, op. cit., pp. 349-67.

30. Ibid., pp. 147-48.

31. Previous efforts to scale event types (Kegley, Jr., "General Empirical Typology," op. cit.) suggest that this interpretation is plausible.

32. Some contend that such "findings" are pedestrian or obvious. The problem is that we find different observers positing, on the basis of common sense, contradictory "self-evident" truisms. As W. Runciman has suggested, in Social Science and Political Theory (Cambridge: Oxford, 1965), the job of the social scientist is to determine which of two competing notions is correct. That both are obvious truisms is immaterial.

33. Charles A. McClelland, "The Beginning, Duration, and Abatement of International Crises: Comparisons in Two Conflict Arenas," in Charles F. Hermann, ed., International Crises (forthcoming); Gary D. Hoggard, "Indicators of International Behavior," paper prepared for annual meeting of the American Political Science Association, September 5-8, 1969, New York.

34. See Karl R. Popper, Objective Knowledge (London: Oxford, 1972).

35. For a discussion of methodological procedures for the validation of theories, see Donal T. Campbell and Donald W. Fiske, "Convergent and Discriminant Validation by the Multi-Trait Multi-Method," Psychological Bulletin 56 (March 1959), pp. 81-105.

36. For discussions of the procedure, and rationalizations for it, see Gary D. Hoggard, "Preliminary Report on a Procedure for Monitoring International Interaction" (mimeo; University of Southern California, November 15, 1970), and his related "Status Report on International Interaction" (mimeo; University of Southern California, December 15, 1970). For a report that develops this idea through the "normal relations range" concept and applies it to research, see Edward Azar, "Conflict Escalation and Conflict Reduction in an International Crisis: Suez, 1956," Journal of Conflict Resolution 16, no. 23 (September 1972).

37. This recommendation is developed fully, and related to various systems theory formulations, in Jerome Stephens, "An Appraisal of Some System Approaches in the Study of International Systems," International Studies Quarterly 16, no. 3 (September 1972), pp. 321-49.

CHAPTER

2

**A COMPARISON
OF THE BLOCS**
Charles Lewis Taylor
and Jack D. Salmon

There is , in a volume such as this, some utility in comparing
the military and economic strengths of the two European blocs. How
powerful is each? How do they compare with each other and with
the rest of the world? How do the countries within each bloc differ
among themselves in terms of economic and military power? We
attempt to answer these questions by using some simple display
techniques and readily available crossnational aggregate data and
then pointing out some reasons why comparison by aggregate
quantitative data must be qualified and accompanied by caveats.

POWER PROFILES

The NATO and Warsaw Treaty Organization (WTO) countries
are, of course, the strongest in the world. Some third world
countries are stronger than some NATO and WTO countries, but
the major bloc countries together have the preponderance of world
power. This can easily be seen in Figures 2.1 through 2.4. Over
four-fifths of the world's defense expenditure, almost half of its
men under arms, three-quarters of its gross national product, and
over four-fifths of its scientific authorship are concentrated in the
one-sixth of its countries that are members of either NATO or WTO.
Of the 30 largest military budgets in the world, 14 are of NATO or
WTO countries. Of the 30 largest armed forces in the world, 11 are
NATO or WTO forces. Europe is even more prominent among the
economically powerful. Of the world's 30 largest gross national
products, 21 are in Europe or North America, as are 24 of the
largest gross national products per capita. This economic power
can, of course, be converted into military power. A country with
sufficient economic capability can produce the armaments for warfare and can sustain warfare over a period of time. The measurement

FIGURE 2.1

World Defense Expenditures

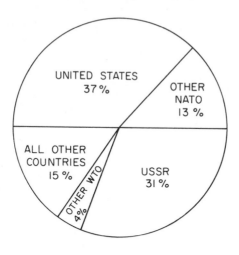

FIGURE 2.2

World Armed Forces

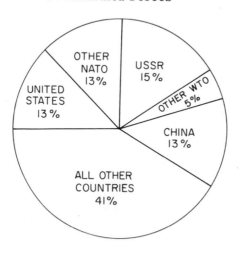

Source for both figures: U. S. Arms Control and Disarmament
Agency, Bureau of Economic Affairs, World Military Expenditures,
1971 (Washington, D. C. : Government Printing Office, 1972), pp. 10-13.

FIGURE 2.3

World Gross National Product

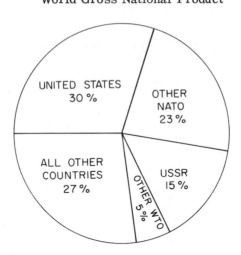

Source: U.S. Arms Control and Disarmament Agency, Bureau of Economic Affairs, World Military Expenditures, 1971 (Washington, D.C.: Government Printing Office, 1972), pp. 10-13.

FIGURE 2.4

Contributions to World Scientific Authorship

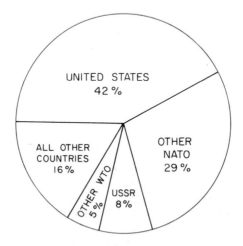

Source: Figures calculated by Derek de Solla Price and published in Charles Lewis Taylor and Michael C. Hudson, World Handbook of Political and Social Indicators (New Haven: Yale University Press, 1972), pp. 322-25.

of military potential can hardly be limited to tanks, guns and men in uniform. Defense expenditure and wealth are closely related; Figure 2.5 demonstrates the relationship for the NATO and WTO countries. Size of armed forces, on the other hand, is more related to eligible manpower; this relationship is represented in Figure 2.6. Figures 2.1 through 2.3 show that the wealthy Europeans and North Americans have a far smaller proportion of the world's armed forces than of the world's defense expenditures, for countries with less economic capability attempt to compensate for low defense expenditures with the resource they do have--manpower.

Exchange rates and methods of national accounting have been the subject of a great deal of debate, so we would hardly argue that our figures are to be strictly accepted. They certainly cannot replace the sources from which they are mostly taken: publications of the International Institute for Strategic Studies and the Arms Control and Disarmament Agency. The data are given here for easy reference within this study. But it does seem clear from the data that some comparisons can be made between the blocs and within them. The United States and NATO are a good deal richer than the Soviet Union and WTO, and the former spend a bit more on defense than the latter. Tables 2.1 through 2.6 also show that relationships within NATO are different than within WTO. France, West Germany, Britain, and Italy form a middle ground between the superpower and the small countries in NATO that has no counterpart in WTO.

QUALIFICATIONS ON THE USE OF AGGREGATE DATA

But the comparison of power between blocs may not be so simple as first appears. For this reason we would like to mention three problems in the use of our tables. The first caveat may be stated in terms employed by Klaus Knorr, who distinguishes actualized power and putative power. Actualized power exists only with respect to getting things done; it is measurable "only in terms of visible changes in behavior patterns." Actualized power is the United States bringing about the Soviet Union backdown in the Cuban missile crisis and it is the Soviet Union changing governments in Czechoslovakia and Hungary without challenge from the United States. By its very nature, it is probably unmeasurable ahead of time. Putative power, on the other hand, is "the ability to coerce." It is the potential cause of behavioral changes. A large number of American missiles surrounding the Soviet Union coupled with an apparent willingness to use them may cause Soviet leaders to rethink their activities in Cuba. The presence of overwhelming Soviet ground forces in Eastern Europe may persuade the United States not to intervene in a Czech or Hungarian crisis.[1]

FIGURE 2.5

Relative Defense Efforts of NATO and Warsaw Pact Countries
in Terms of Defense Expenditures

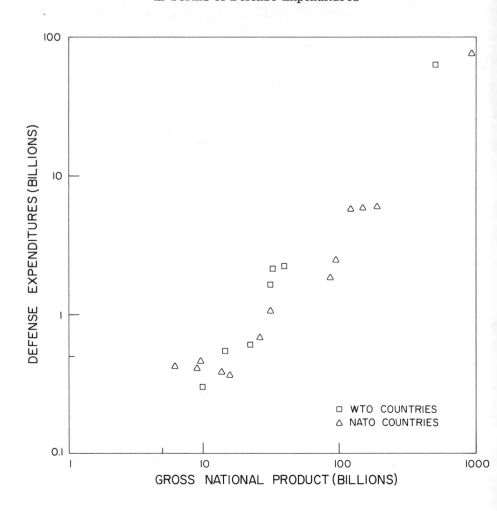

Source: U. S. Arms Control and Disarmament Agency, Bureau of
Economic Affairs, World Military Expenditures, 1971 (Washington,
D. C. : Government Printing Office, 1972), pp. 10-13.

FIGURE 2.6

Relative Defense Efforts of NATO and Warsaw Pact Countries
in Terms of Military Manpower

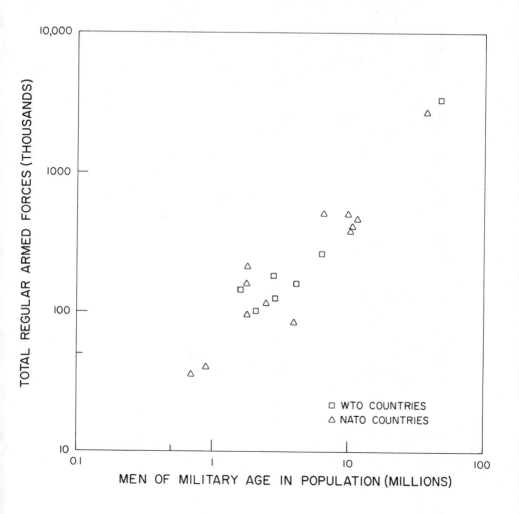

Source: The Military Balance, 1971-1972 (London: International
Institute for Strategic Studies, 1971), as reported in U. S. Congress,
House Subcommittee on Europe of the Committee on Foreign Affairs,
Hearings, Conference on European Security, 92d Cong., 2d sess., 1972,
facing p. 47.

TABLE 2.1

World Ranks and Bloc Standing for Defense Expenditures
(billions of dollars)

World Rank	NATO		WTO	
1	United States	77.80		
2			Soviet Union	65.00
4	West Germany	6.20		
5	France	6.00		
6	United Kingdom	5.90		
7	Italy	2.50		
8			Poland	2.20
9			East Germany	2.20
10	Canada	1.90		
12			Czechoslovakia	1.70
18	Netherlands	1.10		
24	Belgium	0.70		
27			Romania	0.61
28			Hungary	0.58
31	Greece	0.47		
32	Portugal	0.44		
35	Turkey	0.42		
36	Norway	0.39		
37	Denmark	0.37		
40			Bulgaria	0.31
98	Luxembourg	0.01		
119	Iceland	0.00		

Source: U.S. Arms Control and Disarmament Agency, Bureau of Economic Affairs, World Military Expenditures, 1971 (Washington, D.C.: U.S. Government Printing Office, 1972), pp. 10-13.

TABLE 2.2

GNP and Per Capita GNP for the More Wealthy European States, 1970

Rank	State	GNP (billions of dollars)	Rank	State	GNP Per Capita (dollars)
1	United States	976.8	1	United States	4,758
2	Soviet Union	497.0	3	(Sweden)	3,872
4	West Germany	185.2	4	Canada	3,651
5	France	121.0	5	(Switzerland)	3,256
6	United Kingdom	121.0	6	Luxembourg	3,237
8	Italy	91.8	7	Denmark	3,146
9	Canada	78.1	8	West Germany	3,006
11	Poland	39.4	9	France	2,872
14	Spain*	32.4	10	Norway	2,864
15	East Germany	32.3	12	Belgium	2,590
16	Sweden*	31.4	13	Iceland	2,435
17	Netherlands	31.3	14	Netherlands	2,405
18	Czechoslovakia	30.5	15	United Kingdom	2,168
19	Belgium	25.1	16	(Finland)	2,166
21	Romania	22.8	17	Czechoslovakia	2,103
22	Switzerland*	20.5	18	Soviet Union	2,047
23	Yugoslavia*	19.0	22	East Germany	1,889
26	Denmark	15.7	23	(Austria)	1,866
27	Hungary	14.3	24	Italy	1,713
28	Austria*	13.8	26	Hungary	1,388
29	Norway	11.2	27	(Ireland)	1,332
			28	Poland	1,212
			29	Bulgaria	1,153
			30	Romania	1,099

*Indicates nonmembership in NATO and WTO.

Source: U.S. Arms Control and Disarmament Agency, Bureau of Economic Affairs, World Military Expenditures, 1971 (Washington, D.C.: U.S. Government Printing Office, 1972), p. 50.

TABLE 2.3

Defense Expenditures as a Percentage of Gross National Product
in NATO and Warsaw Pact, 1970

NATO		WTO	
Country	Percentage	Country	Percentage
United States	7.8	Soviet Union	11.0
Portugal	6.5	East Germany	5.9
United Kingdom	4.9	Czechoslovakia	5.8
Greece	4.9	Poland	5.2
France	4.0	Hungary	3.5
Turkey	3.7	Romania	3.5
Netherlands	3.5	Bulgaria	3.1
West Germany	3.3		
Norway	2.9		
Belgium	2.8		
Italy	2.8		
Canada	2.5		
Denmark	2.3		
Luxembourg	0.9		
Iceland	0.0		
Average	6.1	Average	9.7

*Depending upon exchange rates and accounting definitions
used by Western economists, figure may range up to 17.6 percent.
Source: The Military Balance, 1972-1973 (London: The
International Institute for Strategic Studies, 1972), pp. 70-71.

Several other chapters in this study deal with actualized
power. Aggregate quantitative indicators are more appropriate to
the measurement of putative power. The latter comes from military
capability as measured by tanks, planes, ships, men under arms,
defense expenditures, and so forth. It also comes from the capacity
for increasing these in times of crisis, which can be measured by
gross national product or its components such as steel, automobiles, or energy production. It also comes from what Knorr calls
military reputation, that is, the apparent willingness to use military
and productive capability for purposes of state power.

The last component of putative power is, of course, the most
difficult to measure. Its measurement involves finding out the
attitudes and expectations of elites in other countries. What they
think of a rival elite's willingness to use its power and its ability
to do so effectively does indeed determine--at least short of actual

TABLE 2.4

Regular Armed Forces in NATO and Warsaw Pact, 1970

NATO		WTO	
Country	Force	Country	Force
United States	2,699,000	Soviet Union	3,375,000
Turkey	508,500	Poland	265,000
France	501,500	Czechoslovakia	185,000
West Germany	467,000	Romania	160,000
Italy	414,000	Bulgaria	148,000
United Kingdom	380,900	East Germany	126,000
Portugal	218,000	Hungary	103,000
Greece	159,000		
Netherlands	116,500		
Belgium	96,500		
Canada	85,000		
Denmark	40,500		
Norway	35,900		
Luxembourg	550		
Total	5,722,850	Total	4,362,000

Note: Iceland is excluded (no standing force).
Source: The Military Balance, 1971-1972 (London: The International Institute for Strategic Studies, 1971) as reported in U.S., Congress, House Subcommittee on Europe of the Committee on Foreign Affairs, Hearings, Conference on European Security, 92nd Congress, 2nd Session, 1972, facing p. 47.

military conflict--the amount of putative power a state has. We have not been able to measure these expectations between East and West.

Our first caveat, therefore, is that our tables compare not the actualized power of the two blocs over the next five years or even their putative power at the moment but only those aspects of putative power that give rise to expectations, on the part of other elites, of power potential. Nevertheless, military and economic power potential is a necessary if not sufficient condition for exercising power over other states and its measurement is worthwhile. States with greater potential will normally be considered those to which other states will pay greater heed in international politics.

Our second caveat is related to the first. If knowing a state's power potential will not let us know the state's actual power over

TABLE 2.5

Regular Armed Forces as a Percentage of All Men
of Military Age in NATO and Warsaw Pact, 1970

NATO		WTO	
Country	Percentage	Country	Percentage
Portugal	12.3	Bulgaria	9.2*
Greece	8.9	Soviet Union	7.0
Turkey	7.8	Czechoslovakia	6.6
United States	7.3	Hungary	4.9*
Belgium	5.3	East Germany	4.2
France	5.1	Poland	4.1
Norway	5.1	Romania	3.8*
Netherlands	4.6		
Denmark	4.5		
West Germany	4.1		
Italy	3.8		
United Kingdom	3.7		
Canada	2.1		
Average	5.8	Average	6.4

Note: Luxembourg and Iceland are excluded (category not applicable).

*Estimated.

Source: The Military Balance, 1971-1972 (London: The International Institute for Strategic Studies, 1971) as reported in U.S., Congress, House Subcommittee on Europe of the Committee on Foreign Affairs, Hearings, Conference on European Security, 92nd Congress, 2nd Session, 1972, facing p. 47.

TABLE 2.6

Military Manpower in Selected NATO and Warsaw Pact Countries, 1971

NATO	WTO	Total Regular Armed Forces (full time)	Para-military Forces	Trained Reservists	Total Forces
	USSR	3,375,000	300,000	2,290,000	5,965,000
United States		2,391,000	--	931,000	3,322,000
France		500,600	73,000	450,000*	1,023,600
West Germany		467,000	18,500	645,000	1,130,500
Turkey		449,000	75,000	612,000	1,136,000
Italy		427,600	86,300	660,000	1,173,900
United Kingdom		372,300	--	429,400	801,700
	Poland	274,000	73,000	490,000*	837,000
Portugal		218,000	9,700	500,000	727,700
	Czecho-slovakia	185,000	35,000	550,000*	770,000
	Romania	179,000	40,000	260,000*	479,000
Greece		157,000	87,500	120,000	364,500
	East Germany	131,000	60,000	200,000*	391,000
Netherlands		122,000	3,200	200,000*	325,200
Canada		84,000	--	22,700	106,700
Total, NATO		5,188,500	353,200	4,570,100	10,111,800
	Total, WTO	4,144,000	508,000	3,790,000	8,442,000

Note: Definitions and duties of trained reservists differ from country to country and figures are not strictly comparable.
*Estimated.
Source: The Military Balance, 1972-1973 (London: The International Institute for Strategic Studies, 1972), p. 72.

the next five years, it certainly will not let us know the areas in which the power will be effected. After all, elites do have some choice in how and where they will put their state's power potential to work. In comparing economic and military data for the two blocs, we are saying nothing about the priorities or targets of either side. Perhaps Western Europe wants to use its military strength to keep Africa in line; perhaps the Soviet Union is far more interested in managing Eastern Europe than in invading Germany or France. If this is true for military potential as such, it is even more true of economic capacity. The economies may be focused on or away from military power. If defense is favored over offense, fewer forces are needed; if neither side perceives the other to be planning offense, little more than ceremonial forces may be needed.

But even within the limited context of defense from each other, there are difficulties in measuring the two blocs' relative power. There are differences in strategy, that is, differences in the ways defensive power is to work. Bernard Brodie refers to this problem when he analyzes the American "insistence on revising the strategy for the defense of Europe to avoid reliance not only on strategical nuclear weapons but on tactical nuclear weapons as well."[2] From the American point of view this is a highly desirable strategy; major conventional forces in Europe would allow possible containment of overt military action to European soil, and at a minimum would allow a pause during which decisions regarding nuclear retaliation could be coolly considered. For a European, this strategy has less to recommend it. It consigns Europe to the horrors of a major conventional war while leaving the two superpowers the luxury of territorial noninvolvement. In such "limited wars" neither side can "win" by traditional standards, with the result that the wars may settle into a pattern of long-term bloodletting until one side or both has had enough. In the context of the NATO-WTO area, this model suggests that a future conflict might last for years and involve a Vietnam-scaled destruction of the political, economic, and ecological basis of European civilization.

If one believes, on the other hand, that the United States and the Soviet Union both accept a current status of mutual deterrence against serious tampering with each other's vital interests, and that each includes European interests as part of its vital interests, then one believes that war in Europe could do no less than explode almost immediately into general world war. In this case, the forces on the ground in Europe are far less important than was the case in former times. Europe has become the fulcrum upon which rests the nuclear teeter-totter in the superpower game, while the balance sits outside. If this is true, problems of the European Security Conference and the mutual and balanced force reductions (MBFR) become less formidable. Therefore, European members of NATO may be willing to contemplate fairly deep conventional cuts, provided U.S. nuclear forces remain firmly committed to NATO. For the Americans this will be a more difficult matter.[3]

From the proposition that deterrence between the superpowers prevents total nuclear war, any self-interested European could conclude that Europe's best choice is a strategy that makes European defense an inseparable part of the American nuclear retaliation plan. From the same proposition, an American would seek to decouple the defense of Europe and the use of nuclear weapons in order to obtain additional protection for the United States. The choice of the most relevant indicators of power to measure may depend upon which strategy is chosen. Therefore, data provided in our figures and tables do not really answer all the questions that, at first glance, they may seem to answer. The context within which each bloc operates, and the fact that the two blocs do not have identical defense perspectives, requires that we consider possible interpretations of the data before attempting any detailed comparisons.

Since both WTO and NATO proclaim their concern to be strictly defensive, we must include in our evaluation the generally accepted military principle that attacking forces require a considerable numerical advantage over defending forces; Henry Kissinger has cited a widely used ratio of three to one.[4] On the basis of current force dispositions, neither WTO nor NATO has reason to be concerned about defensive inferiority or to be confident of an offensive success. On the key central front, NATO is currently outnumbered by about eight to five in combat and direct support troops, by twelve to five in tanks (not counting some 5,000 tanks in NATO reserve), and by two to one in aircraft.[5] Reinforcements from the WTO area could be mobilized and deployed more rapidly than could NATO reinforcements, but the potential NATO power, given the extra time to reinforce, is greater than that of WTO.[6] Furthermore, these figures do not include some 500,000 French troops and equipment. It is probable that France would fight on the NATO side; it is essential that any WTO planning assume France would join NATO. From the perspective of offensive planning, the Warsaw Pact superiority thus becomes an actual insufficiency if there is any justification at all for the assumed three to one attack/defense ratio.

Thus our third caveat has to do with measurement; things are not always what they are assumed to be. The dangers and possibilities of using aggregate data for bloc analysis are very well illustrated by the "conventional manpower problem," which dominated NATO thinking and planning for 20 years and is still quite powerful in policy-planning because of its lingering effects. Alain C. Enthoven and K. Wayne Smith have shown the causes and consequences of this error.[7] From the beginning NATO planners accepted the figure of approximately 175 divisions of Soviet troops as the size of the enemy. This figure remained almost constant throughout the 1950s and 1960s and was the cause of despair in NATO: Since NATO has never had more than 30 divisions on the central front, the strategic planners and political leaders assumed that NATO could not possibly provide a conventional defense of Europe; at best, NATO could enforce a "pause" before the Soviet wave swept on to the sea. NATO conventional forces would function as a trip-wire that would, if triggered, call forth a U.S. nuclear retaliatory response.

This entire analysis was based on an unwillingness to look at the data or consider its implications. Figure 2.2 shows that NATO has an edge on the Warsaw Pact in the very area in which the latter was assumed superior: men under arms. Table 2.4 further shows that even if 2.4 million American troops not actually stationed in Europe are excluded from the total, NATO and WTO forces are not all that unbalanced. Moreover, Table 2.5 shows that NATO states have a smaller percentage of eligible men under arms than do the WTO states; the GNP data of Table 2.2 suggest that NATO would find it much easier to support large military forces than would WTO. Figure 2.3 shows that the NATO allies actually control over half the world's economic capacity compared with WTO's 20 percent, and Figure 2.1 and Table 1.1 show that NATO spends a great deal more for defense than does WTO.

Clearly there was something wrong with NATO assumptions: The actual troop strength was not greatly disparate, and NATO spent more money. Either Soviet military systems were far more efficient than NATO's or the NATO perception was not founded on reality. Secretary of Defense Robert McNamara's Systems Analysis Office reviewed the assumption of WTO superiority and found that the assumed 175 divisions included a number of training and cadre divisions; that WTO divisions were based on a Soviet division model of approximately 10,000 men while NATO division structure was closer to 15,000 men per division and up to 19,000; that WTO divisional firepower and logistic support were less than their NATO equivalents. Additional findings of disparate organization and effects have been made: The WTO stresses armor, in accord with Soviet doctrine, but NATO has a clear superiority in antitank weapons; WTO aircraft are more numerous but NATO aircraft can perform a greater variety of combat roles, and readily transferable NATO aircraft outside the NATO region could redress the numerical imbalance.

We do not wish to say, at one stroke of analysis, that NATO is rendered equal or superior to WTO. Steven L. Canby has argued that NATO's potential is at least as great as WTO's, but that WTO force planning is better and WTO capabilities are perhaps greater because NATO is organized for the wrong kind of war. NATO's heavy divisions, with luxuriously equipped supply lines and a broad range of support troops, are the type used by the United States in the latter stages of the long, relatively slow-paced World War II and Korean conflict. WTO forces are smaller units designed for high impact and short-term combat; they might be able to pull off a blitzkrieg before the NATO potential could be brought to bear. Moreover, the offensive orientation and equipment of U.S.-type divisions is perhaps poorly suited, and at best an expensive luxury, in view of NATO's stated defensive aims.[8] American capabilities will undoubtedly change in the aftermath of the Vietnam war, but it is not yet clear how that change will apply to Europe and NATO.[9]

Another aspect of comparison that greatly complicates the interpretation of aggregate data is the role of geographic structuring of requirements and restrictions upon the two military forces. WTO is generally conceded to have the best military geography, with all its members geographically contiguous, interior and overland lines of communication, and the superpower partner close at hand. NATO is by comparison highly fragmented by sea and land. Italy, for example, is connected by land to only one other NATO state (and that one the oddly in-but-out France) and is isolated from land contact with the WTO nations by two neutrals, Switzerland and Austria. Greece and Turkey are even farther away. The superpower partner is a full ocean away--a fact the WTO nations have noted with their frequent suggestions that non-European powers have no business in European affairs.

The fundamentally different geographic contexts of the two blocs complicate many otherwise reasonable-sounding proposals. The frequently discussed "neutral zone" in central Europe, for example, would mean that WTO forces might still be well deployed in an area large enough for maneuver with protected communications lines, while NATO forces would be reduced to a narrow shelf on the continent with hardly enough room for anything in the context of modern conventional war and a veritable "fish in the barrel" position in nuclear war. Moreover, NATO may discuss military and political measures such as MBFR while secure in the knowledge that the WTO poses the only important threat to direct NATO interests; WTO must operate with the constant presence on its superpower's borders of a China that is, at the minimum, not friendly. Various estimates assign between 25 and 35 percent of Soviet military power to the task of guarding the 5,000 miles of Sino-Soviet border against a major land power that is rapidly acquiring nuclear weapons. The Soviet Union must contemplate and plan against the eventuality of a two-front war with a combination of powers far outweighing WTO in manpower and at least equal in all other military areas. Were there no other complications in deriving formulas for military equivalents, this one factor would be enough to introduce a wide range of error.

Much of Western reluctance to enter MBFR negotiations has been due to looking at aggregate data without thinking about what they measure and without thinking clearly about purposes. After 20 years of rhetoric and planning based on assumptions of overwhelming inferiority, NATO, and particularly the United States, finds it difficult to contemplate a further reduction of forces unless WTO reduction is even greater. But if Canby's analysis is correct, NATO has bought troops and equipment that it does not really need; if our analysis is correct, the problem is nowhere near that of somehow offsetting abysmal inferiority, but rather that of adjusting more minor imbalances that presently are poorly understood. It is possible, to combine the two views, that a defensively oriented force designed to force a rapid halt to WTO penetrations could well be smaller and cheaper than present NATO forces; it is further possible that such a force would have no less deterrent power than presently exists.[10]

NOTES

1. Klaus Knorr, Military Power and Potential (Lexington, Mass.: D.C. Heath, 1970), pp. 2-3.

2. Bernard Brodie, "How Not to Lead an Alliance," The Reporter, March 9, 1967.

3. General Maxwell Taylor (USA-Ret.) has found the United States and NATO military plans for a conventional war in Europe to rest upon "self-delusion," and recommends greater reliance upon deterrence plus a revision in the capabilities of a reduced American force. See "Rational National Security," Parameters: The Journal of the Army War College 2, no. 2 (Carlisle Barracks, Pennsylvania, 1972), pp. 12-21.

4. Henry Kissinger, The Necessity For Choice (New York: Doubleday-Anchor, 1962), p. 88.

5. Based on Trevor Cliffe, "Military Technology and the European Balance," Adelphi Papers No. 89 (London: Institute for Strategic Studies, 1972), Appendix A. The figures given in the Military Balance, 1972-1973 (London: The International Institute for Strategic Studies, 1972) differ only slightly.

6. Cliffe, op. cit.

7. Alain C. Enthoven and Wayne K. Smith, How Much Is Enough? (New York: Harper and Row, 1971), and "What Forces for NATO? And from Whom?" Foreign Affairs, October 1969.

8. Steven L. Canby, "NATO Muscle: More Shadow than Substance," Foreign Policy 8 (Fall 1972). See also Norman Polmar, "Alarmist vs. Realist," The Atlantic Community Quarterly 10 (Fall 1972).

9. The United States is currently experimenting with a new type of army division called TRICAP (triple capability). When this division type becomes operational, will it be equivalent to 1.0, 1.5, 2.0, 2.5 or even 3.0 WTO divisions? See Brooke Nihart, "Army Triple Threat Division at Ft. Hood," Armed Forces Journal, May 3, 1971.

10. If Europe is in fact a stabilized area, it is due to the two superpowers' mutual deterrent posture far more than to the capabilities of conventional ground troops in Europe. However, such troops form part of the political context and must not be considered for their military value only. See the somewhat contrasting views of Eugene V. Rostow, "What's To Be Done?" The Atlantic Community Quarterly 10 (Fall 1972), and Curt Gasteyzer, "Europe and America at the Crossroads," The Atlantic Community Quarterly 10 (Summer 1972).

PART

II

MILITARY ISSUES

3

MILITARY CONSTRAINTS
IN EAST-WEST RELATIONS
Richard F. Staar

The purposes of military alliances traditionally have included (1) maintenance of collective security to discourage aggression; (2) a specifically aknowledged obligation to render mutual assistance; and (3) legitimization, in case of necessity, to intervene on the territory of an ally.[1] In the specific cases of the Warsaw Pact and NATO, a general disparity of interests between the respective superpower and its allies comes to the surface when the former undertakes unilateral action that seemingly indicates that military effort on the part of the latter remains unnecessary. A monopoly or near-monopoly over weapons of mass destruction is the reason for this phenomenon.

On the other hand, an alliance does exercise control functions and may serve to prevent fragmented relations. Such restraints can be and are resented by smaller allies since there are bound to be differing perceptions of the threat.[2] An example of this in Eastern Europe occurred when Romania did not joint the other Warsaw Pact armed forces during the August 1968 military occupation of allied Czechoslovakia. The regime at Bucharest, probably not consulted in advance, went to the extent of publicly condemning the invasion. More recently at the preliminary talks in Helsinki preparatory to a conference on European security, the Romanian spokesman attempted to obtain a guarantee from all and for all 34 participating states against force or the threat of force "in any form and under any pretext."[3]

Another question that brings allies into conflict deals with the high costs for maintenance of garrisons abroad and purchase of advanced military hardware. Who decides how to distribute obligations proportionately? Both the superpower and members of the respective alliance system will desire maximum benefits at minimum cost. Romania allegedly has complained about its share of the costs for stationing Soviet troops in other East European countries.[4] The U.S. attitude toward NATO differs markedly in this context from

49

that of the Soviet Union vis-a-vis the Warsaw Treaty Organization. In the American view, an alliance remains ineffective without a mutuality of interest, which is the cement that binds the allies together: NATO will fall apart once credibility in the Soviet threat disappears.

Already in the 1950s, with U.S. encouragement, Italy and Germany began assembling F-104G Starfighters from parts produced by France, the Netherlands, and Portugal. More recently, European coproduction has begun on the multipurpose two-man MRCS-75 attack/reconnaissance aircraft with a British engine, a German body, and Italian spare parts;[5] some 800 to 900 will be built during the 1970s. In another case, the United States bid for construction of the "Atlantique" patrol aircraft and lost. By contrast, the USSR does not allow its allies to engage in sophisticated military production; an East German four-engine turbojet aircraft, already in the testing stage, was discontinued.[6]

On the military side, it is interesting to note also that the WTO has neither a command function nor any logistics establishment apart from the Soviet high command. The pact remains useful to the USSR because administrative headquarters within the defense ministry at Moscow coordinate allocation of resources, training,[7] and military policies of the East European member states. None of this involves nuclear weapons, which remain the prerogative of the Soviet Union and one that is guarded jealously by the Kremlin.

Control over tactical nuclear warheads on the territory of Western Europe, on the other hand, since 1964 has been within the purview of a special committee under the NATO Council, based on an American commitment to consult with allies. Information has been shared on strategy and guidelines for possible use of these weapons, with the U.S. defense secretary personally attending meetings. A separate NATO nuclear defense affairs committee has 13 members; France does not belong by its own decision. A special nuclear planning group of eight, with three or four seats rotating every 18 months (Belgium/Netherlands, Greece/Turkey, Norway/ Denmark), is useful in satisfying the need for information.[8]

STRATEGIC DETERRENCE AND CENTRAL BALANCES

Surprising little on the subject of strategic deterrence and central balances appears in overt Soviet military publications. The essence of deterrence, of course, is that neither side will attack for fear of retaliation in the form of a second strike by the opponent. Today, mutual deterrence or "functional parity" means that both the United States and the Soviet Union are considered to have an assured destruction capability.

In the past maintence of larger U.S. strategic forces was predicated on the assumption that these would convince the USSR it could never survive a second strike under any circumstances. The corollary American commitment to defense of Western Europe, together with an arsenal of 7,000 tactical nuclear warheads stored on the territory of NATO allies,[9] has concentrated essentially on neutralization of Soviet medium- and intercontinental-range ballistic missiles as well as short-range ballistic missiles.

Deterrence in general remains operative only regarding objectives considered vital to the United States or the USSR, that is, those for which either government would risk complete devastation. This suggests many problem areas in crisis situations. For example, what represents an adequate response in case general-purpose forces remain insufficient but a full nuclear attack would not be appropriate? What if the United States is unable to convince the USSR that it will risk a strategic nuclear conflict over West Berlin? It would be highly dangerous to become maneuvered into a position where the only options left are total war or surrender of previously announced vital interests.

From the Soviet point of view, preparations have been made for both defensive and offensive operations against NATO as well as wars at different levels: conventional, limited, and general. The use of simulated nuclear explosions plus the large concentration of tanks and surface-to-surface missiles during maneuvers indicate that WTO forces are organized for both conventional and nuclear warfare. In recent war games, NATO troops were assumed to have entered Czechoslovakia from West Germany and through neutral Austria.[10] Counterattacks included the use of Antonov transport planes to airlift friendly forces. The "enemy" was contained and then eliminated in the Sumava forest along the southern and southwestern borders of Czechoslovakia.

In terms of conventional strength, WTO disposes of 94 ground divisions (of which 48 are Soviet) compared with 61 for NATO (see Table 3.1). The disparity between armored components is even greater. The Warsaw Pact has some 21,200 tanks (including 11,600 Soviet) against 8,100 in Western Europe. Tactical aircraft attached to WTO total 5,390 faced by only 2,914 NATO planes. Only at sea is the Western alliance stronger, except for diesel-powered submarines and attack cruiser/destroyers.[11]

These conventional aspects will assume crucial importance during negotiations that began at Geneva in January 1973 on mutual and balanced force reductions (MBFR). In this connection, Soviet spokesmen have already given notice that they will reject so-called asymmetrical reductions. An alleged NATO model suggests that for every troop unit withdrawn 3,000 miles across the Atlantic to the United States, there should be a corresponding withdrawal of six units to the Soviet Union which is only 500 miles away. USSR

TABLE 3.1

Ground Formations, NATO and Warsaw Pact

| Category | Northern and Central Europe | | | Southern Europe | | |
| | NATO | Warsaw Pact | | NATO | Warsaw Pact | |
		Total	of which USSR		Total	of which USSR
Ground forces available to commanders in peacetime (in division equivalents)						
armored	9	31	21	6	8	3
infantry, mechanized and airborne	15	36	20	31	19	4

Source: The Military Balance, 1972-1973 (London: The International Institute for Strategic Studies, 1972), p. 87.

spokesmen argue that the geographical factor should be replaced by a global correlation of forces concept, since a conflict in Central Europe inevitably would escalate to world war level.[12]

A EUROPEAN DEFENSE SYSTEM?

According to Yu. Kostko, a scholar at the Institute for World Economics and International Relations in Moscow, the USSR and its allies have put forth a plethora of proposals. They are broken down by category as follows:

1. Politico-military
   a. non-use of force
   b. measures to reduce the probability of military incidents
   c. nonaggression pact between NATO and WTO
   d. dissolution of military organizations
   e. annulment of treaties (NATO and WTO)
   f. collective security agreements

2. Nuclear weapons
    a. cessation of testing
    b. nuclear nonproliferation
    c. creation of nuclear-free zones
    d. limitation of the arms race
    e. prohibition of nuclear weapons
    f. nuclear disarmament

3. Conventional weapons
    a. closing foreign military bases
    b. withdrawal of troops from foreign countries
    c. reduction of national armed forces and military budgets
    d. general and complete disarmament[13]

At a Warsaw Pact political-consultative committee meeting, held in Czechoslovakia during January 25-26, 1972, the participants reiterated their support for the principle of disarmament and declared a readiness to examine the question of reducing armed forces plus weapons (both foreign and national) in Europe.[14] As emphasized by Kostko, the principle of a parity reduction seems to be the only possible one the East will accept. Two preliminary conferences clearly set the groundrules on this matter: (1) the so-called multilateral preparatory talks, which began on November 22, 1972, at Helsinki and (2) the MBFR talks, which opened on January 31, 1973, at Geneva.

The multilateral preparatory talks, at the level of ambassadors already accredited to the government of Finland, included 32 European delegations plus Canada and the United States. It discussed principles concerning: (1) relations among states; (2) possible renunciation-of-force agreement; (3) economic and technical cooperation; and (4) freer movement of people, ideas, and information.[15] The successful conclusion of these talks was followed by the Conference on Security and Cooperation in Europe (CSCE). Only item 2 above has relevance to military relations.

These preliminary talks at Helsinki, as noted, have provided an opportunity for the Romanians to bring up indirectly the subject of the Brezhnev Doctrine, which asserts a Soviet right to intervene militarily whenever Moscow perceives a threat to the communist system in any of the Warsaw Pact member states. Despite the resultant non-bloc character of CSCE, the Romanians have not been successful in again raising the issue of the Brezhnev Doctrine with the Soviets except in the most general terms. The USSR has continued to treat the issue as one of relevance for the "socialist commonwealth of nations" only. Apart from Romania, the Yugoslavs at one time indicated some apprehension of Soviet interference after Tito passes from the scene and a possible struggle for power ensues.

Reportedly, it took three years to arrive at a tough Western position vis-à-vis the USSR. Reasons behind this procrastination involved the fear that any conference would create the illusion that the cold war had ended forever, confirm Soviet control over Eastern Europe, and strengthen the impression that U.S. troops were no longer needed in Europe.[16] Although items on the proposed NATO agenda remain secret and the sessions are closed to the press, one report claimed that they would include proposals for an "agreement on advance notification of military maneuvers and an exchange of observers at these maneuvers."[17]

The nature of these preliminary talks affected the nature of the MBRF negotiations. The Soviet reason for agreement to these two-pronged talks may have originated in the perception of Western Europe as a double threat: (1) continued existence of NATO might force the USSR to fight on two fronts, the other being China; (2) prosperity and freedom in the West attracts the East European countries and tends to draw them away from Moscow.[18]

The proposed permanent European Security Commission,[19] without any American representative, could only become operative in case of gradual U.S. disengagement and withdrawal of troops from Germany. What such a neutralization (or "Finlandization") of Western Europe would be like can be seen from the example of Finland. Soviet ambassadors at Helsinki have forbidden access by a particular political party to a government coalition and even banned the showing of films. A European Security Commission might thus be used as a vehicle for USSR interference with regard to individual states or even integration within the enlarged European Economic Community of nine.

MUTUAL AND BALANCED FORCE REDUCTION

The impetus behind the MBFR negotiations from the American point of view is to reduce the cost of maintaining some 310,000 U.S. troops in Europe (another 466,000 are in West Germany). Senate Majority Leader Mike Mansfield certainly expressed no isolated opinion when he suggested that a million men facing one another in each camp did not represent a normal situation more than 25 years after World War II. U.S. defense expenditures total 7.8 percent of GNP. No other ally even approaches this magnitude of gross national product spend on the military; percentages range from a low of 0.9 for Luxembourg to a high of 6.5 for Portugal, with Britain at 4.9 and West Germany at 3.3 percent.[20]

Although figures for Soviet equipment are unavailable (and perhaps meaningless even if they were available), some idea of costs may be gleaned from the price tags on NATO hardware.[21]

The projected A-X fighter will cost an estimated $3.5 million (compared with $2.76 million for a Starfighter), whereas the F-15 Eagle superiority fighter which passed its flight tests in November 1972 is $7.5 million. Tanks can be produced for $225,000 to $350,000 each. Even antitank guided missile launchers mounted on armored vehicles may cost $100,000 per unit. The portable and disposable Redeye, fired by one man against low-flying aircraft, runs at $5,000 each.

This means that a small country with limited allocations for defense will have to make decisions on what kind of technology to buy. For example, some $15 million will purchase either 50 medium tanks or 800 light launchers together with 4,000 missiles or vast quantities of much less expensive minelets and bomblets for antitank operations.[22] Most members of NATO in Europe have total defense budgets of up to half a billion dollars. This is hardly enough for financing any kind of weapons modernization program.

Again using NATO as an example, with none from the Soviet side because of data scarcity, a huge investment exists in new weapons systems. Both the United States (Lance) and France (Pluton) will have new tactical nuclear surface-to-surface missiles operational prior to 1975. A new American main battle tank, the M-60 A2, has been introduced, with the West German Leopard II scheduled after 1975. Antitank guided missiles forcast in the 1973-75 time frame include Dragon (United States), Milan and HOT (France/West Germany), and ACRA (France). Tactical aircraft for 1973-78 are the Jaguar (Britain/France); F-5E Tiger, F-15 Eagle, A-X, CL-1200 Lancer, and P-530 Cobra (United States); Alpha Jet (France/West Germany); HS-1182 (Britain); MRCA (Britain/Italy/West Germany); Mirage G-8 (France). Other illustrations can be given from tactical air defense weapons systems and antiaircraft artillery.[23]

Interestingly enough, the USSR probably contributes even more in terms of percentages to the Warsaw Pact: Its defense production for WTO allegedly comprises three-fourths or even four-fifths of the total.[24] Estimates of defense expenditures (without including those hidden under industry, research and development, or space) would tend to support the foregoing (see Table 3.2).

The Soviet contribution is almost 87 percent of the estimated military outlays for the Warsaw Pact area. If it were possible to obtain accurate figures rather than those officially released, and to relate them in terms of GNP, this could represent a basis for negotiating meaningful reductions in defense expenditures between WTO and NATO.

Once this has been accomplished, the conferees might be in a better position to take up specifics. Referring to previous agreements between the Soviet Union and the United States, a former cabinet member has testified:

TABLE 3.2

East European Defense Costs, 1971
(billions of dollars)

Country	Cost
USSR	51.80
Poland	2.35
East Germany	2.24
Czechoslovakia	1.86
Romania	0.73
Hungary	0.56
Bulgaria	0.28
Total	59.82

Source: The Military Balance, 1972-1973 (London: The International Institute for Strategic Studies, 1972), pp. 9-13.

they do not apply to bombers, they do not apply to MRBM's and IRBM's targeted on NATO and our forces in NATO, nor to our own forward defense systems in the NATO area. They do not have anything to do with the number of warheads or megatonnage or the qualitative race, which is still left open, or money or surface ships firing missiles from the oceans.[25]

Some of this unfinished business will be taken up at SALT II, perhaps some at the MBFR talks.

The USSR may not be willing to discuss such specifics as bombers versus ballistic missiles at Geneva. A possible approach for Moscow would be to bring up issues that appear vulnerable to exploitation from the Soviet point of view. If the USSR can play on the fears of the West Europeans and attempt to convince them that the United States does not have the will to use nuclear weapons in their defense, pointing to the results of SALT I as evidence, this should add to the friction among the NATO allies.

Another issue of a related nature, which the Soviets or East Europeans are certain to bring up, is that of establishing nuclear-free zones. One need only recall the Adam Rapacki plan for Central Europe, Walter Ulbricht's "sea of peace in the Baltic," Todor Zhivkov's plan for the Balkans, and others for the Mediterranean.[26] The West Europeans have held different attitudes toward these ideas in the past. It is not inconceivable that Willy Brandt's government would find a nuclear-free zone covering both Germanys as well as Czechoslovakia and Poland attractive, but this would necessitate withdrawal of American nuclear warheads now stored in the Federal Republic of Germany.

It is no secret that the USSR also wants a treaty that would prevent first use of nuclear weapons against a conventional attack. Such an issue could very well be brought up at Geneva, limiting the proposal to Europe. Here, of course, the Warsaw Pact already has overwhelming superiority in both quantity and quality. For example, NATO aircraft comprise 35 varieties, with very few less than ten years old. A "no first use" agreement would give WTO a substantial advantage.

During negotiations that led to the SALT I treaty, the Soviet Union argued that U.S. forward base systems should be considered strategic. It is almost certain that the USSR will bring up during SALT II talks the 700 American bombers stationed in Europe.[27] This matter could also be considered in the course of MBFR and the "quick reaction aircraft" of NATO discussed in connection with Soviet MRBMs and IRBMs targeted against Western Europe.

Finally, it is possible that the talks at Geneva may also include British and French nuclear capabilities. The Soviet Union attempted to raise this issue in the course of SALT I, but apparently did not succeed in having it discussed. Although a residue of distrust and suspicion against the French still exists within NATO, the French may take the initiative during 1973 toward nuclear cooperation with the British. That is the year when the Anglo-American agreement on sharing nuclear information expires. An all-European deterrent is probably the last thing the Soviets desire.

There is some doubt whether the USSR will enter into serious negotiations for mutual and balanced reduction of forces. Soviet divisions in Eastern Europe (some twenty in the German Democratic Republic, five in Czechoslovakia, four in Hungary, and two in Poland) are stationed there in forward positions (1) to protect the USSR from a possible attack by NATO, (2) to guarantee Soviet influence throughout the area, and (3) to prevent any change in the type of regime governing each allied country. Although the USSR probably needs more trade with the West and especially an infusion of advanced industrial technology, it is not likely that any of the three foregoing elements would be sacrificed in exchange. However, even if the short-range prospects do not appear optimistic for a meaningful cutback in NATO/WTO armed forces, long-range considerations should take into consideration the possible development of alternative environments.

ATTEMPTS AT MODEL BUILDING

Even the Soviet Union has engaged in futurology of the model-building kind. Such a report was prepared by Nicolai N. Inozemtsov, a prominent USSR ideologist, for a conference at Varna, Bulgaria, attended by representatives from European international relations institutes.[28] He predicted that preliminary negotiations on force reduction could last several years and, if successful, would establish principles and criteria. The process of reduction, according to Inozemtsov, will be comprehensive and "permit an appreciable drop in the absolute mass of armed forces" on both sides. The same security and absence of unilateral advantage presumably will be maintained due to qualitative improvements. This Soviet spokesman suggests three possible models for developments in East-West relations during the 1970s and ranks them in decreasing order of probability.

The first model is called "Progress of Coexistence," based on the principle of peaceful coexistence between states adhering to different social systems. No modifications would occur in class, social, and ideological antagonism between the two parts of Europe. However, it is possible that an "independent Western Europe" will maintain friendly relations vis-à-vis both the United States and the Soviet Union, without being opposed to the socialist countries of Eastern Europe. Although economic integration will continue, political and military integration based on anticommunism will not dominate these processes.

Regarding troop levels and weapons, Inozemtsov foresees withdrawing a proportion of foreign armed forces as well as reductions of national armies and defense budgets. He also anticipates agreement on nuclear-free, arms-free, and neutral zones plus other unspecified measures toward demilitarization of Europe. Each stage in this process will not affect the security of either side but rather adhere to a balance of armed forces and armaments. An organization established by the conference on European security will assume progressively more important functions of coordination and control.

All of the above presupposes that the qualitative development of strategic weapons systems does not lead to a general imbalance of forces. If the status quo is maintained at this level, a gradual limitation of bloc military functions will take place, followed by an active struggle to create a bloc-less structure. Relations in Central Europe will become normalized as a result of the political settlement between the two German states, recognition that existing borders remain inviolable, and renunciation of force as an instrument of national policy.[29]

Less probable is the second model put forth by Inozemtsov, called "Retarded Detente." It will materialize if rightist forces in various Western countries and Atlantic circles are successful in halting, for longer or shorter periods, the trend toward a European security system. Hence, a definitive settlement could not be achieved. Military confrontations, especially in the Mediterranean, would contribute to unstable East-West relations that might assume dangerous overtones. Western Europe would in effect become a garrison state, a politico-military entity with a policy centered on confrontation and opposed to Eastern Europe. The arms race would continue. In response, the Warsaw Pact would continue building up its military potential[30] and strengthening WTO functions.

The least probable, according to Inozemtsov, is the third model, which he designates simply as "Dissolution of Blocs." Once establishment of a European security system had been achieved, both military and political alignments would disappear. A pan-European institution, based on mutual commitments excluding the threat or use of force, would be invested with powers to implement effective controls. It would have to be tested in all aspects before blocs could be dissolved. Foreign troops would then be withdrawn and reduced levels for national forces agreed upon jointly. Separate economic integration of Eastern and Western Europe would continue, but the latter would drop politico-military integration. Probably close to the ideal for the USSR, this model cannot materialize because "strong and stable trends aimed at blocking the detente process exist in certain Western political and military circles."[31]

Any generalized projection from the Western point of view must begin with certain assumptions: Members of the Warsaw Pact will continue to develop along parallel lines since they remain closely bound to one another and to the Soviet Union; similarities in their post-World War II histories, strategic position, and association with the USSR all would seem to militate against radically different paths of development. Changes are possible, but only within Soviet-allowed parameters (for example, the August 1968 invasion of Czechoslovakia and subsequent displacement of Dubcek, the December 1970 riots along the Baltic coast of Poland and removal of Gomulka, the April 1971 succession to Ulbricht in East Germany). One should anticipate perhaps greater USSR influence on Yugoslavia and even reintegration of that country with the East European bloc once Tito leaves the scene.[32]

One extreme possibility for the future of the USSR and its allies might be called neo-Stalinism, accompanied by closer integration and cooperation through the Warsaw Treaty Organization, which would develop into a supranational military force and directorate. The continued physical presence of Soviet troops could be accompanied by Moscow's designation of certain East European military leaders to key positions with little or no local support. In such an instance, conservative high-ranking officers, especially those loyal to the USSR and trained there, might also have influence on the political decision-making process.

A more likely development may be called the dynamic status quo, without any supranational WTO command. Political penetration of armed forces throughout Eastern Europe might even be reduced somewhat. It is conceivable that the USSR would even withdraw some of its troops from the four countries in which they are stationed currently. All of this presupposes decentralization internally and less dependence on the Soviet Union externally. In the politico-military context, a nuclear-free zone in Central Europe might be attractive to the USSR. The Soviet Union still would maintain nuclear dominance over Europe, since missile sites around Kaliningrad (formerly Königsberg) as well as those in the Western Ukraine are outside the zone yet only 500 miles from the Federal Republic of Germany.

Finally, a third possible development could be in the direction of national Marxism. The Soviet Union may decide that voluntary ties can become more productive than imposed ones. In the event that both German states were neutralized, a condition guaranteed by the United States and the USSR, the former could withdraw from their respective military alliances. Poland and Czechoslovakia might find comparable advantages in neutrality, as might Norway and Denmark in the course of subsequent developments.

Despite the dominant Soviet role in East European developments and imposed limits on possible change, the long-range bloc trend apparently is toward liberalization. Such a projection seems consistent with the pattern of uneven but marked and gradual Soviet relaxation of control since the end of World War II. Certain factors seem to be reinforcing this development. Dilution of domestic Communist party power in the USSR may come from the rise of interest groups that question the rationale for a Soviet system as it operates today; externally, serious disintegration of relations with Peking are fed by differences on fundamental geopolitical issues.

Change in Soviet and East European conditions also turn on such factors as shifts in leadership and international crises which themselves are often the culmination of gradually developing circumstances. Points of change for Eastern Europe are closely connected with the Soviet toleration point: crossing certain established boundaries has triggered and may continue to trigger USSR counteraction. But the standard for judging the threshold of Soviet counteraction should change, thereby increasing the difficulty of predicting the precise stage of the development cycle at which Eastern Europe will be at any given time frame in the future.

CONCLUSIONS

Regardless of which developments actually take place, and admittedly some combination of the foregoing is possible, it behooves the West to negotiate with the East on the basis of certain principles rather than numerical reductions of armed forces.[33] How does one define the balance in terms of foreign and national troop contingents? What is the role of nuclear weapons? Should arms control be applied regionally or functionally? What about verification? All members of both alliances should participate in the negotiations. Some of these principles were agreed upon at Rome on May 27, 1970, by representatives of countries within the NATO integrated defense structure, that is, all except France:

1. MBFR should be compatible with alliance vital interests;
2. Reductions should be based on reciprocity and phased in scope as well as timing;
3. Included should be foreign as well as national troops and weapons systems;
4. There must be verification and control to ensure implementation of MBFR.[34]

Even if the Warsaw Pact were to accept these propositions, many problems would still remain unsolved.

How does one equate tactical nuclear warheads in Western Europe with corresponding Soviet stockpiles which apparently do not exist on the territory of allies in Eastern Europe but are stored in the USSR? The only nuclear delivery systems on the NATO central front and capable of reaching the USSR are aircraft. A corresponding weapons system might be Soviet medium- and intermediate-range ballistic missiles targeted against Western Europe.[35]

Another problem is posed by the difference in size of divisions, those in WTO being approximately half the size of those in NATO. However, the WTO maintains superiority in terms of equipment, especially in tanks and armored personnel carriers as well as fighter aircraft. Measurement also is made difficult when mobilization and reinforcement are considered. If the conflict lasts only a few weeks, the Warsaw Pact would have an advantage here.

Force reductions could be limited to foreign troops, that is, American and Soviet. If indeed the latter are stationed in the four Eastern European countries primarily for control purposes, this might pose a problem. Using a concentric circle approach, overlapping both alliance systems, might surmount this possible obstacle. From the center, where there would be no troops other than border guards, each successive circle would have more arms. WTO has suggested a variation of this approach, restricted to establishment of nuclear-free zones. Apart from manpower reductions, whether on a percentage or geographic basis, one can also examine weapons systems and firepower as the basis for equitable tradeoffs.

Finally, certain criteria must be established in order to maintain the security of NATO:[36]

1. The disposition of troops withdrawn by the USSR from Eastern Europe must be ascertained. If they remain in the south or west of Russia, they would be in positions to reinforce the central front quickly. The situation would be different if they were transferred to the Chinese border or demobilized. In the former case, little advantage would accrue to NATO, and the danger of rapid reinforcement under the guise of manuevers would remain.

2. Thus, a ban on reintroduction of withdrawn units must be guaranteed in some manner. Unless this is agreed upon, no warning can be anticipated. The best example of what might happen occurred in Czechoslovakia, when staff exercises during June 1968 were used as a dry run in preparation for the subsequent invasion.[37]

3. Mutual force inspections would build confidence. However, the USSR has always been opposed to anything of this kind since it has traditionally guarded military secrets. If joint maneuvers are allowed under MBFR, observers should participate from the other side.

4. Finally, the American commitment to Western Europe must be maintained at full strength, together with rapid transport capability. Withdrawal of substantial troop elements from Western Europe, without the foregoing, would erode the faith of other NATO partners in the alliance.

Most of this discussion has dealt with the central front, where the preponderance of troops are stationed on both sides of the line dividing East from West. Some thought must also be given to NATO flanks and communications by sea. Not only Norway and the North Atlantic but also the Mediterranean is vital for importing strategic raw materials such as petroleum to Western Europe. The USSR naval threat remains in the background and continues to grow.[38]

Regardless of MBFR, which may take years to negotiate, three propositions appear basic for U.S. security interests throughout the decade of the seventies: (1) NATO is essential, for otherwise the West would be exposed to Soviet pressure; (2) a collective force must be maintained, for if it disintegrates it will be impossible to reconstitute another; (3) a balanced American military force in Europe remains the sine qua non of an effective and viable NATO.[39]

NOTES

1. Henry A. Kissinger, Nuclear Weapons and Foreign Policy (New York: W.W. Norton, 1969), pp. 197ff of abridged edition.

2. Robert F. Osgood, Alliances and American Foreign Policy (Baltimore: Johns Hopkins Press, 1968), pp. 54-62.

3. "The American Presence in Europe" (editorial), The Christian Science Monitor, December 12, 1972.

4. David Holloway, "Soviet Policy and the Warsaw Pact," Soviet Affairs Symposium (Garmisch, Federal Republic of Germany: U.S. Army Institute for Advanced Russian and East European Studies, 1972), p. 41.

5. Nikolai Kuznetsov, "NATO Military-Industrial Complex Hampers Detente," Pravda, August 12, 1972.

6. Pravda, March 5, 1961. Ostensibly this was a decision taken by the fourteenth Council for Mutual Economic Assistance session in East Berlin.

7. The WTO Military Council, comprising chiefs of staff, met at Minsk during October 17-20 to discuss results of operational and combat training as well as tasks for 1973. Radio Moscow, October 20, 1972.

8. When this group met in London, then U.S. Defense Secretary Melvin R. Laird revealed discussion about more reliance on conventional than nuclear weapons. See Orr Kelly, "Shift to Conventional Weapons Seen," Washington Star-News, November 1, 1972.

9. The Military Balance 1972-1973 (London: International Institute for Strategic Studies, 1972), p. 90.

10. These Warsaw Pact maneuvers from September 12 to 16 involved 100,000 troops, code named "Shield '72," from five WTO member states. Radio Free Europe, "Situation Report," September 20, 1972, pp. 1-3.

11. The Military Balance, op. cit., pp. 87-91.

12. Yu. Kostko, "A Balance of Fear or Safeguarding Real Security?" Mirovaya ekonomika i mezhdunarodnye otnosheniya, no. 6 (May 23, 1972), pp. 87-89.

13. Yu. Kostko, "Military Confrontation and the Problem of Security in Europe," Mirovaya ekonomika i mezhdunarodnye otnosheniya, no. 9 (August 22, 1972), pp. 17-25.

14. "Declaration on Peace, Security and Cooperation in Europe," Radio Prague, January 27, 1972.

15. Richard Neff, "Helsinki Talks Scout Security Route," The Christian Science Monitor, October 27, 1972 (dispatch from Brussels on NATO acceptance of talks).

16. Ibid.

17. "Nato Sets Its Terms," Chicago Tribune, October 16, 1972 (UPI dispatch from Brussels).

18. Anthony Hartley (executive director, Committee of Nine, North Atlantic Assembly), "The American Presence in Europe: Permanency or Transition?," paper presented in Valley Forge, Pa., November 18, 1972, p. 4.

19. Valentin Sakharov, "Scope of the European Conference," Radio Moscow, November 1, 1972.

20. Charles Lewis Taylor and Michael C. Hudson, World Handbook of Political and Social Indicators (2nd ed.; New Haven: Yale University Press, 1972), pp. 326-27.

21. Trevor Cliffe, "Military Technology and the European Balance," Adelphi Papers No. 89 (London: Institute for Strategic Studies, 1972), pp. 52-58, gives unit costs and cites open sources.

22. Cliffe, op. cit., p. 23. The cost of equipment for an infantry battalion has risen sevenfold over the past eight years and the price of a combat plane 200 percent since NATO introduced its last generation of fighter aircraft.

23. Cliffe, op. cit., pp. 36-49.

24. Lt. Col. Engineer Jozef Cavar, "Economy and the Defense of Socialism," Pravda, June 29, 1972, p. 5.

25. Dean Rusk, "National Security Policy and the Changing World Alignment," statement before the U.S. Congress, Committee on Foreign Affairs, June 28, 1972 (mimeo.), p. 11.

26. R.F. Staar, "Warsaw Treaty Organization," Communist Regimes in Eastern Europe (2d rev. ed.; Stanford, Calif.: Hoover Institution Publications, 1971), Chapter 7.

27. Alvin Shuster, "Geneva Quest for Lasting Arms Pact Begins," New York Times, November 23, 1972, p. 15.

28. Nicolai N. Inozemtsov, "A Study of European Prospects," as given in Le Monde, November 18, 1972, p. 6. Inozemtsov was deputy editor-in-chief of Pravda for many years but is now director of the Institute for World Economics and International Relations as well as a candidate member of the Russian Communist party's Central Committee.

29. A treaty was signed in East Berlin on December 21, 1972, by representatives of the two Germanys. It recognizes the territorial status quo, even though a letter transmitted by Bonn at this time reaffirms the political goal of reunification. (New York Times, December 22, 1972), p. 2.

30. There is no indication that this has stopped. See, for example, W.I., "Rüstungsausgaben in Warschauer Pakt steigen," Soldat und Technik, no. 6 (Frankfurt, June 1972), p. 303.

31. Inozemtsov, op. cit.

32. See Milorad M. Drachkovitch, "Yugoslavia," in R.F. Staar, ed., Yearbook on International Communist Affairs 1973 (Stanford, Calif.: Hoover Institution Publications, 1973).

33. Christopher Bertram, "Mutual Force Reductions in Europe: The Political Aspects," Adelphi Papers, No. 84 (London: International Institute for Strategic Studies, January 1972), p. 31.

34. Joseph Harned (rapporteur), Conference on Security and Cooperation in Europe and Negotiations on Mutual and Balanced Force Reductions (Washington, D.C.: The Atlantic Council of the United States, November 23, 1972), p. 35; paraphrased.

35. Ibid., pp. 38-44.

36. Ibid., pp. 47-54.

37. Robin Alison Reminton, The Warsaw Pact: Case Studies in Communist Conflict Resolution (Cambridge, Mass.: The MIT Press, 1971), p. 268.

38. Edward Wegener, Moskaus Offensive zur See (Bonn: MOV Verlag, 1972), p. 128.

39. General A.J. Goodpaster, USA (supreme allied commander, Europe), "Address to Association of the U.S. Army at Heidelberg," News Release No. 30-72 (November 8, 1972), pp. 8-9; SHAFE, Belgium.

CHAPTER

4

AN ANALYSIS
OF THE WARSAW PACT
CONFERENCE PROPOSAL
Robert H. Donaldson

On November 22, 1972, representatives from 34 states--all
the states in Europe except Albania, plus the United States and
Canada--gathered in Helsinki for the opening of discussions on the
preparation of the conference on security and cooperation in Europe
(CSCE)--which is called the conference on European security and
cooperation by the U.S. government and its allies, who emphasize
that the issues, but not all the participants, are "European."
According to current expectations, the main conference--its scope
unprecedented in the annals of postwar Europe--opened in the
Finnish capital in June 1973.

As students of contemporary East European and Soviet politics
are aware, the compaign for the convocation of such a gathering has
served as the centerpiece of Warsaw Pact diplomacy in Europe for
over half a dozen years. Yet the initial response and attention given
to the proposed CSCE--outside official circles--in the American
journalistic and scholarly communities can only be described as
"underwhelming." This is due in part to the fact that American
policy-makers and the attentive public have been focusing in recent
years either on the dangerous and often puzzling developments in
areas of the third world, most especially Indochina and the Middle
East, or on the eye-catching events of triangular summitry. At the
same time, that part of the globe diplomatic historians have long
considered the "main arena"--Europe, the very spawning ground
of the cold war--has receded dramatically from public (and, it
sometimes seems to Europeans, from official American) notice.

Moreover, this lack of attention to the CSCE proposal is also
attributable to the fact that many American and NATO officials have
shown pronounced skepticism toward the Warsaw Pact initiative.

The author wishes to express his appreciation to Konrad
Kressley for research assistance.

Some have regarded it as a propaganda ploy about which the Communists themselves are hardly serious. Terms such as nebulous, imprecise,. and "a great waffle" have been used by State Department officials referring to the proposed conference. Others had treated the conference initiative as though it were some poisonous snake, poised to aim a lethal strike at Westerners who wander near it; one NATO personage has dubbed it the "European Suicide Conference."

Despite the skepticism, fears, and better judgment of many in the West, the CSCE has engaged the attention of European and American diplomats, as well as larger sectors of their publics, for many months to come. This chapter seeks to provide a comprehensive assessment of the Warsaw Pact conference proposal. The first section will trace the long evolution of the proposal, noting the changes and adjustments in Soviet and East European statements in the face of both Western reaction and changing European circumstances, most notably events in Germany and Czechoslovakia. In the light of this historical survey, we will then undertake an analysis of the issues--both those it is proposed that the CSCE consider, and those raised by the conference proposal itself. The third section will examine the objectives that the conference and the campaign to convene it have been intended to serve--most especially those of the Soviet Union but also, and to the extent they diverge, those of other Warsaw Pact states. Because the focus throughout will be on Soviet aims and activities, this final section will also include a brief summary of the present Soviet assessment of global politics, the larger context within which the conference campaign has been developed.

EVOLUTION OF THE PROPOSAL

The present campaign for a conference on European security is actually a revived and altered version of a proposal first put forth by the Soviets early in 1954. In February 1954 at the Berlin Conference of Foreign Ministers, V.M. Molotov tabled a draft all-European collective security treaty (in which the United States and China would participate as "observers"), along with a plan for reunification of Germany on the basis of a coalition government. At the end of March the Soviets called for a conference on European security which would arrange, among other things, for the admission of the USSR and several allies to NATO. These initiatives were clearly taken in an effort to forestall the integration of West Germany into the Western defense efforts. After the conclusion of the Paris agreements providing for the Federal Republic's admission to NATO, the Soviets called again for a conference--this time actually holding it, in Moscow in November. Attended only by the Soviet allies in Europe, the conference resulted in its participants agreeing to form an eastern military alliance if the Paris arrangements were implemented.[1]

Thus the Warsaw Treaty was signed on May 15, 1955. But only two months later Prime Minister Bulganin was promoting, at the Geneva summit, a new draft treaty to be adopted by an all-European conference. This one called for a nonaggression pact between NATO and the Warsaw Pact, to be followed by the dissolution of the two blocs. Although the "spirit of Geneva" represented a markedly improved atmosphere, no substantive agreements on Germany or European security were achieved and the conference proposal went into a decade of dormancy.

It was an eventful decade, marked by both internal upheaval in Eastern Europe and a series of crises over Berlin, culminating, with the erection of the Berlin Wall, in the long-delayed consolidation of Communist power in East Germany. Yet there was a sense of "plus ça change, plus c'est la même chose," for when the conference proposal reemerged it was again in the context of Soviet efforts to forestall further West German military integration in NATO. First enunciated by Polish Foreign Minister Rapacki in December 1964 at the United Nations, and then adopted by the Political Consultative Committee (PCC) of the Warsaw Pact the following month, the proposed conference would consider a denuclearized zone in Central Europe and a NATO-Warsaw Pact nonaggression pact. Appearing in the wake of the American proposal for a multilateral force (MLF) for NATO, the new conference campaign was designed to torpedo this project and forestall the acquisition of nuclear weapons in any form by the West German "revanchists." But when the MLF project collapsed of its own weight, the European Security Conference proposal seemed once again to wither without bearing fruit.

This time, however, its dormancy was much briefer. Allusions were made in Brezhnev's speech to the twenty-third party congress in March 1966 to the need for an "appropriate international conference" to discuss arms reduction and other European security measures, and Gromyko's speech on the same occasion indicated that the central target of such measures should be "the influence wielded by a large non-European power." The full-fledged reblossoming of the proposal for a security conference took place a few months later at a meeting of the PCC in Bucharest. And although the Soviets have cultivated it with varying intensity and differing emphasis since the July 1966 meeting, this hybrid variety of the conference idea seems likely finally to bear fruit.

Against a background of simmering tension within Eastern Europe, as the Soviets and Romanians sparred over Moscow's efforts to tighten its military and political controls within the Warsaw Pact, the Bucharest declaration on European security represented a Communist attempt to seize the initiative in continental diplomacy. In language often identical to that used by Brezhnev and Gromyko at the Soviet party congress, the declaration began with an attack focused on the "aggressive," interfering, and divisive European policy of the United States and of its chief ally, the "militaristic and revanchist" circles of the Federal Republic. Although the United States was apparently beyond redemption, the states of Europe, acting "without outside interference," were capable of acting jointly to construct a peaceful and secure order, based on the principle of the "inviolability of the existing frontiers." However, the interests of security demanded that Bonn give up the Hallstein doctrine and accept the existence of two German states, abandon its territorial claims, and accept the "constructive proposals" of the GDR.

According to the signatories of the declaration, the following were the "main directions" for the strengthening of European security:

1. Development of "good neighborly relations" among European states on the basis of the "principles of independence and national sovereignty, equality, noninterference in internal affairs, and mutual advantage founded on the principles of peaceful coexistence between states with differing social systems." Stemming from this would flow strengthened cooperation in the realms of trade, science and technology, and culture--conditioned, however, on the renunciation of political and economic discrimination and the normalization of relations among all states, including both Germanys.

2. To overcome the division of the world into military blocs and achieve the relaxation of military tension, the states of the Warsaw Pact--a "defensive" alignment concluded only in reply to the formation of the "military aggressive" NATO--called for the "simultaneous dissolution" of the two alliances, or at least the abolition of their military organizations.

3. As "partial measures toward military relaxation" in Europe were cited the abolition of foreign bases, "the withdrawal of all forces from foreign territories to within their national frontiers," phased reduction of the armed forces of both German states, establishment of nuclear-free zones, and an end to the intrusion into European territory of "foreign" submarines, ships, and planes carrying nuclear weapons.

4. Exclusion of the possibility of access by Bonn to nuclear weapons "in any form--directly or indirectly."

5. Recognition by all states of the existing frontiers, "including the Polish frontier on the Oder-Neisse" and the East-West Germany frontiers.

6. A search for a German peace settlement proceeding both from the "reality" of the existence of two German states and from the refusal of both to possess nuclear weapons. As for German reunion, the path lies through a "gradual rapprochement" and

agreements between the two sovereign states, through agreements on "disarmament in Germany and Europe," and on the basis of the principle that "the united German state would be truly peaceful and democratic and would never again be a danger to its neighbors or to peace in Europe."

7. "Convocation of a general European conference to discuss the questions of ensuring security in Europe and organizing general European cooperation would be of great positive importance." Agreements reached "could" be expressed in the form of a "general European declaration, open to all interested states, on cooperation and the settlement of disputes by peaceful means." Convocation of such a conference "could contribute to the establishment of a system of collective security in Europe" and could take place "at any time convenient" to interested neutrals and members of NATO. The agenda would be decided upon "by all participating states together, bearing in mind the proposals submitted by every one of them."[2]

Although the Bucharest declaration appeared in some respects to be an echo of Soviet proposals and propaganda themes from the previous decade, its tone and thrust indicated a perception on the part of its sponsors of favorable opportunities in two directions: (1) the recognition, legitimization, and consolidation of the status quo in Eastern Europe, including the separate status of East Germany; (2) a change in the status quo in Western Europe, by means both of a further reduction of American influence in Europe and an encouragement of Gaullist and neutralist tendencies in Western Europe (as NATO approached its twentieth anniversary possibilities for the withdrawal of member states). The general prospect, then, was one of ending the military division of Europe into opposing blocs while retaining the ideological and political division and continuing the struggle between the two sides according to the ground rules of peaceful coexistence.

But this favorable picture was soon clouded by developments that called into question the evident Soviet assumption that fissiparous tendencies and the consequent opportunities for exploiting them would develop primarily in the Western half of Europe. President Johnson's call for an American policy of bridge-building in Eastern Europe, contained in a speech delivered in October 1966, was followed two months later by the formation of the Grand Coalition in Bonn and the adoption of an Ostpolitik full of seductive diplomatic and commercial initiatives toward the states of East Europe. The speed with which the Romanians responded to Bonn's overtures (establishing diplomatic relations in January 1967) raised for Ulbricht the prospect of further isolation and loss of leverage and for Brezhnev and Kosygin the specter of a joint American-West German fishing expedition in the Soviet sphere. Instinctively, the Soviets moved during 1967 to head off the Western initiatives. During March the Polish-Czech treaty was renewed, and East Germany concluded two new bilateral treaties with Poland and Czechoslovakia. By the end of the year all of the Warsaw Pact states except Romania had concluded new bilateral mutual assistance pacts with the Ulbricht regime and had renewed their bilateral treaties with Moscow.

It was in this atmosphere that a conference of 24 European Communist and Workers' parties assembled in Karlovy Vary, Czechoslovakia, at the end of April 1967. Problems of European security shared the agenda with a consideration of Soviet efforts to isolate Peking in the international Communist movement, and it is likely that substantial differences with the Soviet approach to both items kept the Romanians (as well as the Yugoslavs) away from the conference. The statement issued by the assembled parties, again pointing to the United States as the "main force of aggression and reaction" and the Bonn "revenge-seeking and militarist forces" as its chief European mainstay, noted the existence of increasing "contradictions" between these forces and the national interests of the West European states. Despite its avowed peaceful intentions, the new Bonn coalition was said to have shown no signs of abandoning its "imperialist goals."

The statement explicitly cited the coming expiration of the 20-year "period of validity" of the Atlantic Pact, and called for a wide-scale movement against its extension. The parties endorsed the Bucharest declaration's call for a Europe without military blocs, singling out the need for an "immediate agreement" on liquidation of the military organizations of the two pacts. Also echoed was the earlier call for a system of collective security, based on the same conditions with respect to inviolability of frontiers and recognition of "realities" in the German situation. The parties called for an all-European treaty on renunciation of force, noninterference, and peaceful resolution of disputes, accompanied by partial disarmament. But these measures were not specifically linked to a European security conference; indeed, the statement of support for the convocation of this conference lacked any sense of urgency and was somewhat diluted by an accompanying call for a "conference of representatives of the European parliaments."

The Karlovy Vary statement differed from the Bucharest declaration in several other respects: It omitted any mention of eventual German reunion or of force reductions in Germany; it specified areas where denuclearized zones might be established (Central Europe, the Balkans, the Danubian territories, the Mediterranean, and Northern Europe); and, most significantly and most easily attributable to the absence of the Romanians, it substituted a phrase on the withdrawal of "foreign troops from the territory of European states" for the language of the Bucharest declaration, which more clearly referred to all forces stationed outside their national frontiers.[3]

Thus the Karlovy Vary conference ended without contributing either specificity or a sense of urgency to the European security conference campaign. Nor were either of these elements added in the ensuing months, as almost two years passed without another collective affirmation of the conference proposal by the European Communist states or parties. Although the Soviets did explore the proposal in bilateral contacts with Western and neutral governments, the issues of U.S. and West German participation in the conference caused difficulties.

Publicly, very little was said about the conference by Soviet leaders. Brezhnev made only a passing reference to European security in his lengthy speech on the fiftieth anniversary of the revolution.[4] Kosygin, in a major speech in Minsk in February 1968, dwelt at some length on the sins of West German revanchism, but again only briefly mentioned the Warsaw Pact proposals.[5] The most noteworthy mention of the idea during this period came late in June, when Gromyko emphasized it in his review of foreign policy. And although the Soviet foreign minister stated that his government was ready for preparatory discussions with European governments "which understand the need and urgency of pooling efforts for this purpose," he neglected to mention in this context the simultaneous abolition of NATO and the Warsaw Pact.[6]

No formal reply to the conference proposal was forthcoming from NATO organizations during this period. Rather, the NATO foreign ministers formulated a counterproposal calling on the East European countries to join in discussions on mutual force reductions. Meeting at Reykjavik, Iceland, in June 1968, the ministers issued a declaration affirming the need for a "balance of forces" between NATO and the Warsaw Pact, and advancing the proposition that NATO's military capability should not be reduced "except as part of a pattern of mutual force reductions balanced in scope and timing." These mutual reductions were to be governed by the following principles: They should be reciprocal and balanced; they should represent a "significant and substantial step," maintaining present security at reduced cost while not risking destabilization of the situation in Europe; they should be "consonant with the aim of creating confidence in Europe generally and in the case of each party concerned"; they should be "consistent with the vital security interests of all parties."[7] As we shall see, the progress of the dialogue on this issue became intimately linked with the discussions between the two sides about the convocation of a European security conference.

The relegation of all-European "collective security" matters to a place on the Warsaw Pact's back burner during this period is not difficult to explain. Shortly after the gathering at Karlovy Vary, the attention of the Eastern bloc and the entire world was diverted to the Six-Day War in the Middle East and its tension-filled

aftermath. And the spring of 1968 saw the simultaneous development
of a minor crisis over Berlin and major departures from Soviet-style
Communism in Prague. The former event never assumed serious
proportions, but the latter developments soon became the all-
consuming concern of Czechoslovakia's "fraternal" allies in the
Warsaw Pact. Dubcek's course of action was regarded with increasing alarm in East Germany, Poland, and the USSR, and with varying
degrees of sympathy in Hungary, Romania, and Yugoslavia. And not
only was the "Prague spring" seen in some circles as confirmation
of the subversive intentions of assorted "revanchists" and
"imperialists" toward East Europe but the subsequent invasion by
the five Warsaw Pact states was itself a source of considerable
divisiveness within the Eastern sphere. A detailed analysis of the
Czech crisis is beyond the scope of this study; let it suffice to
mention briefly several of its effects. The crisis both preoccupied
the Warsaw Pact states and diverted them from further detentist
initiatives; it heightened Soviet concern over the stability and cohesion of the "socialist commonwealth," as the expression of the
Brezhnev Doctrine sharply illustrated; it provoked second thoughts
about the offer to dissolve the alliance; and at the same time it
profoundly altered the assumptions and security perceptions of many
NATO governments. Thus among the costs Moscow incurred in
reasserting its control over its errant ally was the galvanization of
the opposing alliance, whose cohesion it had earlier been working to
undermine.

     In an effort to regain the diplomatic initiative in Europe, the
Political Consultative Committee of the Warsaw Pact, meeting in
Budapest in March 1969, resumed its campaign to convoke an all-
European conference. This East European summit was held in an
atmosphere characterized both by the increasing seriousness of the
Sino-Soviet conflict (as Soviet and Chinese troops waged a battle on
the Ussuri earlier in the month, and as the Soviets were stepping
up their preparations for a world Communist conference to deal
with the Chinese heresy), and by attempts to repair the damage
wrought in East Europe by the Czech crisis (including efforts to
reform the structure of the Warsaw Treaty's defense organization).
In both areas, the Romanians appeared to have been successful in
pressing their objections to Soviet projects, including a reported
attempt by Brezhnev to gain Warsaw Pact condemnation of Chinese
"aggression" and to recruit "symbolic military detachments" to
be sent from each member country to the Sino-Soviet border.[8]

     In this context, the conference appeal issued from the meeting
also appeared to contain signs of compromise. Reportedly the
product of a lengthy session of deputy foreign ministers working
from a Hungarian draft,[9] the document was significantly milder in
tone (and even less specific in content) than were the Bucharest or
Karlovy Vary statements. In contrast to the earlier versions,

there were no specific references to either the United States or NATO in this new Budapest appeal, but only a vague allusion to unnamed "forces" fomenting tension and seeking to maintain division in Europe. Despite the opposition of such forces to the call for a European conference, the statement said, "not a single European government has opposed the idea," and in the opinion of the signatories "there are no weighty reasons whatsoever for opposing it." Thus, the Warsaw Pact called for a "meeting at the earliest possible date" of representatives of the states of Europe in order to establish procedure and determine the agenda.

The aims and content of the conference were only vaguely stated. The conference would "find ways and means" leading to an end to Europe's division into military groupings and establishment of peaceful cooperation. Preconditions for attainment of European security were said to be: (1) inviolability of existing frontiers, (2) recognition of the existence of two Germanys, and (3) renunciation by Bonn of the possession of nuclear weapons and of claims to represent the entire German people. Reaffirming (without specific repetition) the "steps and provisions" contained in the earlier Bucharest declaration, the Warsaw Treaty states declared that the creation of a system of European security would open possibilities for major joint projects "in power ingineering, transport, water and air space, and the health services."[10]

The effect of the conciliatory tone of this Budapest appeal upon NATO states was greatly diminished by the issuance the following month of a harsh and polemical statement by the Soviet government on the occasion of NATO's twentieth anniversary. This statement accused NATO not only of being the main support of West German revanchism and "all reactionary regimes . . . throughout the world" but also of counterrevolutionary efforts to subvert the socialist camp; it also maintained that "extremely dangerous results" would be entailed by the continued existence of the alliance.[11] Although the statement reaffirmed the necessity of calling an all-European conference on security, its practical effect was to lessen the chances of a serious NATO response to the Budapest appeal. That this result might indeed have been the intention of the Soviet statement is suggested by Harlan Cleveland, who noted that its release was timed to hit the Washington ministerial meeting of NATO just as a discussion of the conference proposal was beginning. "The Soviet statement fell like a great stone" into the meeting, amid "whispers of shock and disbelief. I could almost feel the temperature drop," Cleveland reported.[12]

Whether intentional or not, the Soviet blast did serve to deflate the efforts of those NATO representatives who favored a positive response to the Warsaw Pact proposal. The communiqué released by the Washington meeting made no mention of the Budapest appeal, although it did pledge its signatories to an exploration with the USSR and its allies of "concrete issues" that might "best lend themselves to fruitful negotiation and an early resolution." The "specific practical measures for disarmament and arms control" mentioned in the Reykjavik document were reaffirmed as NATO objectives, although special emphasis was given to the need for close consultations among the allies before and during such talks with the Communists. Moreover, the Washington communiqué clearly signaled that the NATO states had no intention of allowing the Brezhnev Doctrine to remain unchallenged in future talks: "Bearing especially in mind the situation in Eastern Europe," the signatories stressed that lasting improvement in international relations "presupposes full respect for the principles of independence and territorial integrity of States, non-interference in their domestic affairs, the right of each people to shape its own future, and the obligation to refrain from the threat or use of force."13

Despite NATO's continued coolness, some movement toward the conference occurred in May, when the Finnish government endorsed the holding of a "well-prepared" conference on European security and offered to sound out other governments concerning preparations and to host preparatory meetings and the conference itself. But the Finnish plans were not entirely in accord with previous Warsaw Pact specifications, for the Helsinki note--indicating that all states "whose participation is necessary for achieving a solution to European security problems" should have the opportunity to take part in discussions--was sent to the United States and Canada as well as to all European governments.14

That this was not in keeping with the thrust of Communist plans was confirmed the following month, when the communiqué of the Moscow conference of Communist and Workers' parties stressed the need to guarantee to European peoples "their sovereign right to be masters of their continent without interference from the USA." While endorsing the Warsaw Pact's "concrete program" for creating a system of European security, the communiqué added a new wrinkle suggesting that the security conference itself was not perceived to be of as great utility as the agitation on its behalf: "The organization of a broad congress of European peoples, which would prepare for, and facilitate the holding of, a conference of states, is the most important of all these peace initiatives."15

Although both the Soviet government statement of April and the subsequent emphasis on a "people's congress" cast doubt on the seriousness of the Soviet desire for a conference of states, new momentum to the conference campaign was supplied by the October meeting in Prague of the Warsaw Pact foreign ministers. Following by a few days the establishment of the new Brandt-Scheel government in Bonn, those present at the Prague meeting welcomed the Finnish initiative and noted that the positive response to the conference proposal by the European states had created "practical possibilities" for a speedier convening of the all-European conference, which "might in their opinion be held in Helsinki in the first half of 1970." Toward this end, the Warsaw Pact states proposed that the following questions be included in the agenda of the conference:

1. The ensuring of European security and renunciation of the use of force or threat of its use in the mutual relations among states in Europe.
2. Expansion of trade, economic, scientific and technical relations on the principle of equal rights aimed at the development of political cooperation among European states.[16]

Although the question of participation remained unresolved and the agenda proposed was full of ambiguity (omitting, for example, any mention of the dissolution of the two alliances), the tone of the communiqué was nonpolemical and businesslike. Yet further doubt about the degree to which the Warsaw Pact states seriously sought a conference was raised only a few weeks later when a communiqué issued by a summit meeting of party and state leaders in Moscow devoted only fleeting attention to the conference initiative. The leaders added nothing new to the conference campaign, limiting themselves to an expression of "satisfaction" at the extensive international support their proposals were receiving. Rather, it appeared that the summit meeting, held on December 3 and 4, was more directly linked to the new possibilities for bilateral talks arising out of the new Bonn government's version of Ostpolitik. Citing as a positive feature the Federal Republic's signing of the nuclear nonproliferation treaty and noting the growth of tendencies in the direction of "realism," the participants nonetheless expressed the "unanimous view" that sober vigilance was required in the face of "unceasing dangerous manifestations" of revanchism and neo-Nazism in West Germany. This--along with the emphasis on the need for all states to "establish equal relations with the GDR, on the basis of international law," and to recognize the finality of existing borders--indicates that the summit conference was devoted primarily to consultations on the response to be taken to the initiatives of Ostpolitik.[17] Indeed, within the month the Soviet and Polish governments announced that they had undertaken negotiations with Bonn, and the GDR proposed a treaty between the two German states recognizing their separate existence under international law. These bilateral dealings and their ramifications were to preoccupy the states involved for months to come.

Simultaneous with the Moscow meeting was a gathering of NATO foreign ministers in Brussels which resulted in the allies' first specific response to the Warsaw Pact conference proposal. The Brussels declaration restated the principles on which "real and lasting" improvement of East-West relations was said to be based; although they were similar to the list contained in the Washington statement, the principles contained in the Brussels declaration more specifically challenged the validity of the Brezhnev Doctrine by specifying "non-intervention in the internal affairs of any state by any other state, whatever their political or social system." The allies recalled their proposals contained in the Reykjavik declaration, noted the lack of positive response, and called for further studies on mutual and balanced force reductions (MBFR) and other measures, including advance notification of military maneuvers and exchange of observers at such maneuvers.

In evaluating the prospects for future negotiations on security and cooperation, the Brussels declaration said that "great weight" would be attached to the East's responses to Bonn's proposals as well as to the problem of obstructed access to Berlin. Thus, progress in bilateral and multilateral discussions "which relate to fundamental problems of European security" would help to ensure the success of any eventual conference on European security. Moreover, such a conference would require "careful advance preparation and prospects of concrete results," and the United States and Canada would, of course, be participants. Finally, the NATO governments added that cultural exchanges and the prospects of "freer movement of people, ideas and information" between East and West, as well as cooperation in the field of human environment, should be included among the subjects of future negotiations.[18]

Secretary of State William Rogers enunciated the U.S. reaction, which underlined the cautious approach of the West toward the proposed conference, in a speech at the Brussels meeting. Warning against the danger of being lulled "into a false sense of détente" through an "unrealistic and premature exercise," Rogers termed the Warsaw Pact's agenda "nebulous and imprecise," not dealing with the fundamental questions.[19] Progress in bilateral negotiations on Germany, a demonstration of Soviet willingness to improve the Berlin situation, and a positive Warsaw Pact response to the MBFR proposals were listed by Rogers as three "tests of sincerity" for the East. Rogers also stressed that the United States did not intend to participate "in a conference which has the effect of ratifying or acquiescing in the Brezhnev Doctrine."

Although the United States was thus indicating its unwillingness to participate in an early conference, the Soviets pointed out in January, at an unusual press conference in the Soviet foreign ministry, that the issue of the possibility of American participation at a European security conference had been settled favorably, through an assurance from Ambassador Dobrynin, prior to the Brussels meeting. At the same time, L.M. Zamyatin indicated that the Soviets now reckoned that the conference could be held in the second half of 1970.[20]

After the NATO foreign ministers' meeting in Rome in May 1970, their Warsaw Pact counterparts assembled in Budapest the following month to issue their reactions to the NATO proposals. Rejecting the notion of "preliminary conditions" to the holding of the conference, and noting officially that the question of participation had been "clarified," the Budapest memorandum agreed to the inclusion of environmental questions within the second item of the agenda proposed at Prague, and added a new third item: "Establishment at the all-European conference of an organ for questions of security and cooperation in Europe." In the interests of time and of productive discussions, the "question of the reduction of foreign armed forces on the territory of European states" could be discussed in such an organ. This formulation was clearly nonresponsive to NATO's "test of sincerity" on two counts: (1) reduction of "foreign troops" was hardly the same MBFR, and the discussion of this issue--which the Warsaw Pact states originally linked to the European security conference itself--would <u>follow</u> the all-European conference. Indeed, the Budapest memorandum stated that its signers now favored "a number of all-European conferences." In their opinion, preparations for the initial one should be placed "on a practical basis in the near future," with such preparations including both bilateral and multilateral forms.[21]

Progress in bilateral negotiations was soon forthcoming with the initialing on August 11, 1970, of the Soviet-West German treaty on renunciation of force. The treaty between Bonn and Warsaw was signed later in the same year, but Chancellor Brandt made it clear that ratification of the two treaties would depend upon the satisfactory conclusion of four-power talks concerning Berlin. Both treaties were cited by the Soviets as contributions toward an early convocation of the all-European conference. Further progress toward that goal was achieved in October at the conclusion of French President Georges Pompidou's visit to Moscow, when he joined Brezhnev in supporting a "properly prepared European conference" to be held "outside the framework of bloc politics."[22]

However, the other NATO states--those participating in the integrated defense program--"reemphasized" in December the "importance they attach" to MBFR and "noted that the Warsaw Pact countries [had] not directly responded" to their call for exploratory talks on this question. Moreover, the French joined the other NATO states at Brussels in declaring that despite "some progress" on the German issue, "their hope had been that more substantial progress would have been recorded," especially in the talks on Berlin and in the realm of bilateral East-West German negotiations, "so that active consideration could have been given" to multilateral contacts dealing with a European security conference.[23]

Representatives of the Warsaw Pact, meeting in East Berlin the same month, also expressed "hope" that the Berlin talks would result in a "mutually acceptable agreement" meeting not only the interests of detente but the "lawful interests and sovereign rights of the GDR" as well. Nevertheless, the East Berlin statement, condemning the actions of "aggressive NATO circles," revanchist and militaristic forces in Bonn, and "opponents of relaxation of tension," stressed that "sufficient pre-conditions" for holding a security conference had already been created:

> There are no reasons whatever to delay the convocation
> of the conference or to advance any preliminary terms.[24]

Two months later, in a communiqué from Bucharest, the Warsaw Pact foreign ministers attacked those "opponents of détente" who suggest "different preconditions" aimed at complicating work toward convening a conference, and who place "serious obstacles" in its path by "linking" the organization of a conference with other problems. Still, the communiqué stated that "it seems necessary to adopt additional measures" in order to avoid these obstacles; in the opinion of the ministers, it was "both possible and necessary to tackle the concrete problems in a practical and constructive spirit" so that the organization of an ECSC could be accelerated. This language--together with the communiqué's stress of the importance of establishing "equal relations" between East Germany and other states and relations based on international law between East and West Germany, and its urging of the admission of both German states to the U.N.--suggests that the East Germans, in return for the emphasis on the "sovereign rights" of the GDR, may have been forced to give ground to their colleagues on the Berlin issues, thus creating the "possibility" of constructive progress on "concrete problems" holding up the conference.[25]

As the four-power talks on Berlin proceeded, the Soviets moved in the spring of 1971 toward the resolution of another issue delaying the convocation of the ECSC. The "program of peace" included in Brezhnev's speech to the twenty-fourth party congress included a reaffirmation of Soviet readiness to have a "simultaneous annulment" of the North Atlantic and Warsaw alliances "or, as a first step, dismantling of their military organizations," along with the following statement:

> We stand for the reduction of armed forces and arma-
> ments in areas where military confrontation is especially
> dangerous, above all in Central Europe.[26]

Six weeks later, noting that some NATO countries were displaying "appreciable interest" and even "nervousness" in connection with this proposal and inquiring whether foreign or national forces and nuclear or conventional arms were included, Brezhnev responded:

> Do not such curious people resemble a person who tries
> to judge the taste of a wine by its appearance alone,
> without touching it? If there is any vagueness, this can
> certainly be eliminated. All that is necessary is to
> muster the resolve to "taste" the proposals that interest
> you, which, translated into diplomatic language, means
> to enter into negotiations.[27]

Secretary Rogers, stating that "we want to know if it is sweet wine
or sour," instructed American Ambassador Jacob Beam to seek
clarification of Brezhnev's speech. Gromyko reportedly replied
that the Soviets were willing to discuss reductions of both "foreign"
and "national" troops.[28]

Despite these signs of progress, which led the NATO ministers
to announce their willingness to appoint representatives to conduct
further exploratory talks on arms reduction, the Lisbon ministerial
session of NATO in June continued to insist on a completed Berlin
agreement as a precondition for talks about the European security
conference itself. The Soviets, insisting that the Berlin talks could
proceed simultaneously with conference preparations, continued to
accuse NATO of seeking to foil plans for a conference.[29]

Soviet attacks increased after the four-power agreement on
the fundamentals of a Berlin settlement was reached in September,
for the NATO states still insisted that the agreement be finalized
through the successful conclusion of a bilateral East-West German
agreement on Berlin, prior to preparatory talks on the CSCE.
Secretary Rogers confirmed this stand in a speech on December 1,
although he stated more positively than before Washington's willingness to actually enter into preparatory talks after the conclusion of
a Berlin agreement.[30]

But the Berlin issue was not the only remaining obstacle to
preparations for the conference. The Warsaw Pact foreign ministers, meeting on the same day as Rogers' speech, issued a
communiqué expressing "satisfaction" with West Germany's
"businesslike and constructive position" in the Berlin talks and
appealing for the ECSC to be held in 1972, but failing altogether to
mention the issue of force reductions.[31] Now it was Washington's
turn to express official disappointment. President Nixon, under
pressure from the Congress on troop reductions in Europe, had
gone on record as stating that "we expect" NATO's representative,
Manlio Brosio, to be received in Moscow by December 3.[32]

The Soviet failure to conform to this expectation was a consequence of Moscow's refusal to deal with the force reduction issue
on a "bloc basis." According to Pravda commentator G.A.
Zhukov, Moscow preferred to start the European conference first
and then to carry on arms reductions talks in an agency to be
established by this broader forum.[33] This opposition to bloc

negotiations was reconfirmed in January 1972 by the Prague declaration of the Warsaw Pact PCC, which stated that the resolution of the question of force reductions "should not be the prerogative of the existing military-political alliances in Europe." However, the declaration did not insist that the CSCE or its agencies was the only possible forum; rather it suggested that "an appropriate agreement" could be reached on the "procedure for conducting talks on this question."[34]

At its foreign ministers' meeting in Bonn at the end of May, NATO acknowledged the death of the Brosio mission and sought to formulate an alternative position. Secretary Rogers, fresh from the Moscow summit, assured his colleagues that the Soviets were in earnest about force cuts and were ready to talk "without undue delay." The members participating in the integrated defense program thus proposed that multilateral explorations on MBFR "be undertaken as soon as practicable, either before or parallel with multilateral talks on a conference on security and cooperation in Europe." But, at French insistence, the final communiqué also called for consideration of "appropriate measures, including certain military measures aimed at strengthening confidence and increasing stability" by the ECSC itself.[35]

After the finalization of the Berlin accords in June, the Finnish government formally proposed that preliminary talks on the ECSC open on November 22. But the NATO states delayed a response until assurances were won from the Soviets that force reduction talks would begin at about the same time. Such an agreement was achieved during Henry Kissinger's visit to Moscow in September. According to the Moscow compromise, the negotiations, which would not technically be "bloc to bloc discussions," would not be formally linked to the ECSC but would be held "parallel" to them.[36] With the last "test of Soviet sincerity" fulfilled, the way was finally cleared--after a six-year process of negotiations--for preparatory talks on the ECSC to begin in Helsinki.

ANALYSIS OF THE ISSUES

Having surveyed the development of the conference proposal, we shall now focus on the question: What will the CSCE do? At the start of the preparatory meetings, neither side had indicated with much precision what the concrete tasks of the conference would be. Indeed on the Western side, especially in the U.S. government, the conference is still regarded largely as a propaganda exercise, unlikely to deal with real security issues at all. One State Department wag has likened the European security conference to the Holy Roman Empire: It is neither European, nor about security, nor a conference. Another official has suggested that the three items on the agenda might be labeled: The Meaningless (vague declarations on renunciation of force), The Inevitable (increased East-West trade), and The Inconceivable (Soviet troop withdrawals from Eastern Europe).[37]

Soviet commentators, on the other hand, are frequently rhapsodic about the conference's potential: It is said to mark the termination of the "drawn-out" era of consolidation of the results of World War II and to open the way toward a new era of "détente, elimination of the threat of war, consolidation of neighborly relations and peaceful coexistence, and extension of cooperation."[38] Thus, the main task of the conference itself is "to stabilize the situation in the European continent, to consolidate the climate of confidence . . . and put into operation an effective collective security system." Soviet observers have said it will not only secure the existing situation but at the same time undertake the building of a new future.[39]

But such sweeping claims are not entirely without qualification. Rather, Soviet commentators perceive the security conference not as the vehicle for ending the East West struggle but as a means of ratifying certain results and proceeding toward a new form of struggle. In the words of Izvestiia commentator A. Bovin, "no one expects miracles" from the conference, for ahead lies a "stubborn, lengthy struggle--essentially class in nature--a struggle against political conservatism, suspicion, mistrust and rigid thinking."[40] And in the view of Y. Rakhmaninov, "it goes without saying" that the establishment of a European security system would not eliminate the "basic contradiction" but "merely lend a peaceful form to the historical contest between socialism and capitalism."[41]

Thus, when the Soviets call for the "abolition of blocs" and "ending the division of Europe," they are giving these phrases a special meaning. In the words of Vikenti Matveyev, "the division of Europe into military-political groupings is one thing, and the existence of states with different social systems is another."[42] The Warsaw Pact and its military organization, which was from the beginning "purely defensive and open," can be disbanded simultaneously with NATO. But the division of Europe "on social and political lines" is a "natural result" of advancement along the road of social progress, and it is "historically irreversible." Such division can and will be overcome "in the long term," but only as the result of the transformation to socialism in the West; only then will there "be true grounds to speak of a united Europe, in the broadest and fullest sense of the word."[43]

Simply put, the Soviet stance is: What is mine is "historically irreversible" and what is yours is open to "inevitable" transformations. Political and social change is admissible, but only in the direction of socialism. It follows from this that the NATO

formulation, calling for "non-intervention in the internal affairs of
any state by any other state, whatever their political or social
system," is absolutely unacceptable to the Soviets. Matveyev says
it must be remembered that such a formulation is sponsored by a
bloc that has been carrying on an aggressive fight against socialism
in Europe: The 1968 events in Czechoslovakia were proof of NATO's
"feverish" intervention and its "clandestine acts for the purpose of
changing the social and political status quo in Central Europe." The
NATO formulations are not "accidental"; rather,

> they are aimed against the principle of fraternal
> solidarity of the socialist countries and their mutual
> assistance in safeguarding their common interests in
> the face of open and camouflaged attacks by the belli-
> cose forces of imperialist reaction.[44]

The Soviet message could not be clearer: Neither the legitimacy of
the social systems of East European states nor the validity of the
Brezhnev Doctrine--asserting the right of intervention by the
"socialist commonwealth" in the internal affairs of its member
states in order to forestall "imperialist subversion" and "counter-
revolution"--were open to question at the European conference.
The opposing sides are far apart on this issue, for NATO has made
it equally clear that it does not intend to acquiesce in any "ratification" of the social and political status quo that leaves the Brezhnev
Doctrine unchallenged. The persisting bitterness with which the
Soviets viewed the issue was underlined one month before the
opening of the preparatory talks, when a Pravda commentator
denounced the "impudent and defiant 'list of concessions'--now
public knowledge" that NATO reportedly intended to exact from the
Communists at the conference. "What is involved here," he wrote,
"is essentially an attempt to interfere in the internal affairs of the
socialist countries."[45]

The Western proposals to seek agreement at the conference
on the "freer movement of people, ideas and information" between
East and West have evoked a similar Soviet defensiveness, and
further assertions that Eastern Europe must remain closed to
Western attempts at political or cultural "bridge-building." A
recent article declared that the socialist countries had done much
in the realm of "genuine cultural and information exchange," by
which its author meant translating books, encouraging tourist
trade, and so forth.[46] The Western proposals, however, fell outside
the realm of "normal exchange." Rather, the imperialists sought
to open up the socialist frontiers for "exporting the vicious
products of bourgeois 'culture' and misinformation to the socialist
world." To allow the dissemination of such vile, slanderous, and
even treasonous material, aimed at inciting aggression and war,

would be in open violation of the sovereignty and laws of the socialist countries. Peaceful coexistence was unthinkable without strict observation of the principles of state sovereignty and noninterference in domestic affairs, but what the imperialists proposed was precisely such "arrant interference" in the socialist camp.[47]

The position of the Soviet Union, broadly shared by its Warsaw Pact allies, is that "peaceful coexistence" does not extend into the ideological realm. Indeed, as détentist tactics are pursued in the military-political realm, the struggle against alien ideas will necessarily intensify. As Mikhail Suslov put it in June 1972:

> The struggle in the field of ideology, the field in which there is no, and cannot be any, peaceful coexistence between socialism and capitalism, has sharpened.[48]

When the present campaign for a European conference commenced in 1966, the issues of achieving recognition of the legitimacy of the existing borders in Europe and of obtaining commitments, especially from the German "revanchists," on renunciation of the use of force in the settlement of disputes, were especially prominent in Warsaw Pact statements. But the intervening years have produced a series of bilateral treaties calling for recognition of existing borders and renunciation of force between Bonn and Moscow and Warsaw, as well as a bilateral pact between East and West Germany moving toward the normalization of their relations. In the authoritative view of N.N. Inozemtsov, these treaties "signify recognition of the fixity and inviolability" of borders and the "renunciation of all territorial claims whatsoever," thus striking "a very powerful blow at the revanchist elements in the FRG."[49] In the view of N.I. Lebedev, the effect of these treaties, together with the four-power agreement on Berlin, is that Bonn and the three Western powers "have essentially recognized the state borders and the sovereign rights of the GDR," although some parties still nurture "futile hopes of doing away with the GDR under the pretext of 're-uniting' Germany."[50]

Despite the recognized progress achieved through bilateral diplomacy, the Warsaw Pact states did not consider the matter of Germany wholly settled. The Prague declaration of January 1972 noted that "full normalization" of Bonn's relations with the socialist countries and the "deepening" of the European détente required that the Federal Republic establish relations with the GDR "in accordance with the norms of international law" (that is, de jure recognition) and, as the Czechs were demanding, recognize the invalidity of the Munich agreements "from the beginning" (thus abandoning German claims in Czechoslovakia).

Nor did the signatories slacken their efforts for the multilateral conference or alter their position on the need for an all-European agreement on these matters. For one thing, of course, the Warsaw Pact states hope to transform East Germany's "equal" participation in the conference and in its work of constructing the future "collective security" system into a general recognition of its "sovereign" rights. Warsaw Pact statements since the GDR's "fraternal" concessions on Berlin have emphasized the necessity of the recognition, and admission into the U.N., of the GDR. Brezhnev said in March 1972 there "cannot be any effective normalization of the European situation that does not take fully into account the status of the GDR as an independent, sovereign socialist country."[51] Moreover, the Warsaw Pact states apparently see some value in achieving in a multilateral framework what Bonn has already agreed to in the bilateral treaties; they argue that the treaties supplement but do not replace the multilateral agreement. Thus the Prague declaration called for the "creation of a series of commitments ruling out any use of force or the threat of its use among the states in Europe, a system giving all countries a guarantee that they will be safeguarded against acts of aggression."[52]

Concrete details about the Soviet conception of the future security system are sparse. The Prague declaration did not add much in the way of specificity when it spelled out the following seven basic principles of European security and relations among states: (1) inviolability of borders; (2) renunciation of the use of force; (3) peaceful coexistence among states belonging to different social systems; (4) good-neighborly relations on the basis of the principles of independence and national sovereignty, equality, noninterference in internal affairs, and mutual advantage, all of which will facilitate the overcoming of "military-political" divisions on the continent; (5) mutually advantageous economic, scientific-technical, cultural, environmental, and tourist ties among states; (6) general and complete disarmament, along with implementation of measures for limiting and ending the arms race; and (7) support for the United Nations.

In the view of one Soviet scholar, these principles will be embodied in a regional security system through a whole series of agreements and the establishment of mechanisms for implementing them. The first agreement "or treaty, or declaration setting out definite international legal norms in the form of binding rules" for coexistence will include collective commitments renouncing the use or threat of force and agreeing to settle disputes by peaceful means. Raising the possibility of "a formula for mutual assistance and also for sanctions against potential violators," S.I. Beglov concluded that for the time being the question was unsettled. However, he cited the provision of the U.N. Charter for collective measures to eliminate threats to the peace, as well as the provisions of the draft treaty on collective security proposed by the Soviets in 1954, as precedents favoring the inclusion of such features. However, he added,

One thing is clear, and it is that a regional all-European
agreement must be equipped with an effective mechanism
for settling disputes by peaceful means.

The agreement might include the procedure of consultations between
signatories in the event of a threatening situation; this "may in fact
be the shortest way of taking concerted action" in the event of a
threat to the peace.

Beglov also proposed that there should be set up a mechanism
which, "as arms and armed forces are cut back, would take over the
function of safeguarding the continent" from the threat of accidental
war or "deliberate fabrication of an armed incident." A permanent
agency would assume some of these functions, while ancillary agencies might be required for others.

Earlier, Soviet commentary had described this permanent
mechanism as a link facilitating the convocation of subsequent conferences, examining problems at the conference's request, and
coordinating various measures "aimed at consolidating peace and
cooperation." Comprised of government representatives of the states
concerned, it would be empowered to adopt decisions based on unanimous agreement, and "could eventually provide the basis for a
regional European organization."[53] The formula proposed by Beglov
in this context was as follows:

The greater the extent of general security and détente
achieved, the broader the range of practical questions
to be tackled by agencies authorized by the governments
to express their collective will.[54]

Membership in the future security system, in the view of
another analyst, would be open to all states, big and small, those
currently aligned and those presently neutral The new system not
only would be an alternative to the current "military-political
groupings" but also would obviate the need for "any other combinations, alignments and groupings" in the region.[55]

In this context, it is necessary to note Moscow's insistence
that the future Europe be "European in the full and proper sense of
the word,"[56] that is, that it be "a European, not an Atlantic,
Europe."[57] The Soviets do not admit the legitimacy of American
interests on the European continent; in the view of Pravda, the
position of the United States, which "invaded" Europe in the postwar
period, "is alien to the fundamental interests of the European
states."[58] As an editorial in the Soviet journal International Affairs
put it, Washington has "good grounds for apprehension [about]
losing the means for applying pressure on its West European
allies."[59]

Not only does the proposed Soviet system reject the "Atlantic"
notion of European security but it also excludes the alleged scheme

to transform the European Community into "NATO's economic basis" and to intensify "its military-political role."[60] Articles in the Soviet press have warned against alleged attempts to freeze progress toward the all-European conference until integration of the European Economic Community (EEC) has taken final shape, as well as against the assertions of some EEC spokesmen that it should be recognized as acting on behalf of its members in certain matters.[61] Such schemes, in the Soviet view, constitute an inadmissible perpetuation of the bloc approach.

Of course, it is not only the political-military "designs" but also the economic practices of the EEC that concern the Communists. Recent pronouncements of the Warsaw Pact states have emphasized the need for the "elimination of discrimination, inequality and artificial barriers" in interstate relations. Such statements have been accompanied by articles in the press identifying the Common Market as the major participant in such activity and warning that its "discriminatory character is bound to be intensified" by its coming enlargement.[62]

Turning to the question of the formal agenda for the ECSC, it is appropriate to recall the evolution of the Warsaw Pact's position on this question. Both the Bucharest declaration of March 1966 and the Karlovy Vary statement of the following year included in the context of their proposals for a conference issues of disarmament and arms limitations or reduction. But such topics were absent from the Budapest appeal of 1969 and the Prague communiqué of the same year, which finally formulated a two-point agenda. The Budapest memorandum of the following summer incorporated the Western suggestions of environmental and cultural issues (although, as we have seen, the latter point was understood quite differently), and added the third item proposing a permanent conference mechanism, which could take up the consideration of force reductions.

In the Soviet view, the Warsaw Pact agenda has taken account of Western proposals. The socialist countries' approach to the agenda matter is described as stemming from a twofold concern: (1) that the initial conference take up problems "whose successful discussion and solution would leave a deep imprint in the minds" of the European peoples, thus consolidating détente, creating confidence, and paving the way for examination of "more involved" issues; (2) in line with the "main objective, which is to achieve concrete results," care should be taken to avoid placing on the agenda questions that either "cannot be solved" at an all-European conference or that lie "outside its competence." Included in this latter area were "the situation in West Berlin" (judged to be the responsibility of the four powers) and the situation in the Mediterranean.[63] Thus, the agenda should not be overloaded with questions "too complicated" or "not yet ripe" for solution. Such questions could be left to future conferences, or to the permanent mechanism.[64]

Questions of disarmament and force reductions have been included by the Soviets in recent years as among those which would "overload" the agenda of the CSCE.[65] After the Prague agenda was drawn up, the Soviets argued that the Geneva disarmament talks were the proper site for discussion of such questions.[66] Later they seized on the notion of the "permanent mechanism" of the ECSC as the proper vehicle. Moreover, discussion of military issues should follow the general affirmation at the first conference of the suggested "basic principles of security and cooperation"; such an agreement would serve as a "necessary precondition" for discussions of force reductions.[67]

Of course, the NATO states were hardly insisting on a discussion of force reductions at the proposed security conference; rather, the NATO approach from 1968 has been to seek bloc to bloc negotiations on MBFR with the Warsaw Pact. But the Soviets, interested precisely in combating the bloc approach, at least for the West, had insisted (until the September 1972 Kissinger trip to Moscow) on the broader forum. The arrangements worked out in Moscow call for the United States, Britain, Canada, West Germany, and the Benelux countries to invite the USSR, Czechoslovakia, Hungary, and Poland to preliminary talks in January 1973 on Central European arms reduction, and for Bonn to issue a separate invitation to the GDR. The Soviets agreed in addition that the flank countries of NATO--those lying outside the Central European area and having no troops stationed there--could participate in the talks on a rotating basis (one country at a time from each flank). But the agreement on holding these separate and parallel discussions does not preclude the possibility that other states (France and Romania are likely candidates) may insist on discussion of force reductions at the ECSC itself.

Nor does the agreement on parallel talks on force reductions obviate the great complexity of the issues involved. The initial American decision to seek talks on mutual and balanced force reductions was taken as a result of growing pressures within the Congress for unilateral U.S. troop reductions in Europe. After two years of study of the issues, American officials reportedly concluded not only that the question was more complex than SALT I but that, no matter how the problem was war-gamed, it "always works out against NATO." According to one State Department official, large amounts of time and money were spent "to reach the common sense conclusion that stability in Europe can best be maintained by doing nothing."[68] Involved in the negotiations will be such complex issues as figuring the equivalency of NATO and Warsaw Pact units of different size, organization, mission, and distance from home base; discussing whether to include navies and air forces as well as ground forces; deciding whether to disband or merely redeploy the affected units; working out arrangements for verification; and apportioning the cuts among the member states of the two alliances.[69]

The issue of force reductions raises many of the same complex problems for the Soviets as well, although the war-gamers in Moscow are apparently less practiced than their American counterparts. NATO officials were reported to have been puzzled at the absence of evidence that Soviet officials were giving serious study to the complex issues involved.[70]

The Soviets have made it clear that they are not well disposed toward the idea of "balanced" reductions, that is, imposing higher reduction coefficients on the Warsaw Pact states because of the "so-called geographic factor." A Soviet analyst has argued that the vast distances of the USSR and its need to maintain substantial forces on far-distant eastern and southern borders makes the USSR no more proximate geographically to Central Europe than is the United States. In his view, it is impossible to consider the ratio of forces in Central Europe apart from the global ratio, or to consider the ratio of conventional forces apart from the strategic ratio. Although this analyst believes that "objective coefficients" could probably be worked out in the course of negotiations, he argues that "the principle of parity reduction is the only possible principle" in accord with Brezhnev's stated condition of "no detriment to the states taking part in such a reduction."[71]

OBJECTIVES OF THE CONFERENCE

Having assessed both the historical unfolding of the Warsaw Pact's conference proposal and the issues associated with it, we shall now turn to an assessment of the objectives--those the USSR and its allies have sought to achieve in the campaign for a conference, and those they hope to fulfill as a result of the conference itself. Since the Soviets exercise the predominant weight in the Warsaw Pact, and since their superpower status endows them with certain global responsibilities and purposes over and above those in the European theater, we will begin with a brief look at these larger issues.

By the end of the 1960s the gap in the strategic capabilities of the United States and USSR, which the current leaders had inherited from Khrushchev, had narrowed substantially. With an increasing global capability, both strategic and conventional, with the United States mired in Vietnam and undergoing a domestic debate from which a continuation of American globalism was unlikely to emerge, with the Western alliance in seeming disarray, and with the Chinese undergoing a severe internal crisis that put a virtual halt to their own foreign activity, the Soviet leaders entered the decade with a greater confidence than their earlier limited capabilities and low-profile policy had allowed.

As the authoritative (and pseudonymous?) observer A. Sovetev wrote in 1972, international relations were at a turning point. The global structure was radically altered and the balance had changed in favor of socialism, although further improvements would come only through struggle. Recent events had shown that the imperialist alliance was no longer the moving force; the initiative had been "completely and forever grasped from the hands" of the imperialists.[72]

In the view of Georgi Arbatov, another observer, the Moscow summit--resulting from "years of persistent and patient effort" by Soviet diplomacy and "resolute rebuffs" to imperialism--had led to a recognition of "objective realities" on the part of the United States.[73] The summit documents proclaimed a shift on the part of the United States away from "cold war manifestations [of] positions of strength" and striving for superiority toward positions of peaceful coexistence. Political rivalry, "principled idological struggle," and economic-scientific-technical competition would of course continue, but in Arbatov's opinion, this struggle would take the form of negotiation and peaceful competition rather than crisis and war. Arbatov, citing the possibility of "situations in which all sides are winners," thus pictured the international arena in mid-1972 as one in which the United States and Soviet Union, in a state of acknowledged parity, would dominate the strategic sphere, existing in a limited adversary relationship in which agreements promising mutual advantage were possible.[74]

Indeed, the conclusion at the summit of the first-stage SALT agreements, setting limits on further quantitative developments of strategic weapons, did appear to signify a choice by the Soviet leadership not to attempt, for the present, the achievement of strategic superiority vis-à-vis the United States. Justifying the decision, V. Viktorov stressed that the arms agreements--based as they are on the principle of "equal security"--do not harm either party but rather "help each to strengthen its national security in full conformity with its national interests." Moreover, by preventing the pouring of resources into deployment of additional defensive or offensive missiles, the agreements are "bound to benefit the peaceful economic development of both states."[75]

In positing that the Soviets have chosen, after some debate, to accept a position of strategic parity for the immediate future, we must make two additional points quite explicit. First, this choice by no means relegates the Soviets to foreign policy quietism or to a position as a "satisfied power." Although their policy could hardly be described as "revolutionary global expansionism," the Soviets will yet be capable of engaging in "fishing expeditions" on the Eurasian continent and in the Middle East. In the course of such efforts they may fully expect their new-found status of nuclear equality--in a world in which "imperialism" is perceived as a declining force--to bring political advantages in crisis-bargaining situations; a world of parity is not necessarily a world in which risk-taking is forsworn.

To put it another way, the Soviets expect that their rivalry with the United States will continue, even though the Moscow summit may have established some important ground rules for the conduct of the rivalry. Buttressing this expectation are quite concrete needs of the Soviet leadership stemming from its ideological commitments and from the continuing necessity to utilize the struggle with the imperialist enemy as a justification for its policy choices, and its very rule, at home. As evidence of this tendency we might recall Suslov's post-summit exhortation, cited above, against relaxation of the struggle against "bourgeois ideology."

The second point concerning this new relationship involves the nature of a limited adversary situation in a world that is no longer strictly bipolar. It is quite correct to point out, as Arbatov did, that the absence of a zero-sum situation may allow both parties to make gains (or suffer losses). Yet the Soviets are also quite aware that the burgeoning presence of a third major party to the relationship complicates the question of relative gains still further. Thus, the Soviet leaders were by no means unmindful of China as they took steps to increase the USSR's military capabilities: Soviet forces on the Sino-Soviet border trebled between 1968 and 1971. And although relations between the two sides have improved since the low point of 1969, both Soviet and Chinese decision-makers still consider the other side a major security threat. That neither side judges it likely that there will be any imminent return to "fraternal" relations is evidenced by the Soviet acceptance of the Chinese formulation to the effect that their relations should be based on the principle of "peaceful coexistence--a term reserved in Leninist parlance for the relations of states of different social systems.

The Chinese, of course, have not been inactive of late in the conduct of their own dipolmacy, and that fact has brought the dispute more squarely into the international arena and made life even more complicated for the Soviet leaders. An article in International Affairs, assessing the new Sino-American relationship, suggested that China's anti-Soviet policy was compensation to the Western states for their aid in developing China's economy and "turning China into a state capable of realizing its territorial claims on the Soviet Union, and of bringing under its influence the neighboring states in East and Southeast Asia." Mao, who had covertly sought to improve relations with the United States since 1964-65, was seen as the "Trojan horse of imperialism in the international revolutionary movement, this forming the essence of the intensified diplomatic flirtation" between Washington and Peking.[76]

Because their interests are more directly and concretely in conflict, it is the Soviet and Chinese leaders who must most fear being "odd man out" as they perceive the new triangular relationship--Washington, Peking, and Moscow--as a struggle on two fronts.

If, to borrow Michel Tatu's framework, China perceives the USSR as
adversary number one and undertakes to reduce its antagonism to
the United States in order to more effectively struggle against the
Soviets, then this in turn alarms the Soviets and causes them also to
appeal to the Americans.[77] So long as the Chinese and Americans
were simply not in contact, the Soviets occupied the advantageous
position. Far from having to offer concessions to the West in return
for cooperation, they were able to use the Chinese "threat" as a
lever with which to attempt to exact concessions from the West.
Thus, in a campaign for a security conference and recognition of the
status quo in Europe, the Soviets have taken no pains to deny the
impression that such a quieting of the Western front was in the common interests of both East and West in Europe, since it would allow
the Soviets to defend the alleged interests of Western civilization
more effectively against the "Chinese menace." In fact, as Tatu has
suggested, the reverse was actually the case: The Soviets had
consciously moved at the end of 1969 to ease tensions on the Sino-
Soviet border in order to pursue a more active policy in the West.
But the continued sorry state of their own relations with Peking,
together with their perception that the Americans and Chinese are
teaming up in anti-Soviet maneuvers, may well put the Soviets in a
more disadvantageous position in this triangular relationship.

But while the new international relationships may thus have
complicated the situation, apparently they have not altered the Soviet
purpose. Having won recognition as the military and negotiating
equal of the United States, the Soviets will continue to seek containment of China, the protection of their East European "commonwealth," and the expansion of their own influence into Western
Europe. And it is to further these latter basic purposes that the
campaign for a security conference enters the picture. Indeed, to
some curious extent, the conference campaign is perceived as part
of the struggle against China. Articles have cited alleged Chinese
plans to spur on the integration of capitalist Europe, to give "NATO
chiefs" cause to think they have a free hand to step up tension, to
make common cause with the West German "revanchists," and to
try to persuade West European leaders to unite in a common stand
against the USSR.[78] That the Soviet claims of Chinese efforts to
torpedo the security conference are not pure fantasy was confirmed
by Chiao Kuan-hua's speech to the U.N. General Assembly, in which
he dubbed the "European insecurity conference . . . only another
name for the division of spheres of influence between the two superpowers."[79]

To return to the level of Soviet objectives, we may first cite
certain propaganda benefits that have already been derived from the
long, noisy campaign on behalf of the conference initiative. For
through the struggle for the ECSC, the Soviets have communicated,
to audiences throughout Europe, both the image of the socialist

states as the major initiators and proponents of peace and stability on the continent, and the image of assorted "NATO chieftains," "European capitalist circles," and "revanchists" (most recently meaning primarily the West German opposition parties) as the opponents of these same laudable goals. In the wake of the Czechoslovakian invasion, the images of the Soviet Union and Warsaw Pact were in great need of refurbishing in both Eastern and Western Europe, and it was precisely in that period that the appeal to the European "masses" and emphasis on an all-European "popular congress" was heaviest. The European Communist parties and international "front" organizations (especially the World Peace Council) have been intimately involved in the effort to build a popular base for the security conference campaign. These efforts, which culminated in the holding of an "assembly of representatives of public opinion for European security and cooperation" in Brussels in June 1972, were likened by one Soviet writer to the "Stockholm appeal" of the early 1950s.[80]

The Soviets not only wished to improve their image following the Czech crisis but they also sought to ensure that such upheavals within Eastern Europe would not recur. Thus, especially in the post-1968 phase, the security conference has been viewed in large part as a defensive tactic. The insistence on multilateral recognition of the "inviolability" of the borders of the GDR, Poland, and other East European states stems not so much from a fear of Western military attack (although the renunciation of force agreement seeks to make that even less likely) as from a desire to gain legitimization and Western acceptance of the finality of East European Communist systems.

That this will have a stabilizing effect on the domestic level in these states is understandable only in light of the Soviet assumption (probably quite genuinely held) that the peoples, and occasionally the leaders, of these states engage in "counterrevolutionary" activity only with the encouragement and support of outside forces. In this context, it is worth recalling the vehemence of Soviet objections to Western "bridge-building" policies and to the "subversive" designs felt to be contained in NATO's proposal for the "freer movement of people, ideas and information."

In light of the increased emphasis on defense of the "socialist commonwealth" since the Czech crisis and enunciation of the Brezhnev Doctrine, it is logical to question Soviet seriousness in proposing that the Warsaw Pact, or its military organization, be dissolved simultaneously with NATO. Since the Warsaw Pact provides much of the rationale for the stationing of Soviet troops in Eastern Europe, and since it is the primary vehicle for "coordination of its members' foreign and defense policies, could the Soviets afford to dissolve it? In fact, the answer to this question is probably not an unequivocal "no." For it must be remembered that the

Soviets (unlike the United States) have erected a complete network of bilateral treaties among all the active members of the Warsaw Pact, and these treaties--together with the Council for Mutual Economic Assistance (CMEA) and whatever other "coordinating" mechanisms the Soviets might wish to devise--could probably serve to ensure continued Soviet domination of the area. If the benefits to be gained from the abolition of NATO are perceived to be great enough (and they probably are), the Soviets might well be prepared to "sacrifice" the Warsaw Pact. (It might also be noted that in an emergency the Warsaw Pact could probably be reconstituted much more rapidly than NATO.)

Related to the "status quo" purposes of the CSCE proposal is the goal of acquiring international recognition of the "sovereign equality" of the GDR, ratifying the finality of Germany's division. The very fact of the GDR's full participation in the CSCE may be perceived as progress toward the achievement of this long-sought status for the East Berlin regime.

The initial Warsaw Pact unwillingness to acknowledge the possibility of U.S. participation in the CSCE, and the continued reluctance to recognize that the Americans have any legitimate role in Europe, is an indication that the Warsaw Pact campaign has sought to bring about a lessening of American political and military presence in Europe. The Soviet emphasis on the need for reduction of "foreign" (non-European) troops, and the insistence on a "European" rather than "Atlantic" Europe are further signs of the Soviet desire to remove this "alien" presence and exclude the United States from any role in the future European security system, leaving the Soviets as the dominant power on the continent. The dissolution of NATO, if achieved by a CSCE, would of course re-move much of the basis for a continuing American military presence in Europe.

Short of achieving this admittedly "maximalist" goal, the Soviets have been and will continue to be sensitive to opportunities inherent both in the conference campaign, and in the staging of CSCE itself, for accentuating the divisions among the NATO member-states and capitalizing on the unwillingness of some NATO countries to support continued heavy defense expenditures. The "unreliability" of security under the American umbrella will con-tinue to be a favorite Soviet theme. The French have been a particular target of such Soviet diplomacy, both inside and outside the conference campaign framework. The Soviet press has held up the alleged "benefits" to France of nonmembership in the inte-grated defense program of NATO as a model for other NATO members. It will indeed be difficult for NATO to present a united front at the CSCE, especially with the popular pressures building in the West in favor of steady progress toward détente, and the Soviets are not likely to repeat past mistakes and make this process of coordination any easier.

As indicated above, the Soviets are no more enthusiastic about a European Community bloc than they are about NATO, and thus the conference campaign and CSCE itself are also aimed at reversing the trend toward expansion and tighter integration of the Common Market. The attempt to gain recognition for "nondiscrimination" as one of the principles of European cooperation has been an integral part of the Warsaw Pact effort to increase East-West trade. As an inducement to equality of treatment, Soviet Premier Kosygin has held out a long list of projects--from creation of a unified power system to pooling research on heart disease and cancer--on which "broad cooperation" might be possible as a result of the CSCE.[81]

This is not to suggest that such developments as increased trade and scientific exchange, or even the signing of renunciation of force agreements, are not valued by the Warsaw Pact states for their own intrinsic value. The point is that most of these can be more appropriately obtained through existing bilateral and multilateral channels. Nor is it to suggest that the Soviets are not seriously interested in increasing security in Europe. But the fact remains that the most central and controversial issues affecting European security have been ruled out by the Soviets as (quite appropriately) incompatible with the conference setting. Thus the conclusion must be reached that the objectives mentioned above are those most central in the Soviet drive for a conference on European security.

To concentrate, as we have so far, on Soviet objectives for the CSCE should not cause us to overlook the possibility that the other states of the Warsaw Pact may not share the Soviet purposes in equal measure, or may have independent and/or conflicting objectives of their own that they hope to realize through the campaign for a conference. Of course to some extent the various statements and communiqués of the alliance are themselves the products of compromise and the coordination of national objectives. In light of Soviet objections to bloc diplomacy by the West, it is of interest that the Soviet press has put stress on the virtues of the close policy coordination the Warsaw Pact mechanisms promote.[82]

As Peter Bender points out, the East Europeans generally fear the West more for its political-ideological threat than as a result of any real perception of military threat.[83] Although for the GDR, Poland, and Czechoslovakia the war danger from the West-- and particularly from the FRG--is more real because of questions of territory or national reunification, the bilateral treaties with Bonn certainly lessened the perceived threat, and multilateral recognition of the inviolability of their frontiers at an ECSC might further lessen their fears on this count. Even the members of the southern tier of states, more removed from the Federal Republic and lacking any territorial conflicts with the West, must to some extent share their northern neighbors' hopes for settlement of the frontier issues, if only because they are obligated to participate in any conflict resulting from these disputes. Moreover, for all the East European regimes (if not for their peoples), ratification of the legitimacy and inviolability not only of boundaries but more especially of their social systems--to the extent that it can be achieved at a CSCE--could serve to enhance their stability.

But this latter point is itself debatable since, as Bender observes, "the absence of danger can itself become a danger" to the extent that increasing détente and East-West cooperation raise the risks of "ideological infection." Such softening up can be perceived as dangerous not just by ideological dogmatists but by East European politicians who feel it raises the specter of Soviet intervention. But even for those leaders who have their internal political situations well enough under control, and who are able to interact with the West without fear of "infection," the security threat from the East still arises, if Moscow perceives such interaction as defiant behavior. This is the current dilemma in Romania, where the internal stability of Ceausescu's regime is in part the product of his independence of action and assertion of Romanian national interests in an anti-Soviet direction.

Nevertheless, despite the dangers of détente, East European leaders may see in the CSCE--and in its potential achievement of agreements on renunciation of force or principles of nonintervention, and especially force reductions or regional disarmament--the possibility of weakening the effect of the Brezhnev Doctrine and thus lessening Moscow's domination while retaining its protection. Bender, for one, is skeptical that such possibilities will be realized for, as he puts it, "if it endangers the Soviet claim to dominance in the other Warsaw Pact countries, the Soviet Union will not agree to it."[84]

Judging from the behavior of the East European states during the years of the conference campaign, the Romanians are the most likely practitioners of an independent line at the ECSC. Bucharest has continued to employ the formulations of the Bucharest declaration with respect to both the withdrawal of all troops to their national territories and the dissolution of the Warsaw Pact, even when these formulations were out of favor with the other Warsaw Pact states. As Ceausescu declared in July 1967 in a speech to the Romanian Grand National Assembly:

> There is no doubt that the withdrawal of the non-European troops from Europe, the withdrawal of all troops from the territory of other states to within their national frontiers, the dismantling of foreign military bases and the abolition of military blocs would have a particularly positive effect.[85]

Also worth noting is the Romanian emphasis, evident in the same speech, upon the need for middle-sized and small countries to act with "militancy and vigor in defense of their legitimate interests and rights." And in fact Romania has served notice, from the very beginning of the preparatory talks for the CSCE, that it intends to exercise a militant and vigorous role at the conference. Declaring that they would move to place the issue of mutual force reductions on the conference agenda, and insisting on open meetings, the Romanians warned against adoption of a bloc attitude at the conference. In an incident that may yet prove typical, the Romanian delegate insisted that all should participate equally, "regardless of whether or not they belong to an alliance." To this the Soviet delegate is said to have replied that the phrase would have no legal value, for there was no reason to say that membership in an alliance limits a country's independence. "For example," he said, "the Soviet Union belongs to an alliance, but its independence is not limited."[86]

Official American skepticism that either concrete achievements in the realm of security or even genuine manifestations, rather than just the appearance of détente, can emerge from a conference of 34 nations is probably justified. While the Soviets expect that Warsaw Pact states will demonstrate a higher degree of discipline than will their NATO counterparts, Moscow still runs the risk that the conference will expose and accentuate fissiparous tendencies within the "socialist commonwealth," especially now that the Bonn "revanchists" are no longer credible bogeymen. Whether the opportunities perceived by either side will indeed prove more lasting than were the risks they ran is yet to be determined. At any rate, the conference on security and cooperation in Europe, seven years in the making, will likely have a continuing impact throughout the rest of the decade.

NOTES

1. For an account of this period, see Thomas W. Wolfe, Soviet Power in Europe, 1945-1970 (Baltimore: The Johns Hopkins Press, 1970).

2. "Declaration on Strengthening Peace and Security in Europe," Bucharest, July 1966. The full text is in Pravda, July 8, 1966, and excerpts are found in Michael Palmer, The Prospects for a European Security Conference, European Series No. 18 (London: Chatham House, June 1971), pp. 77 82.

3. "Statement Issued by the Conference of European Communist and Workers' Parties," Karlovy Vary, Czechoslovakia, April 24-26, 1967. The text is available in Timothy W. Stanley and Darnell M.

Whitt, Détente Diplomacy: United States and European Security in the 1970's (New York: Dunellen--University Press of Cambridge, Mass., 1970), pp. 137-44.

4. Pravda, November 4, 1967, pp. 2-6.

5. Sovetskaia Belorussia, February 15, 1968, pp. 1-3.

6. Wolfe, op. cit., p. 332.

7. "Reykjavik Declaration on Mutual Force Reductions," June 24-25, 1968. The text is found in Stanley and Whitt, op. cit., pp. 119-20.

8. Wolfe, op. cit., pp. 497-98.

9. A. Ross Johnson, The Warsaw Pact's Campaign for "European Security," a report prepared for U.S. Air Force Project Rand (Santa Monica, Calif.: Rand Corporation, 1970), p. 21.

10. The Budapest Appeal is reproduced in Stanley and Whitt, op. cit., pp. 149-52.

11. "Aaiavleniia Pravitel'stva SSSR," Pravda, April 10, 1969, p. 1. Examples of similar Soviet attacks on NATO appearing at the same time are Sergo Mikoyan, "NATO, the Soviet Union, and European Security," Orbis, 13 (Spring 1969), pp. 59-67; N. Polyanov, "Europe: Peace Zone or Hotbed of War?" International Affairs (Moscow), no. 5 (1969), pp. 5-8.

12. Quoted in Stanley and Whitt, op. cit., p. 86.

13. Communiqué of the North Atlantic Council, Washington, D.C., April 1969. Extracts may be found in Palmer, op. cit., pp. 87-88.

14. Aide-memoire of the Finnish government, Helsinki, May 5, 1969, in Palmer, op. cit., pp. 88-89.

15. Documents Adopted by the International Conference of Communist and Workers' Parties, Moscow, June 5-17, 1969 (Moscow: Novosti, 1969), p. 56.

16. The Prague communiqué is contained in Stanley and Whitt, op. cit., pp. 153-54.

17. Ibid., pp. 155-56.

18. Final communiqué and declaration of the NATO foreign ministers meeting, Brussels, December 4-5, 1969, in Stanley and Whitt, op. cit., pp. 121-26.

19. Quoted in Stanley and Whitt, op. cit., p. 35.

20. "Press Conference at the Soviet Foreign Ministry," New Times, no. 4 (1969), pp. 16-17.

21. Quoted in Palmer, op. cit., pp. 97-98.

22. Franco-Soviet declaration, Moscow, October 1970, in Palmer, op. cit., p. 101.

23. Communiqué of the North Atlantic Council, Brussels, December 1970, in Palmer, op. cit., pp. 102-5.

24. "Statement of Questions of Strengthening Security and Developing Peaceful Cooperation in Europe," East Berlin, December 1970, in Palmer, op. cit., pp. 105-6.

25. The communiqué is excerpted in Palmer, op. cit., pp. 106-7. For an analysis, see R. Waring Hedrick, "European Detente and the Bucharest Meeting of the Warsaw Pact," Radio Liberty Dispatch, February 24, 1971.

26. New Times, no. 15 (1971), p. 34.

27. Pravda, May 15, 1971, p. 2.

28. Bernard Gwertzman, "U.S. Tells Soviet it Favors Parley," New York Times, May 18, 1971, pp. 1, 7.

29. N. Polyanov, "European Realities and Prospects," International Affairs, no. 9 (1971), pp. 3-10, 18.

30. Bernard Gwertzman, " Rogers Ties Security Talks to Berlin Pact," New York Times, December 2, 1971, p. 16.

31. Pravda, December 3, 1971.

32. Bernard Gwertzman, "Soviet Disappoints U.S. on Troop Cuts," New York Times, December 4, 1971.

33. G. A. Zhukov in International Affairs, no. 11 (1971), pp. 85-86.

34. "Deklaratsiia o Mire, Bezopasnosti i Sotrudnichestva v Evrope," Pravda, January 27, 1972, p. 1.

35. Drew Middleton, "NATO Set to Talk with East on Arms," New York Times, June 1, 1972, p. 6.

36. Tad Szulc, "Soviet Said to Agree on European Talks," New York Times, September 21, 1972, pp. 1, 21.

37. "After Cold War" (editorial), New York Times, November 21, 1972. See also Secretary Rogers' speech of December 1969, cited in Stanley and Whitt, op. cit., p. 35.

38. N. Novikov, "New Phase in the Struggle for European Security," International Affairs, no. 6 (1972), pp. 3-7.

39. I. Aseyev, "Europe 1972: Time of Hopes," International Affairs, no. 10 (1972), pp. 18-20.

40. A. Bovin, "Mezhdunarodnyi Obzor," Izvestiia, July 4, 1972, p. 3.

41. Y. Rakhmaninov, "Towards Lasting Peace in Europe," International Affairs, no. 3 (1972), pp. 4-6.

42. Vikenti Matveyev, "European Security and NATO," International Affairs, nos. 2-3 (1970), pp. 91-92.

43. E. Novoseltsev, "Europe Twenty-Five Years Later," International Affairs, no. 7 (1970), pp. 21-22 (emphasis in original).

44. Matveyev, op. cit., pp. 91-92.

45. Vladimir Yermakov, in Pravda, October 26, 1972, p. 5.

46. V. Sobakin, "Peaceful Coexistence and Ideological Struggle," New Times, no. 45 (1972), pp. 18-19.

47. Ibid.

48. Izvestiia, June 21, 1972, p. 3. For abundant documentation of the views of other Soviet and East European officials on this issue, see the three dispatches by Jean Riollot entitled, "The Free Flow of People, Ideas and Information and European Security," Radio Liberty Dispatch, July 10, October 17, and November 2, 1972.

49. N. N. Inozemtsov, "Printsipial'nost' i Deistvennost' Sovetskoi Vneshnei Politiki," Pravda, June 9, 1972, pp. 4-5.

50. N. I. Lebedev, "The Maturing of the Objective Prerequisites for an All-European Conference," International Affairs, no. 5 (1972), pp. 67-69.

51. Pravda, March 21, 1972, p. 3.

52. "Deklaratsiia o Mire . . . ," op. cit., p. 1.

53. "New Stage in Preparations for All-European Conference," International Affairs, no. 9 (1970), p. 4.

54. S. I. Beglov, "European Security System: Content and Ways of Ensuring It," International Affairs, no. 11 (1971), pp. 66-67.

55. Novoseltsev, op. cit., pp. 21-22.

56. Aseyev, op. cit., p. 19.

57. Bovin, op. cit., p. 3.

58. Boris Dmitriyev, "From a Europe of Conflicts to a Europe of Lasting Peace," Pravda, May 11, 1971, p. 4, in Current Digest of the Soviet Press (hereafter CDSP) 23, no. 19, p. 6.

59. "The Urgent Task of Consolidating Peace in Europe," International Affairs, no. 3 (1971), p. 25.

60. V. B. Knyazhinsky, "Variants of the Bloc Approach to the Conference," International Affairs, no. 5 (1972), pp. 90-91.

61. V. Kravtsov, "Time for Decision," New Times, no. 36 (1972), p. 5; Sh. Sanakoyev, "Lasting Peace, Effective Security for Europe," International Affairs, no. 8 (1972), pp. 9-13. For a statement of the European Community's view, see Michael Palmer, "The European Community and a Security Conference," The World Today 28 (July 1972), pp. 296-303.

62. "Deklaratsiia o Mire . . . ," op. cit., p. 1; Yu. N. Kapelinsky, "Forum," International Affairs, no. 11 (1971), pp. 71-72.

63. V. Shakhov, "European Security System: Soviet Effort," International Affairs, no. 5 (1971), p. 34.

64. V. Shatrov and N. Yuryev, "Key Problem Today," International Affairs, no. 4 (1970), pp. 59-62.

65. "For a Military Détente in Europe," International Affairs, no. 1 (1972), p. 66.

66. Johnson, op. cit., p. 35.

67. Yu. Kostko, "The 'Balance of Terror,' or Ensuring General Security," Mirovaia Ekonomika i Mezhdunarodnye Otnosheniia, no. 6 (1972), pp. 87-89, in CDSP 24, no. 40, pp. 8-9.

68. Bernard Gwertzman, "U.S. Aides Now Foresee Peril in Mutual Troop Cut for Europe," New York Times, January 31, 1972.

69. Stanley and Whitt, op. cit., p. 62. The authors advance a very rudimentary four-stage plan as a proposal for MBFR negotiations.

70. Drew Middleton, "Soviet Bloc Held Lagging on Talks," New York Times, August 1, 1971, p. 9.

71. Kostko, op. cit.

72. A. Sovetov, "The Leninist Policy of Peace and the Future of Mankind," International Affairs, no. 7 (1972), pp. 3-10.

73. Y. Nikolaev, "USSR-USA," International Affairs, no. 8 (1972), pp. 3-8.

74. Georgi Arbatov, "The Strength in a Policy of Realism," Izvestiia, June 22, 1972, pp. 3-4, in CDSP, 24, no. 25, pp. 4-6.

75. V. Viktorov, "Agreements of Historic Importance," International Affairs, no. 8 (1972), pp. 14-20.

76. D. Vostokov (pseud.?), "The Foreign Policy of the People's Republic of China Since the 9th Congress of the CPC," International Affairs, no. 1 (1972), pp. 23-25.

77. Michel Tatu, "The Great Power Triangle: Washinton-Moscow-Peking," Atlantic Review, no. 3 (December 1970).

78. O. Ivanov, "With Whom, Against Whom: A Look at Certain Modifications of Peking Policy," New Times, no. 35 (1972), pp. 4-5; Y. Usov, "Peking West European Policy," New Times, no. 43 (1972), pp. 18-19.

79. Peking Review, no. 41 (1972), p. 7.

80. Y. A. Lomko, International Affairs, no. 11 (1971), p. 87.

81. April 6, 1971, speech to the twenty-fourth party congress, in CDSP 23, no. 16, p. 10.

82. See, for example, Sh. Sanakoyev, "Socialist Countries' Struggle for European Security," International Affairs, no. 4 (1972), pp. 3-10; A. Bovin, "The Coordination of Foreign Policy," Izvestiia, August 17, 1972, pp. 2, 4, in CDSP 24, No. 33, pp. 14-15.

83. Peter Bender, East Europe in Search of Security, trans. by S. Z. Young (Baltimore: Johns Hopkins Press for the International Institute for Strategic Studies, 1972). I am indebted to Bender's analysis for several points made here.

84. Ibid., p. 140.

85. Nicolae Ceausescu, Report to the Session of the Grand National Assembly of the Socialist Republic of Romania (Bucharest: Agerpres, July 24-26, 1967), pp. LIV-LV.

86. "Conference Planning May Require Unanimity," Associated Press dispatch in The Tennessean (Nashville), November 25, 1972.

PART

III

ECONOMIC ISSUES

5

ECONOMIC CHANGE
AND EAST EUROPEAN
REGIONAL INTEGRATION
William A. Welsh

Relations in the next decades between the nations of Eastern and Western Europe will be significantly affected by the parallel processes of integration within each of the two areas. Thus an understanding of the issues surrounding regional integration in Eastern Europe is important to an assessment of likely future developments in East-West relations.

Viable definitions must always precede meaningful discussion, and perhaps especially when the topic is the "integration" of national political units. There has been considerable debate over the appropriate way to define integration, and this is not the place to rehash these definitional issues. However, it is worth explicating a definition of regional integration in order to provide some points of reference. Integration is seen here as involving three developments:

1. Some delegation of authority from national units to international decision-making units, accompanied by the actual implementation of collective choice-taking through the latter,

2. Increasing levels of interaction among the national units, not only in absolute terms but also relative to the levels of interactions between the constituent national units and national units not part of the integrative mechanism,

3. At least non-negative attitudes on the parts of political leaders in the involved national units toward authoritative international decision-making and toward levels of economic interaction.

Two additional aspects of the concept of integration bear elaboration. First, there is no reason to believe that integration

---

Several people have contributed a great deal of time and effort to the preparation and analysis of the several data collections on which this chapter is based. I am especially grateful to Chia-hsing Lu for programming assistance and to Barbara A. Gilbert and David Pfotenhauer for assistance in data preparation.

necessarily involves a willingness on the part of elite or mass to give up or diminish a sense of national identity or national loyalty. Indeed, it seems reasonable to assume, as does Leon Lindberg, that support for integration may come largely because of the perception that national objectives can most effectively be pursued through new international mechanisms.[1] Second, it cannot be assumed that the perceived or real impact of integration on the constituent units is invariant for all levels of integration. That is, some integration might be considered desirable by elites in all the involved units, but the attractiveness of integration might decrease differentially for different sets of leaders with increasing levels of integration. Thus although integration may be viewed as a process in which there are increasing levels of interactions among the constituent units, there is undoubtedly a series of threshold levels beyond which the integrative process would become counterproductive for the member units. One of the important tasks facing students of international integration is the identification of these differential threshold levels.

There is a good deal of conventional wisdom in currency on the subject of Eastern European integration. It is undergirded by a series of assumptions, some of them problematic, about the extent to which Soviet interests and Eastern European interests are similar. Broadly, these premises seem to stipulate that the Soviet Union is rather more interested in Eastern European integration than are most (or perhaps all) of its Eastern European partners, several of which are usually pictured as decidedly skeptical about the likely results of increasing integration. These conventional notions may well turn out to be correct, but they are worth examining closely.

A useful strategy in trying to broaden our perspectives on the subject is to develop and refine new data collections and modes of analysis that might be useful in studying phenomena relevant to regional integration. This chapter tries to take some initial, and very tentative, steps in this direction by attempting to tie together information on three categories of events and behaviors: (1) systemic change, especially economic change, (2) leadership perceptions of how these systemic changes ought to be handled, and (3) the perceived implications of these methods of handling change for the future of integration in Eastern Europe. The research strategy is first to identify patterns of economic change since 1956 in two Eastern European countries, Bulgaria and Hungary, selected because of the apparently substantial differences in the structure and functioning of their economies. Second, the major dimensions of difference between the two countries in patterns of economic change will be linked to leadership perceptions of how economic reform can contribute to the solution of economic and social problems. Third, leadership statements on these specific elements of economic reform--that is, the elements of reform directly related to the dimensions of economic change that most clearly distinguish between the two countries--will be related to leadership statements about the integrative/counterintegrative implications of economic change and reform.

PATTERNS OF CHANGE

Although economists have given careful attention to the analysis of change for some time, other social scientists have continued to treat the concept of change with a remarkable lack of rigor. Political scientists have begun to devote some attention to the conceptual and operational problems involved in the longitudinal comparison of observations, but it remains the case that a substantial majority of the comments made about social change are highly descriptive and impressionistic, and show little understanding of what economists have long since learned, i.e., that the study of change introduces several perplexing methodological issues not encountered when one is dealing with cross-sectional data. Because the temporal dimension is so important in causal explanation, the study of how social units and patterns change over time is especially important.

A variety of statistical techniques is available to serve as systematic bases for explanatory statements about the process of change. Our strategy here will be to use system-level indicators of economic and social change in an effort to map patterns of change. The data generally are time series of interval or ratio-scale measures. Since our interest is in identifying patterns of change and their salient dimensions, we will employ techniques designed to identify and give form to such patterns, rather than using more powerful techniques, such as multiple regression, that are designed to account for variation or unit changes in a specified dependent variable.

Conventionally, factor analysis is used to identify clusters of relationships among subsets of variables. Factor analysis is used in this analysis, but it has a distinct limitation when used in studying change. When applied to time series data, factor analysis simply treats the different observations for a given variable (that is, observations for sequential years) as a set of discrete observations rather than as components of a temporal sequence. That is, the transitional dimension, or change dimension, is inadequately handled in factor analysis.[2] Consequently, the present analysis is extended through the use of a form of pattern analysis, which takes into consideration both the vertical distance and the transitional distance between curves, that is, both the difference in magnitude between corresponding entries (here, standard scores) on two curves, and the extent to which two curves are moving in the same direction between each sequential pair of observations (from one year to the next).[3]

The results of the factor analyses (principal axes, varimax rotation) of 36 variables for the period 1956-69 are summarized in Tables 5.1 and 5.2. (The loadings, especially for Hungary, are "inflated,"[4] both because the solution is overdetermined and because of the very high intercorrelations among certain subsets of variables; these factor solutions are therefore of suggestive use only.) There are only a few surprises, but they do merit attention. In Table 5.1, nearly all import commodities are clustered with the variable of imports from non-Communist countries. Remembering that the "cases in this analysis are time units, we can explain this finding by inferring that the most significant increases in imports of these important materials occurred in years in which imports from non-Communist countries were increasing. (Factor 2 does not imply that Bulgaria imports most of its raw materials, for example, from non-Communist systems.) Still, the suggested linkage is important in that it implies that imports from outside the bloc have played a

TABLE 5.1

Factor Analysis of Socioeconomic Data on Bulgaria

F_1		F_2		F_3	
Popdens	-0.2391	Impnocm	0.2369	Econactv	0.3089
Indprod	-0.2478	Foodimp	0.2829	Earnings	-0.3112
Agrprod	-0.2445	Rawimp	0.2869	Cemaexp%	-0.4363
Retail	-0.2498	Metlimp	0.2888	Expussr%	-0.4553
Prices	-0.2486	Chemimp	0.2875	Esu%Cema	-0.2485
Grosexp	-0.2430	Bldimp	0.2936	Rwfdimp	0.2281
Expussr	-0.2357	Machimp	0.2898	11.3%	
Grosimp	-0.2416	Conimp	0.2439		
Cemaimp	-0.2420	22.2%			
Impussr	-0.2433				
47.5%					

F_4		F_5		F_6	
Livcost	-0.6022	Popincr	0.4006	Urban	-0.6764
Arrest	-0.3189	Econbir	0.4819	Popplbir	0.6287
Revolutn	-0.3067	Anmlimp	0.4593	3.1%	
Cemaexp	0.2700	Cemaimp%	0.4014		
Expnocm	0.3399	6.7%			
Expnocm%	0.3692				
9.3%					

TABLE 5.2

Factor Analysis of Socioeconomic Data on Hungary

F_1		F_2		F_3	
Popdens	0.9258	Anmlimp	0.5729	Econactv	0.7017
Urban	0.9296	Foodimp	0.9611	Arrest	0.8185
Agrprod	0.8853	Rwfdimp	0.6818	17.8%	
Retail	0.8079	Rawimp	0.9907		
Prices	0.4618	Metlimp	0.8846		
Revolutn	0.6649	Chemimp	0.9045		
Econbir	0.7932	Bldimp	0.9486		
Grosexp	0.9566	Machimp	0.8930		
Expussr	0.9602	Conimp	0.8976		
Cemaexp	0.9627	19.3%			
Expnocm	0.9251				
Cemaexp%	0.8352				
Expussr%	0.8838				
Esu%Cema	0.9180				
36.1%					

F_4		F_5		F_6	
Indprod	0.8427	Popincr	0.8537	Cemaimp%	0.9470
Livcost	0.8439	Expnocm%	0.5377	Popplbir	0.9645
Grosimp	0.8277	9.2%		6.8%	
Cemaimp	0.8156				
Impussr	0.7912				
Impnocm	0.8241				
10.7%					

relatively important part in Bulgaria's increases in imports of critical items since 1956.

Significantly, Table 5.2 reveals no such linkage between these import commodities and the value of imports from non-Communist systems. In the Hungarian case, imports from non-Communist systems loads highly on the same factor (factor 4) with imports from the USSR and the Council for Mutual Economic Assistance (CMEA), that is, as part of a general factor of increasing import volume. This factor also includes industrial production for Hungary. In the Bulgarian case, industrial production is also linked to higher imports, as suggested in factor 1.

As mentioned above, factor analysis has its limitations when applied to time series data. For our purposes, a form of pattern analysis presented by Zaninovich is more useful. We shall use this technique in two ways. First, the statistical concepts on which pattern analysis is based, mean vertical distance (MVD) and mean transitional distance (MTD), will be used to draw univariate comparisons between curves of 21 time series for the two countries. Second, the statistical concepts will be used to derive a pattern of relationships among 16 economic indicators for each country. These patterns can be defined in terms of peripheral variables, focal variables, and "constellations" of variables.[5] These salient elements of each pattern, in turn, permit us to compare the patterns of economic change for the two countries, and to determine which dimensions of economic change are most salient for generating explanations of differences in attitudes toward economic reform between Bulgarian and Hungarian leaders. For our purposes, peripheral variables are of greatest interest since they focus our attention on aspects of economic change that are out of pattern with other indicators and therefore might be expected to receive greater attention in the course of planning reforms.

Table 5.3 summarizes the "functional distances" (MVD + MTD) between 21 pairs of curves for the two countries. The FDs for at least six of these time series seem substantial. Two of these have to do with characteristics of the political leadership: proportion of party central committee members who have been arrested for political activity (arrest) and proportion who took part in revolutionary activity before 1944 (revolutn). Two of the curves with high FDs are economic indicators having to do with the consumer welfare sector, average hourly earnings in manufacturing (earnings), and the retail price index (prices). The other two curves with high FDs are exports to non-Communist systems as percentage of total exports (expnocm%) and an indicator of the annual magnitude of fluctuations in volume of imports (% chimp). (The last may be viewed as an indicator of the "stability" of overall import activity.) We can focus distinctly on the findings summarized in Table 5.3 by glancing at the standard-score curves for the six variables with high FDs. These curves are presented in Figure 5.1. Briefly, they reveal the following inter-country differences:

1. The Bulgarian leadership, although including a higher proportion of persons with backgrounds of political arrest and revolutionary activity, has seen these proportions decline more consistently over time than is the case in Hungary.

2. Prices have risen more consistently in Bulgaria than in Hungary. By contrast, average earnings have fluctuated much more in Bulgaria than in Hungary.

3. Very generally speaking, exports to non-Communist countries have been relatively decreasing for Bulgaria and increasing for Hungary.

TABLE 5.3

Functional Distances Between Curves for Bulgaria and Hungary (all years, 1956-69)

	MVD	MTD	FD*
Revolutn	1.7500	1.1375	2.8875
%Chimp	.9855	.5825	1.5680
Expnocm%	.8821	.6769	1.5590
Prices	.9600	.5913	1.5513
Earnings	.9592	.4313	1.3905
Arrest	.6767	.6650	1.3417
Expussr%	.6507	.5023	1.1530
Cemaexp%	.5900	.4846	1.0746
Conimp$	.4520	.2203	.6723
Popincr	.5346	.1075	.6421
Impnocm$	.3800	.1932	.5732
Machimp$	.2936	.2270	.5206
Urban	.3400	.1700	.5100
Agrprod	.3233	.1723	.4956
Rawimp$	.2436	.1495	.3931
Metlimp$	.2490	.1225	.3715
Indprod	.2200	.1036	.3236
Cemaimp$	.1929	.0961	.2890
Grosimp$	.1779	.1046	.2825
Grosexp$	.1407	.0715	.2122
Popdens	.0228	.0046	.0274

Notes: As M. George Zaninovich uses the term, "functional distance applies to distances among multivariate data. However, the mathematical basis for calculating these univariate distances is the same, and it does not seem a great misuse of the term to apply it to both univariate and multivariate cases. See Zaninovich, "Pattern Analysis of Variables Within the International System: The Sino-Soviet Example," Journal of Conflict Resolution 6, no. 3 (September 1962), pp. 253-68.

All curves in this table have been converted to standard scores (Z-scores).

It is difficult to determine how "significant" and "non-significant" FDs might be distinguished. For purposes of reference, if we treat the FDs themselves as if they were Z-scores, $Z \geq 1.65$ with $p \leq 0.10$, and $Z \geq 1.29$ with $p \leq 0.20$.

FIGURE 5.1

Curves with Highest Functional
Distances for Bulgaria
and Hungary, 1956-69

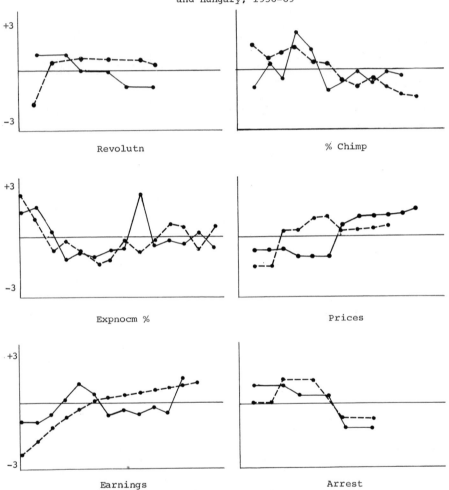

Key: Solid line = Bulgaria; broken line = Hungary.
Note: Curves are represented in standard score units.

These differences, summarized in Table 5.3 and Figure 5.1, may be considered relevant to an explanation of inter-country differences in leadership attitudes toward economic reform, and will be examined in that context.

The analysis of multivariate patterns within each country can be summarized with reference to the principal peripheral variables for each pattern:

Bulgaria	Hungary
Fluctuations in total imports	Fluctuations in total imports
Exports to non-Communist as percent of total	Exports to non-Communist as percent of total
Exports to CMEA as percent of total	
Exports to USSR as percent of total	
Earnings	

Two indicators for both countries seem to show changes broadly inconsistent with other economic changes in the 1956-69 period: fluctuation in total volume of exports and the proportion of total exports going to non-Communist countries. Three other indicators were peripheral for Bulgaria but not for Hungary: earnings, exports to CMEA countries, and exports to the Soviet Union. On the basis of these findings, we would expect both Bulgarian and Hungarian statements to give substantial attention to the stability of imports, as well as to relations with non-Communist countries, in the course of discussing new directions for the economy. If the premise from which this analysis proceeds is correct, and economic dimensions that are out of pattern receive particular emphasis, we would also be led to predict that Bulgarian statements would give more attention to wages and to the flow of exports to other CMEA countries, including the USSR.

CONTENT ANALYSIS

The expectations concerning differences in Bulgarian and Hungarian concerns about economic change and attitudes toward economic reform can be examined by looking at results from a computer content analysis of a considerable body of material published in these two countries during 1968. These materials were selected through a multistage sampling procedure from a universe of approximately 600 documents. The final sample consists of about 30,000 lines of text taken from 147 articles. These documents contain policy statements on the antecedents, nature, and implications of economic reform.[6]

For our purposes here, this content analysis material can help answer several questions suggested by our analysis of economic change.

1. Do the Bulgarians evidence more concern with wages, prices, and citizen standard of living, as would be implied by the out-of-pattern character of these elements of economic change in Bulgaria?

2. Are the Bulgarians more concerned than the Hungarians with their economic relations with the USSR, and with other CMEA countries?

3. Is there any difference between the Bulgarian and Hungarian statements with regard to their references to economic relationships with non-Communist countries--an element that was peripheral to the change process for both countries?

A total of 11 of the 68 categories into which the content of these documents was coded seem directly relevant to answering these questions. With regard to the first question, Table 5.4 summarizes what would have to be called an ambiguous set of findings. Seven themes treated in the content analysis were considered relevant to the general topic area of wages, prices, and standard of living. There are significant differences between the means for the

TABLE 5.4

Mean References to Selected Themes:
Wages, Prices, and Standard of Living

Theme Category	Bulgaria	Hungary	p*
Remuneration	7.864	5.163	nonsignificant
Income and consumption	11.986	9.742	nonsignificant
Consumer demand	1.724	3.482	0.05
Consumer goods costs	1.840	3.053	nonsignificant
Prices	0.930	3.613	0.01
Price controls	3.959	11.659	0.001
Standard of living	53.611	33.301	0.0005

Note: This table shows so-called "catcon" indexes, which correct for the differential overall salience of the documents analyzed. Catcon indexes indicate the references to a particular category as a proportion of the references in a document to the more general concept of which the category is a part.

*These are significance levels for t, 1-tailed test, assessed on the basis of estimated degrees of freedom; that is, it could not be assumed that the two populations had equal standard deviations.

two countries for four of these seven themes. But in three cases the difference is the opposite of that predicted, that is, the Hungarian materials emphasize these themes more than do the Bulgarian. Two of the three nonsignificant differences are in the predicted direction, reflecting greater Bulgarian concern, but the differences are of insubstantial magnitude.

However, the most significant difference between the two sets of documents concerns general statements about the standard of living. Here the relative and absolute Bulgarian emphasis is striking. It appears that the Hungarian statements place relatively great emphasis on specific components of this topic whereas the Bulgarian references are more general. This interpretation is consistent with a broader analysis done of Bulgarian and Hungarian statements concerning the antecedents and likely results of economic reform: The Hungarian documents tend to be concrete, the Bulgarian, general and vague, especially when talking about the consumer sector.

The second and third issues concern perceived problems in foreign economic relations. Bulgarian relations with CMEA were determined to have a high "functional distance" from the pattern of economic change in the 1956-69 period; consequently a greater Bulgarian concern with this problem area was predicted. Relations with non-Communist countries were out of pattern for both Hungary and Bulgaria; thus equally high concerns for this issue area were predicted.

Table 5.5 provides at least a partial basis for answering these questions. The findings generally do not support our expectations. Bulgarian references to CMEA relations (in the context of defining a theme labeled "foreign economic problems") were slightly more frequent than Hungarian references, but the difference is small. More striking is the much greater Hungarian concern with relations with non-Communist countries. Indeed, the Bulgarian documents exhibited slightly greater attention to non-Communist economic relations than to relations with CMEA countries.

TABLE 5.5

Mean References to Relations with CMEA and with Non-Communist Countries as Proportion of Total References to Problems in Foreign Economic Relations

Topic	Bulgaria	Hungary	p
Relations with USSR, CMEA	7.56	6.50	non-significant
Relations with non-Communist countries	9.28	23.52	0.0005

The substantial lack of support for several of our expectations or predictions, based on the pattern analysis, raises the question of the appropriateness of the basic premise underlying those predictions: That is, the pattern analysis identified the functional distances among economic variables. Thus the underlying dimension of coherence, or cohesiveness, of the pattern has to do with the logic of interdependence of economic factors. The prediction that out-of-pattern issue areas would receive special attention in discussions of economic reform is based on the assumption that such variables exhibit high functional distance for economic reasons. If the explanations for the out-of-pattern character of these variables are non-economic--perhaps political--this would explain the unexpected findings reported above.

One way to check the plausibility of this explanation is to examine the correlation between the incidence of references to foreign economic relations and the wage-price-living standard indicators, on the one hand, and references to political and ideological themes, on the other. Table 5.6 reports these correlations.

There are considerable crossnational differences in these sets of correlations, many of them not directly relevant for present purposes. Perhaps the most important finding in point suggested by Table 5.6 is that there are very few significant positive correlations linking either living standard references or foreign economic

TABLE 5.6

Correlations for Living Standard and Foreign Economic Relations with Political and Ideological Themes

| | Political Themes | | Ideological Themes | |
	Bulgaria	Hungary	Bulgaria	Hungary
Living Standard				
Remuneration	-0.18	0.002	-0.36	-0.13
Income and consumption	-0.16	-0.007	0.03	0.22
Consumer demand	-0.25	-0.13	-0.02	-0.22
Consumer goods costs	-0.04	-0.14	-0.17	-0.22
Prices	-0.28	-0.23	0.23	-0.24
Price controls	-0.07	-0.22	-0.04	-0.21
Standard of living	-0.21	0.09	-0.07	0.25
Foreign Economic Relations	0.12	-0.18	-0.02	-0.13

Note: Table shows Pearson product-moment correlations; underscored coefficients are significant, $p \leq 0.05$ (1-tailed test).

relations to political or ideological themes. Indeed, there is not a single significant positive correlation with political themes, although there are six significant negative correlations, three for each country. There is a significant positive correlation in the Bulgarian case between ideological references and references to prices (not price controls, it should be noted) as an economic problem area. The Hungarian documents show significant positive correlations with ideological themes for references to income and consumption patterns and general references to standard of living. Overall, however, the impression left by Table 5.6 is that the relationship between living standard references and foreign economic relations references, on the one hand, and political and ideological themes, on the other, tends to be inverse rather than direct. Thus, if there are political or ideological themes that help explain high functional distances in patterns of economic change, we can say at a minimum that these themes were conspicuously absent over a large number of discussions of related issues of economic reform.

PREDICTING INTEGRATIVE AND COUNTER-INTEGRATIVE ORIENTATIONS

The final step in our effort to link economic change, attitudes toward economic reform, and attitudes toward regional integration involves seeking the best statistical predictors of integrative/counterintegrative orientations from among other reference themes in the documents being content analyzed. I have elsewhere reported in detail the results of multiple regression analysis and some tentative causal modeling used to identify predictors of attitudes toward integration.[7] The results of direct relevance to this chapter are summarized in Table 5.7.

Two multiple regressions were run. In the first, nine category-level indicators of the "economic problems" concept were the independent variables. These categories included standard of living and foreign economic relations references. In the second regression, the independent variables were three political/ideological categories. The dependent variables were references coded as integrative or counterintegrative.

It might be noted that, as could be expected, Hungarian documents were significantly more counterintegrative than were Bulgarian documents. Worth noting, however, is the fact that the Bulgarian documents were not more integrative than counterintegrative (see Table 5.8).

Of the seven living-standard content themes linked with out-of-pattern elements of economic change, only one is a useful predictor of integrative perspectives. This is the variable of references to income and consumption patterns, which is a respectable predictor

TABLE 5.7

Useful Predictors of Integrative and Counterintegrative Perspectives

	Bulgaria			Hungary		
	Multiple R^2	F-value	$p \leq$	Multiple R^2	F-value	$p \leq$
INTEGRATIVE PERSPECTIVES						
Economic problems	0.2193	1.7789	non-significant	0.1082	0.9422	non-significant
Perform		5.796				
Inccnsmp		4.251				
Political/ ideological	0.7707	70.5754	0.01	0.5856	35.7985	0.01
Ideology		190.073			105.222	
COUNTER-INTEGRATIVE PERSPECTIVES						
Economic problems	0.8703	42.4859	0.001	0.8158	34.4581	0.001
Forgnecn		366.268			261.988	
Inccnsmp		3.793			3.395	
Perform		7.230				
Political/ ideological	0.0405	0.8866	non-significant	0.0261	0.6776	non-significant

TABLE 5.8

Means for Integrative/Counterintegrative References

	Bulgaria	Hungary	$p \leq$
Integrative	42.253	26.596	0.005
Counterintegrative	42.823	55.993	0.02

of both integrative and counterintegrative orientations for the
Bulgarian documents; thus it does not help us distinguish between
the two perspectives.

It is highly significant that references to the need to solve
problems in the foreign economic relations sectors represented a
powerful predictor of counterintegrative references for both countries. This finding reinforces an impression from a casual reading
of the material being analyzed: that both sets of documents were
stressing the importance of broadening and deepening ties with
countries outside COMECON.

Perhaps equally significant is the finding that references to
ideological themes strongly predict integrative perspectives. This
is the case for both Hungarian and Bulgarian documents. This
finding reinforces our earlier impression that there are political/
ideological explanations for out-of-pattern elements of economic
change, perhaps especially for Bulgaria. We need to be wary of
oversimplified conclusion-drawing, especially when dealing with a
substantial body of data and relatively complex analytical techniques.
But the research reported here lends at least some credence to the
notion that the principal pressures toward the increasing integration
of Bulgaria and Hungary into the network of CMEA relations may be
political in nature, whereas the major pulls in a counterintegrative
direction are substantially economic.

NOTES

1. See Leon Lindberg, The Political Dynamics of European
Economic Integration (Stanford, Calif.: Stanford University Press,
1963), p. 6.

2. This terminology is used by M. George Zaninovich, "Pat-
tern Analysis of Variables Within the International System: The
Sino-Soviet Example," Journal of Conflict Resolution 6, no. 3
(September 1962), pp. 253-68.

3. Ibid. These two distances are summed into what Zaninovich
calls a "similarity index" of "functional distance."

4. See R. J. Rummel, Applied Factor Analysis (Evanston, Ill.:
Northwestern University Press, 1970), pp. 260-61, 317-18.

5. Zaninovich, op. cit., p. 262.

6. For a more complete discussion of the sampling and coding
of these data, see William A. Welsh, "Political Implications of
Economic Reform in Eastern Europe: Some Preliminary Findings
from a Computer Content Analysis of Bulgarian and Hungarian
Documents," paper presented at meetings of the American Association for the Advancement of Slavic Studies, Dallas, March 15-18,

1972. The paper is available as Report No. 46 from the Laboratory for Political Research, University of Iowa, Iowa City, Iowa.

7. William A. Welsh, "Content Analysis and the Study of Integration in Eastern Europe," paper presented at conference on trends in integration of the East European Community, The University of South Carolina, Columbia, S.C., April 27-29, 1972.

6

GLOBAL RESOURCES
AND THE
FUTURE OF EUROPE
Dennis C. Pirages

Recognition that population and resources are variables closely related to social and political processes has been implicit in much political science literature. It is impossible to study "who gets what, when, and how" without also looking at what there is to distribute and the limits that population growth places on distributional possibilities.[1] But explicit attention to the relationship between demographic and environmental variables and patterns of political behavior has been lacking. This has undoubtedly been due in part to the dominant position that political scientists educated in industrial societies have enjoyed in the discipline. Beginning with Seymour Martin Lipset there is an extensive literature that equates industrialization with political stability and some form of democracy.[2] "Developing" countries could look forward to a golden future once they made the transition to industrialism. There were exceptions to the rule, but for the most part, according to the prevailing view, industrial man could expect to live in urban areas, be fairly well educated, vote regularly, be ruled by democratic and stable government, and look forward to a progressively better future.[3]

More recently, however, geopolitical and ecological concerns have become much more explicit in political research.[4] This is in part due to the tremendous public consciousness of the importance of population growth and various forms of environmental deterioration.[5] It is also in part due to reports showing that unless human behavior is drastically modified in the near future, the human race might well consume its way to a much less desirable level of living.[6] The economic, social, and political future of advanced industrial democracies no longer seems as bright and optimistic as it did during the 1950s and early 1960s, and research concerns have shifted accordingly.[7]

Adequate supplies of energy materials and other mineral resources are essential for the maintenance of industrial civilization.

Once upon a time major powers were known by the size of the armies they could put into battle. But today large populations, in the absence of an adequate resource base, represent a serious political liability.

Throughout the history of civilization, mankind has utilized ever larger quantities of energy and resources. In traditional societies humans sustained themselves by extracting needed energy from the living environment by hunting and gathering. Almost all energy needed came directly from living plants and animals. In such societies the environment put very visible and direct constraints on the numbers of humans that could be sustained. When there was no game to be hunted or plant food to be gathered, people perished. There was little stored energy available to ward off the ultimate human form of entropy, death, in such subsistence situations.

Industrial man is not so directly dependent upon fluctuations in his immediate environment. The discovery of fossil fuels, energy from living organisms stored in the earth long ago by geologic processes, has enabled industrial man to support numbers far greater than those that could be sustained by dependence on simple ecosystems. This energy subsidy permits much more complicated organizations of human beings to flourish in very intricate social systems. These complex systems contain enough stored energy to buffer their members from immediate scarcities. In this sense industrial society represents an evolutionary step forward, a mechanism for permitting survival of great numbers under conditions of stress.[8]

On the other hand a price has been paid for this immediate security. In order to keep entropy from chipping away at complex social organizations, a constant throughput of energy materials and mineral resources is required. Modern societies now run on petroleum, coal, and natural gas. New dwellings require steel, aluminum, copper, and plastics. As long as there is a readily available supply of these building blocks of industrial civilization, a highly complex social organization can sustain itself. The risk is that industrial man may move too far too fast, well beyond natural systems that adequately supplied him under simpler conditions. If the lengthy lines of supply, characteristic of most industrial societies, are ever disrupted or if the supply of stored energy begins to run out, industrial societies will quickly collapse and only a few persons will survive the transition to more primitive conditions.

Throughout human history homo sapiens has exacted an ever greater toll from the natural environment. Humans feed on "negative entropy" found in organic and highly structured inorganic matter.[9] Demand for negative entropy has grown very rapidly through human history. The most obvious reason is that the planet has witnessed a population explosion of no small magnitude. Today there are nearly four billion people on earth; in 1930 there were only two billion. Only 35 years from now demographers estimate that eight

billion people will occupy the same space.[10] At the present two percent annual rate of population growth, 75 million persons are added
to the human race each year. Even if each person at present required
the same amount of antientropy materials today as his or her ancestors, the total amount needed would have grown considerably.

But there are two other important factors in determining mankind's total demands on the ecosphere. Each person in industrial
society expects much more than his ancestors and thus is a much
bigger environmental burden: "Every application of technology,
every invention, and every discovery requires resources from the
environment. The larger the number of people and the higher their
level of technological development, the greater is likely to be the
range and extent of resources they need or perceive themselves as
needing."[11] In today's world each citizen of the United States has
an impact on the environment approximately 22 times that of each
Chinese.[12] Automobiles, large heated homes, and rapid intercontinental air transport require energy subsidies that are much greater
than anything needed in traditional settings. But in addition, the very
complexity of the society itself requires an additional increment.
There are clear diseconomies of scale in highly complex and densely
populated nations, at least diseconomies from nature's point of
view.[13]

If there was an infinite supply of energy materials and mineral
resources available, these matters would be of little political concern. Political scientists could go right on writing about "who gets
what" without concern for how much of what remained. But recent
studies have clearly revealed that there are limited amounts of these
materials readily available and in many respects economic and
social life is becoming a much more obvious zero-sum game.[14]

Rates of population increase, stocks of available resources,
and growth of technology have been and currently are important both
as objects of policy decisions and as variables influencing political
life. This includes not only relationships between one man and
another in nation-states but also relations among nation-states and
the various regions of the world. Examining historical data, Robert
North and Nazli Choucri have found these variables to be very good
predictors of nation-state behavior. For example, they report that
states with stable populations, growing technology, and adequate
territory tend to be nonaggressive. Those with large and growing
population, growing technology, and perceived resource inadequacies
tend to be centralized, aggressive, and militaristic.[15] Those nations
unable to adequately supply their populations with energy and essential raw materials are characterized by lateral pressures, movement
outward in search of required resources.[16]

At present political leaders in all countries are coming to
realize that foreign policies must be framed so as to insure access
to an adequate resource base. In the last quarter of the twentieth

century previously infinite quantities of mineral resources suddenly appear to be quite finite indeed. Oil-producing nations have banded together in the Organization of Petroleum Exporting Countries to demand higher prices for energy materials. The United States has suddenly expressed interest in natural gas in Soviet Siberia. Japanese shipyards rush to construct tankers capable of doubling or tripling the capacity of the world's fleet of tankers. Increasingly the external, as well as internal, actions of nation-states are predicated upon concern for access to essential resources. If resources cannot be obtained through normal channels, violence may well be the last resort of nations in need.[17]

Experts predict that world demand for energy will continue to increase by at least the present rate of six percent annually over the next decade. Demand for other essential minerals will increase apace. When present known reserves are exhausted, new reserves will be more difficult to tap and less rich in quality. Technologies can and will be developed to dig deeper and utilize less rich deposits of minerals, but society will eventually have to pay the price for these developments. Obviously, resource-poor countries will feel these economic pressures long before they affect those generously endowed with natural resources. The resulting economic pressures will shape the political behavior of nation-states in the future.

THE CHANGING RESOURCE BALANCE

Not more than a decade ago even experts would have scoffed at any mention of a potential worldwide shortage of energy and critical resources. But only a decade ago the world was consuming energy at roughly half the present rate. Only a little over ten years from now, the rate of energy consumption will have doubled once again. The geological processes that created most scarce minerals took millions of years, but mankind can easily wipe out most known resource reserves in a matter of decades.

The most important aspect of the changing resource balance is that consumption is increasing in an exponential rather than linear fashion. Linear growth is usually discussed as amount of increase per unit of time. Thus, in a hypothetical world, refining of petroleum might increase by a constant figure of 500 million barrels per year. Much conceptualization and thinking is done in linear terms, but they do not really apply to problems of world resource consumption. In the real world human consumption of resources is increasing exponentially, by a constant percentage per unit of time. It is estimated, for example, that consumption of petroleum will increase by three to five percent each year in the future. This means that the time it takes for the quantity consumed to double is very short. As a rule of thumb, yearly percentage increase divided into seventy yields an approximate doubling time. Taking the higher estimate for increasing petroleum consumption (five percent annually) yields an estimated doubling time of only fourteen years. Thus, fourteen years from now twice as much petroleum will be extracted from the earth annually, 24 years from now four times as much, and so forth.[18]

Natural populations grow exponentially. Homo sapiens has recently been expanding his numbers at the rate of two percent each year. This means that the component of environmental impact attributable to population alone doubles every 35 years. Obviously population grows at different rates in different areas of the world. In many nonindustrial countries rates of population growth are as high as three percent per year, meaning population doublings every 23 years. In most of Europe, however, a demographic transition has occurred and the portion of environmental impact attributable to simple population growth is very small.* The yearly rate of population growth for all of Europe was only 0.8 percent between 1963 and 1969; the Soviet Union grew at a rate of 1.1 percent during the same period.[19] In Europe, however, per capita impact on the world's supply of resources has increased tremendously. While industrialization has slowed population growth, it has also spurred individual consumption. Even with very low rates of population growth, European energy demands jumped 60 percent between 1960 and 1970.[20]

For the world as a whole, the portion of environmental impact due to simple population growth will continue to increase for the foreseeable future. Demographers estimate that if a replacement-sized family is realized for the developed world by the end of this century, very unlikely from the social point of view, and in the developing world by 2040, the world's population will not stabilize until it reaches 15.5 billion one century hence.[21] The lag time built into these equations results from the age structure of the world's population; since it is composed of a great portion of young people, birth rates will remain high. It is very likely that world population will continue to grow at present rates, about two percent each year.

In the developed nations additional energy and resource demands are due to a combination of increased per capita demand and the problem of servicing complex societies. In Europe, for example, population size will double only every 70 to 100 years. While

---

*Briefly stated, a demographic transition occurs when birth rates fall off in response to industrial development. Traditional societies are characterized by high birth rates as each family strives to ensure that some children will survive by having many offspring. In industrial society, however, survival rates for children are higher and families have fewer offspring.

industrialization has slowed European growth in population, it has spurred individual consumption.

When population growth, increased per capita impact, and a social complexity component are added together, it appears certain that exponential growth in global consumption of resources cannot stop for the foreseeable future. World industrial production is growing at 7 percent each year. Although the rate of increase in demand for each important resource varies, the present yearly world average increase is 4 percent. Demand for some strategic metals is growing much faster. Demand for aluminum, for example, is increasing at nearly 5 percent each year. This means consumption doubles every 14 years.[22]

This is the context within which any examination of the European future must begin. Western Europe, the cradle of the industrial revolution, has now exhausted most domestic supplies of needed resources. Western Europe is now resource poor and has been forced to look elsewhere for vital raw materials. Eastern Europe has fared a bit better, but must eventually face similar problems. Only the Soviet Union remains a resource "superpower" with apparent resource reserves that will last well into the next century if used only to meet domestic demand.[23]

Table 6.1 dramatically illustrates some of the dimensions of the impending resource scarcities for the world as a whole. Some regions of the world possess the greatest portion of these known and potentially exploitable reserves. Other regions have virtually no reserves at all. Table 6.1 is based on two of the best current estimates of future resource consumption as well as potentially available supplies, given present levels of technology. The most interesting data are found in the column labelled 5X. The dates in this column assume that reserves five times the size of those now known will be discovered or opened by new technologies over the next few decades, a very generous assumption. But the dynamics of world resource consumption are such that even this level of exploration and discovery will not significantly alter depletion dates.

Interpreting the data for aluminum and petroleum, both essential resources for industrial societies, yields the following theoretical depletion dates: Given present demands for aluminum and knowable reserves, supplies will be exhausted sometime between 2072 and 2145. But given that demand is increasing at exponential rates, supplies will be exhausted much earlier, sometime between 2001 and 2005. Adding the "discovery" factor (column 5X) only lengthens the projection by about twenty years. The data on petroleum project that it will no longer be available sometime between 1990 and 1995, given exponentially increasing demand, and will disappear around the year 2020 even if the discovery factor is added in.[24]

It is important to interpret the meaning of these figures appropriately and to emphasize that these are "ballpark" estimates.

TABLE 6.1

Key Minerals: Projected Year of Depletion

	Static-1	Exponential-1	5X	Static-2	Exponential-2
Aluminum	2072	2001	2025	2145	2005
Copper	2006	1991	2018	2010	1995
Iron	2210	2063	2143	2370	2045
Lead	1996	1991	2034	1988	1984
Manganese	2067	2016	2064	2152	2020
Mercury	1983	1983	2011	1985	1985
Nickel	2120	2023	2066	2115	2005
Tungsten	2010	1998	2042	2015	2010
Zinc	1993	1998	2020	1985	1983
Petroleum	2001	1990	2020	n.a.	1995
Natural gas	2010	1994	2021	n.a.	n.a.

Note: Columns 1 and 3 are different projections on the assumption that we continue to use resources at present rates of depletion. Columns 2 and 4 are different projections assuming that resource consumption will continue to increase exponentially. Column 5 assumes the same depletion rate as column 2, but also assumes that reserves five times the size of present known reserves will be discovered or opened by new technologies over the next few decades.

Sources: For columns 1, 2, and 5: Donella H. Meadows, et al., The Limits to Growth (New York: Universe Books, 1972). For columns 3 and 4: "A Blueprint for Survival," The Ecologist, January 1972.

Even though dates are projected for the disappearance of key resources, this will never in fact happen. Obviously new technologies for resource extraction will be developed, when it becomes economically feasible. But these new technologies will take time to develop and require a tremendous investment of financial resources. At some future date, for example, new methods of mining and smelting copper ore will make presently low-grade deposits attractive. Rising prices will also encourage further exploration. Similarly, breeder reactors and eventually fusion reactors will begin to supply substantial amounts of electric power. But even the most optimistic estimates, many of which are simply public relations efforts, indicate that such innovations will be extremely costly and that it will be some time before they are "on-line."[25]

In addition, two other things will happen to assure that resources do not simply disappear. Long before resources become depleted, market mechanisms will drive up prices and encourage development of substitutes.* The price of oil and natural gas, for example, has already begun to rise, and indications are that these prices will go much higher.[26] As prices go up, there will be tremendous pressures to find and exploit new deposits. Environmental damage will increase as oil wells are dug deeper and in less accessible places. Presently plans call for oil to be brought down from Alaska's north slope and negotiations have begun for exploiting Soviet natural gas fields in Siberia. (If consummated, the Siberian gas deal would eventually cost the United States $53 billion in hard currency, with an initial investment of $16 billion.) This means that the price of everything from home construction materials to gasoline and electricity can be expected to rise. These prices will obviously rise much faster in the resource-poor countries than in the resource-rich areas. As prices increase there will be more incentives for industry to develop substitutes for scarce materials and to recycle what is presently available. In some cases this will be very practical, but in most cases it will do little to change the underlying dynamics of consumption.

Thus the economics of the situation, rather than depletion dates, have very important political consequences. Over the next few decades the changing resource balance will be an extremely important factor in reshaping and undoing political alliances. Formerly resource-rich superpowers will find themselves hard pressed to maintain existing levels of resource throughput. In addition, the increasing costs of resources will have very important internal political implications in those countries most affected. Industrial development might well be redirected and living standards drastically altered. The "haves" will be in the best shape to endure or even profit from impending shortages. The "have nots" will be forced to maneuver to guarantee continued access to the building blocks of industrial society.[27]

The future of Western Europe is closely tied to the availability of adequate resources. Western Europe has become deficient in almost all critical energy materials and mineral resources. Eastern Europe is in slightly better shape but will be increasingly forced to rely on the Soviet Union for substantial help.[28] The colonial empire once provided needed raw materials, but today access to these

---

*But in many cases there is no adequate substitute for scarce metals. Copper, for example, is a good conductor of electricity. It will be difficult to find an adequate substitute. Similarly, many suggest that plastics will solve the resource problem. But plastics are made from petroleum, which will also be in short supply.

supplies is increasingly restricted by political pressures. These factors will be extremely important in determining the political future of the European continent.

EUROPEAN RESOURCES

The industrial revolution first occurred in Western Europe, and this in part explains many of the resource problems the region now faces. None of these countries has been especially well endowed with natural resources, with the notable exception of coal, and over the decades what did exist has been depleted. The energy for early industrialization was provided by coal and this has proven to be a liability in the second half of the twentieth century. While coal is abundant, it is a dirty and inefficient fuel, undesirable in densely populated urban areas. Petroleum and natural gas burn with a much cleaner flame and a much higher portion of the fuel can be transformed into useful energy.[29]

Since World War II Western Europe has been retreating from coal as a fuel in the interests of industrial efficiency.[30] In 1958 coal and other solid fuels accounted for 71 percent of Western European energy consumption; by 1969 this figure had declined to 37 percent.[31] Since coal is Western Europe's only well-developed resource, these shifting patterns of energy utilization have made the region extremely vulnerable to political pressures. The closing of the Suez canal demonstrated to the world just how dependent Western Europe had become on long lines of supply from former colonial areas. In 1960 Western Europe consumed 831 million metric tons of coal equivalent in energy. By 1970 this consumption figure had grown to 1,348 million metric tons, an increase of 68 percent in ten years. During this same period, however, domestic production of energy materials in the region declined from 563 million metric tons to 557 million metric tons of coal equivalent.[32] The gap has been filled by increased imports from the Middle East and other developing countries.

In the centrally planned economies the retreat from coal has not been quite as rapid. The data in Table 6.2 indicate that most of the countries with very high energy production-consumption ratios are centrally planned economies. Poland, Romania, and the Soviet Union all produce more energy than is consumed domestically. Czechoslovakia, East Germany, and Hungary are nearly self-sufficient. One of the main reasons is that their retreat from coal has not been quite as rapid. About three-quarters of present energy consumption in the region is in the form of coal and other solid fuels.[33] In summary figures, the centrally planned economies consumed 1,348 million metric tons of coal equivalent in 1960. This figure increased to 1,961 million metric tons in 1970, an increase

TABLE 6.2

Energy Balance for Major European Nations

	Production/ Consumption Ratio	Percent Increase/ Decrease in Production, 1965-68	Per Capita Consumption*
Poland	1.14	10	3,826
USSR	1.13	18	4,059
Romania	1.12	19	2,386
Czechoslovakia	0.88	- 1	5,776
East Germany	0.83	- 2	5,387
Hungary	0.75	0	2,816
United Kingdom	0.63	-10	5,004
West Germany	0.61	-10	4,484
Bulgaria	0.58	27	3,322
Netherlands	0.55	67	4,012
Norway	0.48	20	4,259
Austria	0.48	- 7	2,854
France	0.38	-11	3,282
Belgium	0.29	-25	5,236
Switzerland	0.20	23	3,012
Italy	0.20	13	2,215
Sweden	0.14	3	5,360
Finland	0.08	12	3,339
Denmark	0.01	-65	4,690

*Measured in grams per day.

Source: Figures are derived from U.N. Statistical Yearbook 1969 (New York: United Nations, 1970).

of 47 percent.[34] But energy production increased apace, and all this expansion was financed within the Comecon community.

Of greater significance is the abundance of natural resources in the Soviet Union. A recent study has credited the Soviet Union with self-sufficiency in 26 of the 36 minerals essential in an industrial society. The United States, by contrast, is self-sufficient in only 7 of these minerals.[35] There are only two important industrial minerals for which current Soviet imports exceed 20 percent of present consumption. The first is bauxite, for which the Soviets now rely on Yugoslavia and Greece. The only other mineral in this category is tin, which is imported from Great Britain and Malaysia.[36]

Most Western European nations, by contrast, are heavily dependent upon outside sources for almost all important mineral resources. Belgium, Denmark, Finland, Italy, Sweden, and Switzerland all produce less than one-third the energy consumed domestically. No country in Western Europe comes close to matching energy production with energy consumption.

Table 6.3 documents the increase in demand for petroleum and key metals for France, West Germany, and the United Kingdom. In the three-year period 1966-69, petroleum imports by France shot up 37 percent, the United Kingdom by 34 percent, and West Germany by 32 percent. By contrast, the Soviet Union was cutting back on imports of petroleum and had no great requirements for outside metallic ores. In 1958 Western Europe imported a total of 240 million metric tons of coal equivalent in energy materials. By 1970 the total had risen to 853 million metric tons and there are no indications that this outside dependency will be reduced in the near future.[37] In most Western European nations, energy production is not keeping pace with population growth. In eight countries it is not rising at all. Each of these nations will be forced to confront the consequences of these dependencies as energy materials and other mineral resources become more expensive on a global scale.

Looking to the future, one potential answer to Europe's energy dependence is the development of nuclear and thermonuclear power. Although development of such installations will undoubtedly ameliorate the situation, it is not the perfect solution many believe it to be. Nuclear reactors require uranium as fuel, and this also is not abundant in Western Europe. World uranium supplies are finite, just like petroleum and natural gas. Second-generation reactors, so-called breeder reactors, have not yet been proven safe and workable, although they certainly will be on-line within the next decade. But even when they are certified as "safe," breeder reactors present a host of problems that are difficult to solve and bound to limit Western European growth. These reactors will have to be frequently replaced due to radiation effects on structures; the fuels will have to be serviced by technologically sophisticated processing plants; and the reactors will also pollute the immediate

TABLE 6.3

Mineral Demands of Major European Powers
(in thousands of metric tons)

	1966	1969	Percent Increase/ Decrease
East Germany			
petroleum	6,400	9,200	44
metal ores	1,500 (iron)	1,300 (iron)	-13
France			
petroleum	63,000	83,000	37
metal ores	7,000	10,000	43
West Germany			
petroleum	68,000	90,000	32
metal ores	37,000	52,000	41
United Kingdom			
petroleum	71,000	95,000	34
metal ores	18,000	20,000	41
USSR			
petroleum	1,700	1,100	-35
metal ores	negligible	negligible	--
Poland			
petroleum	3,300	6,500	97
metal ores	9,400	11,600	23

Source: U.N. Yearbook of World Trade Statistics 1969 (New York: United Nations, 1970).

environment with low-level radiation. In many areas of the world these plants can be sited far from populated areas and the radiation dangers can be diminished. In Western Europe, however, such isolated areas are extremely difficult to find.[38]

Aside from these caveats, however, Western European leaders have not been in a hurry to make a transition to nuclear power. They have followed short-sighted policies and have failed to construct nuclear facilities since Middle Eastern oil and abundant coal have permitted electricity to be produced more cheaply in conventional plants. In nuclear reactors the price for electricity has proven much higher than originally estimated. Very long lead times are needed for nuclear power plant construction, and the market prices for oil today bear little resemblance to the prices that will be charged ten years from now. The Organization for Economic Cooperation and Development (OECD) has estimated that member countries will be generating 29 percent of their power from nuclear sources by 1980, but present statistics show no such rapid progress.[39] In summary, nuclear power certainly offers Western Europe one way out of the energy dilemma, but development of such installations will be costly, has been lagging because of economic considerations, and will be very dangerous to densely populated areas. Furthermore, nuclear power can do little to lessen Western European dependence on the rest of the world for other mineral resources, including energy materials that cannot be readily replaced by electricity. Electricity consumption is currently only one-quarter of the U.S. energy budget, and less in other countries; conversion of cars, for example, to electric fuel will be extremely difficult and expensive.

RESOURCES AND POLITICS

Dependence on outside sources of supply makes all European nations very vulnerable to political pressure and even blackmail. These pressures have been particularly pronounced in Western Europe, where daily consumption of oil was only 1.2 million barrels in 1950 and is scheduled to rise to nearly 24 million barrels daily by 1980. These imports cost Western Europe an estimated $9.5 billion in 1970. New financial settlements with the OPEC (Organization of Petroleum Exporting Countries) members will add at least $5.5 billion yearly to the European fuel bill. There is no indication that a unified OPEC will not demand and get better settlements in the near future. It is important to note that during the crisis of 1970 Western Europe was caught with only a 60-day supply of petroleum in reserve.[40] Should OPEC members suddenly decide to cut off Europe's supply of petroleum for political reasons, economic activity would come to a grinding halt.

Eastern European nations are vulnerable to political pressures of a different nature. Comecon members have only recently received permission to explore trade ties with the Middle East and Africa. Although levels of self-sufficiency are higher in Eastern than in Western Europe, the Soviet Union is the obvious source for supplies of critical minerals that are lacking in each of these countries. The Soviet Union has a virtual monopoly on bloc production of precious metals, many of which have very early depletion dates, as well as a near monopoly on production of mercury, cobalt, molybdenum, manganese, tungsten, tin, and chromium.[41]

The Soviet Union not only sets explicit political bounds around Eastern European interactions with other nations but also has the implicit control offered by resource monopoly. Eastern European leaders really have little choice but to follow Soviet dictates on resource matters, and they will be even more pressed in a less affluent future. These countries have only small reserves of hard currency with which to shop on world markets. While barter arrangements are a possibility, Eastern European products are generally not as attractive as Western European or American merchandise. Given future resource considerations, OPEC countries are not particularly anxious to make unattractive barter deals.

Looking to the future, Eastern Europe has little choice but to remain firmly tied to the Soviet Union. Western Europe certainly cannot supply CMEA countries with needed resources. Neither can the United States. East Germany, Poland, Czechoslovakia, Hungary, and Bulgaria will be most affected by resource dependence. All these countries substantially increased petroleum imports from the Soviet Union in the mid-1960s.[42] Twenty-five years of economic dependency on the Soviet Union means that pipeline and transport facilities have been set up for trade with the Soviet Union and not with the rest of the world. This dependency cannot be reversed by fiat, especially when there are no obvious economic reasons for doing so.

It is clear that the Soviet Union will play a critical role in influencing the future of European alliances. One of the common wisdoms that still finds support is that the Soviet Union needs Comecon more than these countries need the Soviet Union. Perhaps this was true of the Europe of the past, but it certainly will not be true of the Europe of the future. Eastern Europe would like and deserves more freedom from Moscow's political control, but such freedoms can only be granted by the Kremlin. The exceptions to this rule are Yugoslavia and Romania. It is not unexpected that these two "maverick" states are fairly self-sufficient in natural resources and therefore resistant to Soviet pressures. Any Western efforts to lure members from the Soviet coalition can only work for a short period of time, as in the long run massive foreign aid would be required to meet resource needs.

There are also indications that Russia will be able to use its resource abundance to good advantage in Western Europe. Not only have friendship pipelines been built pointing to the heart of Western Europe, but the Soviet Union has already sold large quantities of oil to Western Europe and Japan. In 1970 estimated sales were 50 million tons. Negotiations for the purchase of Soviet gas have been conducted with Austria, France, Italy, Finland, West Germany, and Sweden.[43] Now that the United States has legitimated a European turn to the East through its own negotiations for Siberian gas, there are no ideological barriers to such activities.

While it is impossible to predict that such trade will eventuate in some form of "integration" or "community building," as these terms are used in the literature, it is certainly true that resource considerations will lead to shifts in European realpolitic. Barring unforeseen political turmoil, the Soviet domination of CMEA will surely increase in the 1970s and 1980s. It is also to be expected that Soviet overtures in Western Europe will bear fruit as the dimensions of the global resource crisis become more apparent in the 1980s. This is not to argue that the Common Market will collapse or that the NATO alliance will disappear, but to stress that the Soviet Union will, for at least the next two decades, certainly have more to offer Western Europe from the resource point of view than will the United States.

Looking to the more distant future, however, there are technological factors that should begin to right the balance by the year 2000. Eventually the Soviet Union will also face the same type of resource constraints that other nations are now facing.[44] Already Moscow seems to have responded to Soviet realities by urging Eastern European countries to establish minimal ties with oil producing countries. This makes good political sense as Soviet reserves can be protected for the future, but it also demonstrates Soviet weakness. In the long run new technologies involving breeder reactors and fusion power will be necessary to maintain coalition predominance. In this respect it is well known that the United States and Western Europe have the edge over the Soviet Union. Despite the fact that the Soviet Union developed the first nuclear reactor in 1954, and despite recent Soviet innovations in fusion power, the United States and Western Europe have a sizable across-the-board lead in development of new technologies. In applications of nuclear power, for example, the United States produced one-fourth of the world's total in 1970, Great Britain one-third, and France one-tenth. Together these countries accounted for over two-thirds of all nuclear power generated.[45]

Resource questions not only will affect the European future in external relationships but also will have an important impact on domestic politics in both Eastern and Western Europe. The flourishing of Western European democracy in the 1950s and 1960s has in

part been a function of economic conditions. Political differences
are easily submerged during periods of abundance. It is easy to for-
get the effect of poor economic conditions in Germany in the 1930s.
It is not at all unlikely that similar political turmoil will take place
in Western Europe in the 1980s as each country attempts to adjust
to the economic realities. Recent rampant inflation on the continent
and labor strife in Great Britain may well be harbingers of things to
come. Available data indicates that some countries have responded
internally to the developing challenges. Although the social mechanisms by which ecological imperatives are transformed into social
and political attitudes are not well understood, there is little question
that there are systematic relationships between resource availability
and demographic statistics. As Tables 6.4 and 6.5 indicate, rates of
population growth are consistently low in those countries most in
need of resource subsidies; the United Kingdom, Austria, Hungary,
and Ireland all have rates of population growth less than 0.5 percent
yearly.

Perhaps the future of industrial societies facing acute resource
shortages is best understood by studying the countries listed as
"mature" societies in Table 6.5. It appears that social mechanisms
are at work preparing these nations for a world in which energy and
mineral resources are no longer freely available. In these countries
population growth as well as industrial growth has tapered off,
seemingly in response to very low energy production/consumption
ratios and decreases in yearly amounts of energy produced. It is
perhaps a bit ironic that the United Kingdom, the country that paved
the way for the industrial revolution, is now the first industrial
power to feel the pains of once again adjusting to living within
nature's constraints. All the countries of Western Europe eventually
will have to make such a transition to a condition resembling what
economist Herman Daly calls a "steady-state" within which the
throughput of new mineral resources is minimized and economic
growth takes place in industries that do not consume natural
resources.[46]

In Eastern Europe political stability has been maintained
largely through economic growth. People who perceive the system
to be performing economically make poor revolutionaries.[47] Where
economic breakdowns have taken place--Czechoslovakia in the mid-
1960s and Poland in the late 1960s--political instability has resulted.
Leaders of Comecon countries must assure access to mineral
resources if such incidents are to be avoided in the future.

From a more theoretical perspective, the global resource
crisis calls into question the whole school of thought that equates
political stability and democracy with industrial development.[48]
This perspective is obviously timebound. When industrial expansion
took place without regard for environmental considerations, there
was such a relationship among these variables, but this relationship

TABLE 6.4

Dimensions of Growth in Europe, 1963-70

	Industrial Production (1963 = 100)	Population (average annual percent increase)
Austria	153	0.4
Belgium	139	0.6
Bulgaria	212	0.7
Czechoslovakia	154	0.5
Denmark	157	0.7
Finland	161	0.5
France	149	0.9
East Germany	153	0.1
West Germany	153	1.0
Hungary	144	0.3
Ireland	152	0.5
Italy	150	0.8
Luxembourg	128	0.7
Netherlands	175	1.2
Norway	145	0.8
Poland	178	0.8
Romania	229	1.1
Sweden	156	0.8
Switzerland	146	1.2
United Kingdom	124	0.5
USSR	168	1.1
Yugoslavia	168	1.1

Source: U.N. Statistical Yearbook 1971 (New York: United Nations, 1972).

TABLE 6.5

Comparative Growth in Europe, 1963-69

	Industrial Growth	Population Growth	Produced/ Consumed	Percent Increase
Late-Developing Nations				
Bulgaria	212	0.7	0.58	27
Netherlands	175	1.2	0.55	67
Poland	178	0.8	1.14	10
Romania	229	1.1	1.12	19
USSR	168	1.1	1.13	18
Yugoslavia	168	1.1	0.78	- 1
Mature Societies				
Austria	153	0.4	0.48	- 7
Belgium	139	0.6	0.29	-25
Czechoslovakia	154	0.5	0.88	- 1
East Germany	153	0.1	0.83	- 2
West Germany	153	1.0	0.61	-10
Hungary	144	0.3	0.75	0
Ireland	152	0.5	0.35	25
United Kingdom	124	0.5	0.63	-10

was anchored in the economic abundance with which political leaders could meet the rising demands of a new middle class. From a different perspective it would appear that in future societies a very high level of industrial development might lead to precisely the opposite outcome. Dean Neubauer has already pointed out that among highly industrial countries there is no relationship between increasing affluence and many indicators of democracy.[49] In the future the superindustrial countries that will be hardest hit by resource problems might well be faced with what Samuel Huntington has termed political decay. Demands built into industrial society might well overload political systems, leading to instability and collapse.[50]

Thus, global resource considerations will be an extremely important factor in determining the European future. In this respect Western Europe offers a laboratory for the study of phenomena yet to be experienced by other industrial societies. Very few countries will be able to avoid some sort of resource crisis during the next few decades. Tremendous political, economic, and social adjustments will have to be made in coming to grips with these problems. Political instability and more centralized forms of government might well result as democratic regimes become hard pressed to meet citizen expectations. These problems will certainly surface first in Western Europe, and the rest of the world should be able to learn much from the European experience.

NOTES

1. Harold Lasswell, Politics: Who Gets What, When, How (New York: Meridan Books, 1958).

2. Seymour M. Lipset, "Some Social Requisites of Democracy: Economic Development and Political Legitimacy," American Political Science Review, March 1959.

3. Seymour M. Lipset, Political Man (Garden City, N.Y.: Doubleday, 1960); Philip Cutright, "National Political Development: Its Measurement and Social Correlates," American Sociological Review, April 1963; Donald McCrore and Charles Cnudde, "Toward a Communications Theory of Democratic Political Development: a Causal Model," American Political Science Review, March 1967.

4. Lynton Caldwell, Environment: A Challenge to Modern Society (Garden City, N.Y.: The Natural History Press, 1970); Richard Falk, This Endangered Planet (New York: Random House, 1971); David Kay and Eugene Skolnikoff, eds., World Ecocrisis: International Organizations in Response (Madison: University of Wisconsin Press, 1972).

5. See, inter alia, P.R. and A.H. Ehrlich, Population Resources and Environment: Issues in Human Ecology (San Francisco: W.H. Freeman, 1970); John Holdren and P.R. Ehrlich, eds., Global Ecology: Readings Toward a Rational Strategy for Man (New York: Harcourt, Brace, Jovanovich, 1971); John Hart and Robert Socolow, eds., Patient Earth (New York: Holt Rinehart and Winston, 1971).

6. Donella H. Meadows, et al., The Limits to Growth (New York: Universe Books, 1972); "A Blueprint for Survival," The Ecologist, January 1972.

7. William Ophuls, "Leviathan or Oblivion," in Herman Daly, ed., Toward a Steady-State Economy (San Francisco: W.H. Freeman, 1973).

8. Robert C. North and Nazli Choucri, "Population and the Future International System," paper presented at the sixty-sixth annual meeting of the American Political Science Association, Los Angeles, September 1970, p. 2 and references cited therein.

9. Ibid., p. 3.

10. P.R. and A.H. Ehrlich, op. cit., Chapter 2.

11. Nazli Choucri and Robert C. North, "Population and Politics: The Interdependence of Ecological and Social Imperatives," paper presented at annual meeting of American Political Science Association, Chicago, September 1971, p. 4.

12. See Dennis Pirages and P.R. Ehrlich, "If All Chinese Had Wheels," New York Times, March 16, 1972. See also Pirages and Ehrlich, Ark II (New York: The Viking Press, 1973), Chapter 7.

13. P.R. Ehrlich and John Holdren, "Impact of Population Growth," Science, March 26, 1971; Ehrlich and Holdren, "One Dimensional Ecology," Science and Public Affairs, May 1972.

14. See Meadows, et al., op. cit.; Preston Cloud, Jr., ed., Resources and Man (San Francisco: W.H. Freeman, 1969).

15. Robert North and Nazli Choucri, "Population and the International System: Some Implications for United States Planning and Policy," paper submitted to the Commission on Population Growth and the American Future, August 15, 1971, pp. 29-32.

16. Nazli Choucri, Michael Laird, and Dennis Meadows, "Resource Scarcity and Foreign Policy: A Simulation Model of International Conflict" (Center for International Studies-Massachusetts Institute of Technology, March 1972).

17. See Nazli Choucri, "Population, Resources, Technology: Political Implications of the Environmental Crisis," International Organization, Spring 1972.

18. For more details on exponential growth and doubling times, see Meadows, et al., op. cit., pp. 25-44.

19. U.N. Statistical Yearbook 1970 (New York: United Nations, 1971), p. 28.

20. World Energy Supplies, United Nations Statistical Papers, Series J, No. 14 (New York: United Nations, 1971).

21. Data on momentum of population growth can be found in Demography, Vol. 8 (1971), pp. 71-80.

22. Meadows, et al., op. cit., pp. 56-59.

23. Lawrence Rocks and Richard Runyon, The Energy Crisis (New York: Crown Publishers, 1972), pp. 136-151.

24. For other estimates and details of methods of figuring depletion rates, see Cloud, Jr., ed., op. cit.; S. Fred Singer, ed., Is There an Optimum Level of Population? (New York: McGraw-Hill, 1971).

25. For reliable estimates, see John Holdren and P. Herrera, Energy (New York: Sierra Club Books, 1972), pp. 100-22. See also P.R. Ehrlich and John Holdren, "Population and Panaceas--A Technological Perspective," Bioscience, December 1969.

26. Earl Cook claims that energy costs in the United States will rise sharply before 1980. His estimates range from a 100 percent increase for natural gas to power plants to 33 percent for gasoline. See "Resource Limits to Economic Growth," paper presented at meeting of the National Association of Manufacturers, New Orleans, November 1972.

27. See data in Pirages and Ehrlich, Ark II, op. cit., Chapter 7.

28. Dennis Pirages, "Energy, Resources, and East European Integration," paper presented at conference on East European integration, University of South Carolina, May 1972.

29. For estimates of fuel efficiencies, see Holdren and Herrara, op. cit., passim.

30. See Richard Gordon, The Evolution of Energy Policy in Western Europe (New York: Praeger Publishers, 1970).

31. U.N. Statistical Yearbook 1970 (New York: United Nations, 1971), p. 66.

32. World Energy Supplies, op. cit.

33. U.N. Statistical Yearbook 1970, op. cit.

34. World Energy Supplies, op. cit.

35. Raymond Ewell, "US will Lag USSR in Raw Materials," Chemical and Engineering News, August 24, 1970, pp. 42-46.

36. U.N. Statistical Yearbook 1969, op. cit.

37. U.N. Statistical Yearbook 1971 (New York: United Nations, 1972).

38. A more complete discussion of nuclear reactors and their hazards is found in Holdren and Herrera, op. cit., pp. 57-86. See also John Gofman and Arthur Tamplin, Poisoned Power (Emmaus, Penn.: Rodale Press, 1971).

39. W.G. Jensen, Energy in Europe 1945-1980 (London: G.T. Foulis, 1967), pp. 95-96.

40. Walter J. Levy, "Oil Power," Foreign Affairs, July 1971, p. 736.

41. Pirages, "Energy, Resources, and East European Integration," op. cit.

42. Robert E. Ebel, Communist Trade in Oil and Gas (New York: Praeger Publishers, 1970), Chapter 8.

43. Ibid., Chapters 6-8 for further details.

44. Ibid. These constraints are discussed pp. 87 ff.

45. U.N. Statistical Yearbook 1971, op. cit., p. 348.

46. Daly, ed., op. cit.

47. For a thorough discussion of economic factors in maintaining political stability in socialist societies, see Dennis Pirages, Modernization and Political Tension Management (New York: Praeger Publishers, 1972).

48. Lipset, "Some Social Requisites of Democracy," op. cit.; Cutright, op. cit.

49. Dean Neubauer, "Some Conditions of Democracy," American Political Science Review, December 1967.

50. Samuel Huntington, "Political Development and Political Decay," World Politics, Fall 1965.

7

EUROPEAN REALPOLITIC I:
EAST BERLIN'S WESTPOLITIK
James A. Kuhlman

Any projection of the future probably will end on a note of caution concerning the distinction between the preferred and the possible. This chapter addresses that issue by presenting a dialectical synthesis of our problem in the consideration of Bonn's Ostpolitik, Berlin's Westpolitik, and Europe's realpolitic. The theoretical and the practical aspects of the "German problem" serve here to focus the attention of scholar and decision-maker alike upon the parallel aspects of normative and empirical approaches to the European problem of bloc relations.

Taking the "German problem" as a means of identifying an issue of relevance to all levels in the European framework, we will use an overall systemic approach within which foreign policy is considered an issue area. The systemic level of analysis employed in facing the issue will be shown to be crucial in relation to the normative/empirical balance in the approach of the scholar and to the theoretical/practical balance in the processes of the policy-maker. The various systemic levels are then outlined with specific attention to the linkages between systems at different levels. The linkages in turn point out the systemic bias involved in the German problem. The mobilization of bias inherent in the interdependence of these systems necessitates an examination of the role of legitimacy in the German state systems of the East and West, at one level, while also demanding attention to the role of integration in the multi-state systems of the East and West at another level. This systemic bias from various levels defines the European realpolitic within which, we submit, Bonn and Berlin, scholar and diplomat of East and West must work.

The need for an issue area typology is obvious in the study of a system's policy-making process.[1] It has been generally recognized as a necessary means to prevent an overly fragmented, idiographic explanation of policy outcomes on the one hand, and to caution an exaggerated structural and functional consistency in system behavior on the other. Issues do make a difference in policy input and output. At the same time policy processes are not emptied of patterned interaction among the variables, both independent and dependent, as the issues change. The most often invoked issue area types are those of domestic and foreign policy distinctions. The obvious difficulty with this dichotomy is that in almost all political systems one can conceive of a third category of issues whose area overlaps with the patterned interaction of variables in the domestic and foreign policy-making processes. Yet the alternative to the domestic/foreign typology threatens a hopeless myriad of issue variability in the policy process, an endless invitation to account for process and outcome by stating that it all depends on the issue. One answer is to distinguish domestic and foreign systems of a nation, as opposed to distinguishing domestic and foreign issue areas of a national system, which then allows the possibility of certain "exceptional" issues that transgress the boundaries between the areas. To consider a case exceptional or deviant, however, is to render that case inexplicable. An alternative answer is provided here by drawing a parallel in issue areas with that in systems analysis in general. As there are identifiable linkages between levels of systems, so we might conceive of a linkage type of issue area.

THE GERMAN PROBLEM AND THE PROBLEM OF LEVELS

In this sense the Ostpolitik of Bonn and Westpolitik of Berlin, foreign policies of the political systems of the German Democratic Republic (GDR) and Federal Republic of Germany (FRG) most certainly overlap with their respective domestic issue areas. The patterned interaction among variables determined by the foreign and domestic issue areas quite likely will outline the boundaries of a linkage issue area. The German problem more suitably belongs to this third issue area rather than within the boundaries of either the domestic or foreign areas of these two political systems. Policies in the linkage issue area will have impact upon other systems at higher and lower levels, as will be shown later. The pattern of linkage variables between systems at various levels may then be seen as formed in particular in relation to the linkage issue area.

Having briefly outlined a relationship among the issue areas involved in the interdependence of the two German states, we need some sort of framework within which to investigate the variables brought to significance by those issue areas. The systems framework or systemic approach is deemed most useful here due to two related tasks: first, we are concerned with identifying linkages among the issue areas involved in the German problem, and these linkages may vary according to the systemic levels at which inquiry proceeds; second, therefore, we must be able to ask our problematic question in a meaningful way at various levels of analysis.[2] Both tasks involve much more than verbal gymnastics. Scholars who choose a level of analysis wholly unsuitable for identifying data required by their hypotheses will invariably engage in a normative discourse about the systems they would want to realize, missing any concrete estimate as to the systems that might actually materialize. As the decision-maker must base his behavior on practical policy considerations, so the scholar must theorize with an empirical assessment of the situation in mind.

The international system as a level of analysis has been ably critiqued from the standpoint of its general inability to provide for specificity and causality, while amply supported on the basis of its ability to provide for comprehensiveness and totality.[3] Simply stated, different levels of analysis may be fruitfully employed at different levels of research--description, classification, explanation, and prediction--depending upon what the investigator wishes to describe, classify, explain, or predict. The levels of analysis problem in research is a particularly vexing aspect of the general scientific problem of the levels of discourse. "Set thinking" restricts the researcher to a single universe of discourse.[4] But keeping straight whether one is discussing birds or people is only part of the problem. One must also make it clear in any single research endeavor whether the discussion involves one bird or person, or a whole flock of birds or a group of people. Properties of the single unit of analysis may or may not be properties of the aggregation. Set and subset thinking may be adhered to in the approach to our problem by systemic and subsystemic frameworks. An explanation of elite behavior will be dulled in the framework of a nation-state subsystem, since impact upon and influence of elites is facilitated by the systems approach at that level but not the why of elite behaviors. If one wishes to explain nation-state behavior, then a regional subsystem model will offer little insight. In attempting to explain bloc behavior by the use of a global systems model, one would be confronted by excessive abstractions.

Within any single framework or explanatory endeavor, a constant level of analysis should be employed. Analytically diagramed, the problem usually is easily solved. Practically speaking, the question itself is not always easy to ask. The German problem begs the question, and it must be asked at several different levels of inquiry. The unit of analysis most explanatory and ultimately predictive of the future in that problem framework might be individual Germans, but it could be the two states or even a single German nation, or quite possibly the two regional subsystems, or even an all-European system or the international system itself. Do Germans identify with their respective states or rather with their common nationality? Will the two states want to reunite? Will the two states be allowed to reunite by their respective alliance systems? Will European unity be achieved in spite or or because of a reunified Germany? What impact will a changing international system have upon the two Germanys? The answer to each of these questions demands a different analytic framework emphasizing a different level of analysis. Any predictability of the future of the German problem in the broad European context ultimately will depend upon establishing linkages between the questions and answers, between the different levels of the problem.

Proceeding from the inside to the outside of the "Russian doll" analogy for systemic levels, the linkages from lower or inside subsystems to higher or outside subsystems may be seen as groups within one subsystem that have ties with the surrounding environment (analytically, the system at another level).[5] For example, management specialists of the several participating CMEA states may identify with regional policies more than with national plan directives. Trade specialists of the European Economic Community (EEC) and CMEA may identify with European trade levels rather than with bloc relations, and so forth. Not only will the number of linkages be significant as we analyze the strength of various systemic levels (that is, the probability of various systemic outcomes) but attention should be devoted to the strength of the ties versus the inertia of the present systemic level, and also how these frequencies and intensities of linkage vary with the policy relevant issue, in our case the German problem.[6]

Alternative strategies for researching our problem could be diagramed as shown in Figure 7.1, which illustrates an approach to our problem from the broadest possible perspective. Data gathered on international systemic actors would at present be minimal and for the most part quite abstract and even conjectural. Potential inputs include multinational corporations in the socio-economic sector, such institutions as the United Nations, man's historical conditions in light of world wars, and elites with global systemic influence. On the output side of the diagram, we may seek evidence that the particular patterning of inputs is conducive to cohesion in the international environment, but these conditions and their consequences as diagramed are likely to be representationally inaccurate to the point of precluding explanation due to the level of abstraction required. In reference to the German problem, little insight will be gained by working at this level of analysis. The elite behavior sector holds most promise for explanation of the role of the international system in the problem, but even elite behavior

FIGURE 7.1

An Approach to the Question:
What Impact Will a Changing International
System Have upon the Two Germanys?

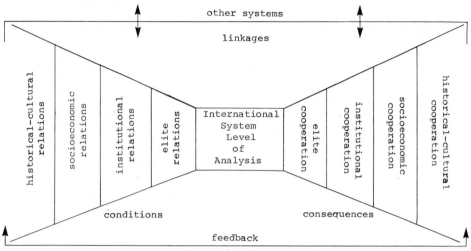

control and communication by world order

FIGURE 7.2

An Approach to the Question:
Will European Unity Be Achieved
in Spite of or Because of
a Reunified Germany?

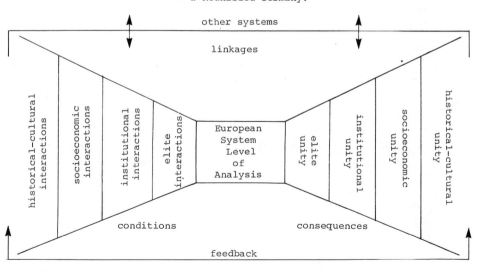

control and communication by European federation

149

defined in terms of international units of analysis will be difficult to identify and measure in some meaningful manner. The systemic level of analysis must be lowered in order to bring the problem into closer focus. However, one might project the desirability of the outcomes indicated in Figure 7.1 without as yet attributing any explanatory power to the model.

Figure 7.2 envisions a system (or subsystem) of the future we have been considering. The major actors may be seen as alliance or bloc subsystemic groups whose interactions comprise an identifiable larger subsystem, a unified Europe, which might be integrated within some sort of federal structure.

Linkages to the higher system could be identified among groups, with ecological interests, for example, whose identities transcend European configurations and bear upon global concerns. Again we are too far removed at this systemic level to derive an empirical position of the German problem in European affairs. European interactions are not yet at a frequency or intensity to provide the necessary, much less sufficient, conditions for European unity. As generally indicated at the level of Figure 7.1, data on European elites and perhaps interactions in the socioeconomic sector will provide indicators for the time being of any systemic formation at the all-European level. At this systemic level, historical and cultural unity may simultaneously be less evident and less necessary than institutional unity. Again, however, little light is shed upon the role of the German problem, and logic indicates another systemic focus is necessary. However, some general indication of the import of a European system for the future of the German states may be found in the linkages with the lower, regional subsystem level. Apparently systemic reality sharpens at the next lower subsystem level, where identifiable groups with common interests are much more easily ascertained. Few groups--these centered mostly in the socioeconomic sector--at the European level may be traced by linkage of interests down below the regional subsystem level. As a matter of fact, the regional subsystems evidence a certain bias toward the maintenance of their East-West distinction, which by linkage is reflected within their respective subsystems, that is, East and West Germany. (It is a general criticism of systems theory that there is a bias of system maintenance as opposed to system change.) With this systemic bias in mind, we proceed next and nearer to our problem with another subsystemic level, as shown in Figure 7.3.

Figure 7.3 represents the empirical framework within which data on several dimensions, economic and military among others, have been presented in previous chapters. Organizations such as the EEC or CMEA, NATO or WTO, provide the regional subsystem frameworks within which transactions occur and develop greater or

FIGURE 7.3

An Approach to the Question:
Will the Two Germanys be Allowed
to Reunite by Their Respective
Alliance Systems?

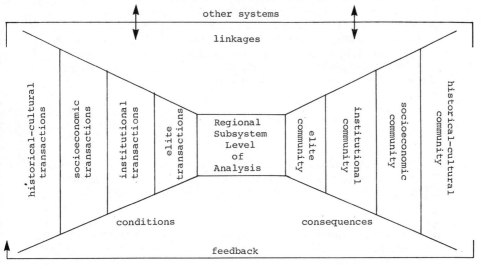

control and communication by bloc organizations

FIGURE 7.4

An Approach to the Question:
Will the Two Germanys Want to Reunite?

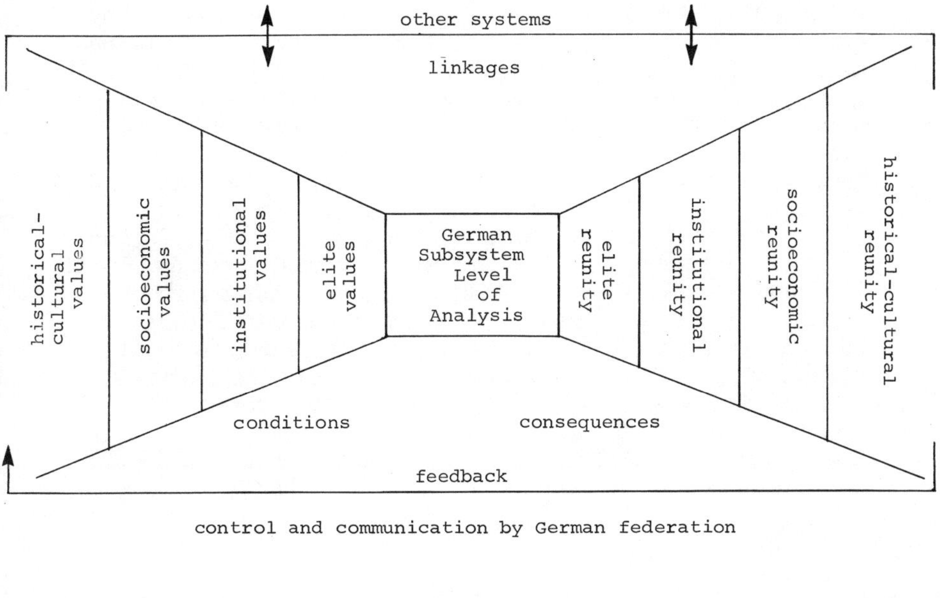

control and communication by German federation

or lesser degrees of community. Projections have been made with respect to the strength of linkages with the Figure 7.2 or European level, in an assessment of the European future. By stressing transactions and interactions at the Figure 7.3 and Figure 7.2 levels, our systems approach comes closer to discering the nature of real systems than would, for instance, an actor-oriented approach. Most of the data on bloc transactions can be found in the socioeconomic sector, although, as indicated, sufficient institutionalization of those transactions has occurred for us to identify real-world communities of a sort for both Eastern and Western Europe.

NATIONAL AND REGIONAL INTEGRATION

Now that our diagram evidences a necessary and perhaps sufficient degree of representational accuracy, our ability to locate the German problem is facilitated. As one must admit, the linkages from this level to the all-European level are minimal; one also looks in vain for linkages downward to the next subsystemic level, that is, an all-German subsystem. To repeat, there is an obvious systemic bias, from both an Eastern and Western bloc point of view, against the appearance of a subsystem that includes components not in its environment. Even when a regional bloc finds an instance of East-West relations to its advantage, such as the special economic interaction between the FRG and the GDR tolerated in the East, the specific relationship is quite likely to remain confined to one area only and not extended, for instance, into relations of another sort (e.g., the publicly stated fear and opposition of the GDR with respect to "free flow of peoples, ideas, and information" as proposed by Western countries at the CSCE). This "free flow" is seen in the East as a threat at the national and regional levels.

The dilemma of German reunification is increased as we proceed to the next lower subsystem indicated in realpolitic. The question as posed now asks for explanations of both state system behavior and individual actor subsystem behavior (see Figures 7.5 and 7.6).

As one could indicate with relative ease in Figures 7.5 and 7.6, there is a subsystem bias against a reunified Germany (Figure 7.4), just as there is a systemic bias from the other direction (Figure 7.3). Sufficient empirical evidence has been gathered to indicate that the individual East German increasingly finds his identity with the GDR state system. Groups of East Germans who perceive their legitimacy within the state system contribute eventually to the goal consensus at that systemic level. From the inside to the outside of the Russian doll (an apt analogy in light of systemic bias and the issue of Soviet power in that bias), then, we

FIGURE 7.5

An Approach to the Question:
Do Germans Identify with Their
Respective States or with
Their Common Nationality?

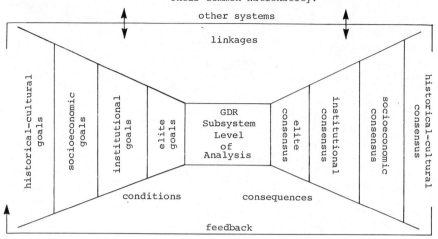

other systems

linkages

historical-cultural goals | socioeconomic goals | institutional goals | elite goals | GDR Subsystem Level of Analysis | elite consensus | institutional consensus | socioeconomic consensus | historical-cultural consensus

conditions   consequences

feedback

control and communication by state system

FIGURE 7.6

A Second Approach to the Question:
Do Germans Identify with Their
Respective States or with
Their Common Nationality?

other systems

linkages

historical-cultural identity | socioeconomic identity | institutional identity | elite identity | Individual Actor Level of Analysis | elite legitimacy | institutional legitimacy | socioeconomic legitimacy | historical-cultural legitimacy

conditions   consequences

feedback

control and communication by group subsystems

153

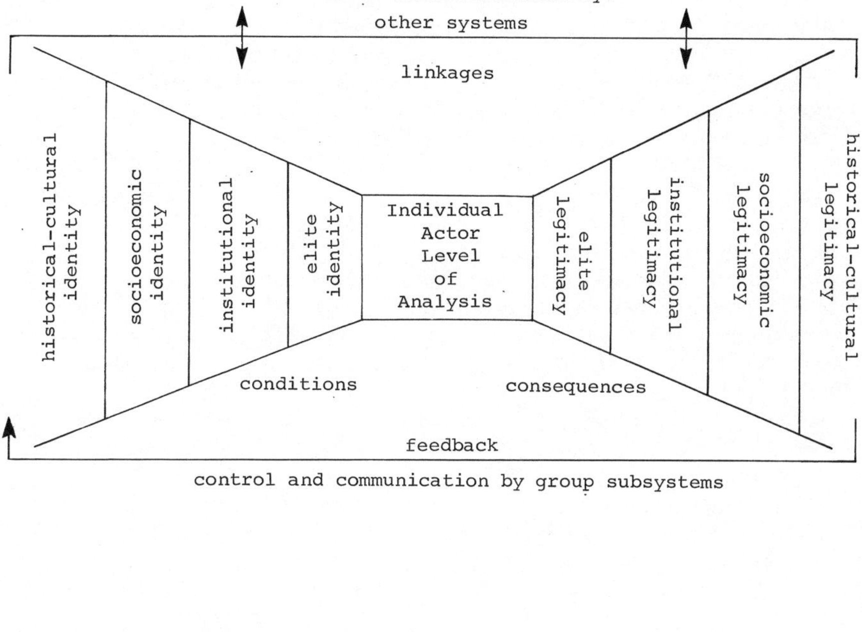

again pass over the realization of Figure 7.4. The process of European integration with which we are concerned might be achieved by a number of different models, but the two most often used, and reflected in Soviet policy and scholarly models respectively, are the neofunctional and the transactional--in more simple terms, integration from above and from below. In either model German reunification is prevented by a systemic mobilization of bias among linkage groups: Figure 7.2 . . . Figure 7.3 . . . (Figure 7.4) . . . Figure 7.5 . . . Figure 7.6. Or, Figure 7.6 . . . Figure 7.5 . . . (Figure 7.4) . . . Figure 7.3 . . . Figure 7.2. Linkages between these systemic levels may provide for integration incrementally, or transactionally, and directly, or functionally, but in both processes German reunification breaks the systemic linkage. Unless one assumes a European federal structure would arbitrarily reunite the two states, an improbable outcome since that system would have been formed out of linkage groups identified by bloc origin, European unity may be conceived without German reunification. Unless one assumes the German states will arbitrarily reunite, an improbable outcome since their respective linkage groups are identified by Eastern or Western systemic legitimacy originally, bloc communities will be formed with the GDR and the FRG in their respective alliances.

Scholarly models aimed at a dependent variable called cohesion, either within bloc subsystems or between regional communities, in the absence of any deliberation or determination of the cohesiveness of subsystems within the larger environment, are confined to normative speculation about a preferred future. Such prescriptions may be valuable in raising the hopes and possibilities of a future order, but they are hardly useful in determining the actual probability of the utopian condition. The issue that confronts us is the European future. Implied in that projection is a model that posits Europe (East and West) as a unit of analysis. However, there is little success as yet in finding input and output variables that explain "European" behavior. And while data has been presented to explain bloc behavior, particular national subsystems are important to the point of separate recognition (by scholars and actors) in the deliberations.

Having determined that a reunified Germany is systemically improbable, the exact positioning of the GDR and the FRG in our problematic framework becomes necessary. Taking the German Democratic Republic as a single subsystem, we might now ask what impact that state has upon its domestic and foreign environments. This line and level of questioning is likely to be far more susceptible to empirical generalizations about the German problem issue area than an approach that, by virtue of a focus too diffused to highlight subsystemic processes, places the regional or European systems in central consideration. It will be argued below that the

issue patterning determinants of cohesion within the state system
of the GDR is one of legitimacy. That issue provides a policy framework within which one may follow the linkages established between
Figures 7.5 and 7.3 to the exclusion of Figure 7.4.

The internal characteristics of the state system of the GDR
will be described and its policy variation from Ulbricht to Honecker
examined. The relationships among determinants of a state's foreign
policy (or domestic policy) may be defined in many ways and may
vary on many dimensions. One simple configuration of policy determinants for a given system is offered in Figure 7.7.[7] Categories
of historical-cultural, socioeconomic, institutional, and elite behavior
variables are seen as funneled into the policy-making point of conversion. Without spelling out in detail the permutations a policy-
relevant issue (from domestic, foreign, or linkage areas) may follow
through the funnel, several key features of the framework should be
pointed out. First, it is assumed, especially when dealing with
centralized, hierarchical systems such as the GDR, but also generally in any policy analysis, that elites are the single indispensable
factor and belong nearest to the point of conversion. In other words,
all determinants flow through the elite behavior sector, which then
consciously acts in accordance or in contrast with such determinism.
While one may view the incremental influence of these factors upon
policy-making, it is important to recognize a reverse direction, or
even reciprocal feedback relationship, among sectors in the funnel.
Elites may shift a nation's socioeconomic development onto a new
pattern or into a new area, as well as themselves reflect in their
decisions the country's socioeconomic capabilities. Socioeconomic
development may give rise to institutional proliferation, which in
turn might effect cultural change in a country.

It is also important to distinguish patterns of policy determination on the basis of issue variability. The domestic issue of industrialization might produce a different pattern of variables (or
substructure of policy determinants) than would the foreign issue of
Soviet power in the determination of the GDR state system's behavior. Contrariwise, one could assume a stable pattern of determination between the two issue areas, which will be shown to be
the case in the GDR. In that event we may label the patterned
interaction among variables associated with the concern for legitimacy as one brought forth by a linkage issue area. Both systemic
and extra-systemic impact would be support for policies geared to
legitimacy of the state. Different rank orderings of the degree of
determination of these policy substructures may occur as policy-
relevant issues change. If such variation is not found from issue
to issue, then systemic reinforcement is predominant. Since it is
the linkage issue area that produces systemic stability in the GDR,
the ties with the bloc subsystem are also reinforced. The systems
approach and framework in Figure 7.7 contains an explicit theoretical

FIGURE 7.7

An Approach to the
Policy Process

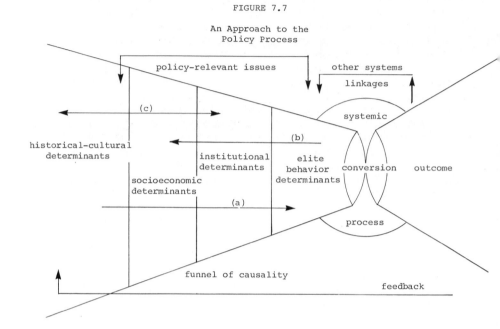

bias with respect to the significance of elites. Without a detailed defense of that systemic feature, a defense that will increasingly become necessary as socioeconomic development proceeds in the GDR, the framework bases its assumption on a reading of the general structural-functional characteristics of Communist polities. One might also add that even comparative analysis of American states' policies has explained little variation on the basis of socioeconomic variables and has itself begun to reemphasize elite/politics variables. Analysis of the changing East German elite should provide the clearest indicators of policy determination in that state. The critical issues to be examined, as explained previously, will be those that overlap with the domestic and foreign areas and relate to other systems. In our assessment of the East German leadership, then, we should identify the relationships of the historical-cultural, socioeconomic, and institutional variable categories with the elite behavior category, on the one hand, and we should attempt to identify issues that produce stability or instability in that policy substructure on the other hand.

Data availability is an ever-present problem in Communist elite studies and is only accentuated when dealing with the GDR. The summary review of elite change here acknowledges a debt to the work of Peter Christian Ludz, while at the same time recognizing that his data analysis should be read within the context of Ulbricht's optimistic model of a "developed social system of socialism."[8] Many of the socioeconomic and institutional reforms to which Ludz relates trends of continuity and change in the elite sector have now been reversed. However, it is not to be debated that the advanced industrialized state of the German Democratic Republic has produced a subtle distinction between a "strategic clique" and an "institutionalized counterelite." Our systems framework implies that the elite is concerned with system maintenance above all other matters, and Ludz's findings confirm this bias in the model by stressing that the new counterelite is not oppositional but simply more open to social change, more willing to rationalize ideologically, and more concerned with economic performance than with political power. Although concentrated within the Central Committee and lower echelons of the party apparatus, this specialized counterelite has managed to effect a "consultative authoritarianism" in contrast to the old totalitarian operational code. In an elaborate statistical analysis of the Socialist Unity Party of Germany (SED) Central Committee, Ludz presents a detailed demonstration of the trend toward an educationally advanced and economically/technically sophisticated elite. Further, he outlines a functional stability within the elite structure, whereby the interchangeability of roles has become diminished, although, as one reviewer has pointed out, little attention is given to any shift in the basic SED cadre policy of continued interchangeability across party, governmental, economic, and other bureaucracies.[9] Ludz also discusses an institutionalized revisionism on the ideological dimension. Such revisionism has manifested itself in "utopian" and "systems theory" variants, with the latter receiving special attention from Ludz as a more "relevant" alternative to traditional Communist ideology than is utopianism.

It should be underlined that the trends outlined by Ludz do not posit a single pattern of determination for policy in a liberal direction. The technical elites themselves seem entangled in an argument over the issue of market versus plan, with one group emphasizing the flexibility provided by liberal reforms while another emphasizes the sophistication provided by advanced mechanisms of control and planning. The New Economic System sponsored by Ulbricht in the 1960s produced an impressive level of economic performance but only heightened fears about legitimacy and authority within the system, which were then confirmed by the Czech events of August.

Thus the reversal of market experimentation in the 1970s and a planning approach to both economic performance and political authority.[10]

The shift in domestic issue area orientation has been paralleled by a shift in the foreign policy issue area. Honecker's assumption of power reflected obvious extra-systemic influences--in other words, from the Soviet/East European bloc, the environment of an all-European security conference, and the environment of détente in the international system itself. Ulbricht's inflexible position, requiring an a priori recognition of his international and internal legitimacy by the Federal Republic as a condition of negotiation, set the scene for his resignation, and a four-power agreement was concluded on September 3, 1971. In the interim Honecker had made clear his move toward greater ties with the Soviet/East European bloc at the twenty-fifth Comecon Council conference in Bucharest in July 1971.

The most obvious fact in the November 1972 state treaty normalizing relations between East and West Germany is that both parties have benefited. Honecker's domestic and foreign policy confirmation of Soviet intentions seems to have gained his authority a degree of internal and external legitimacy.[11] Although the GDR's sovereignty is not total, due to a restatement by the four victor powers of World War II as to their continuing rights in Germany, the theoretical possibility of a reunification is slight indeed.

To complete Figure 7.7 and the systems analysis of the GDR's policy-making process, policy outcome and impact should be considered (see Figure 7.8). As we have used the analogy of a funnel of causality to discuss determinants of that policy, we may now employ the analogy of a projector of effectuality. From the point of conversion outwards--as in the funnel an increasing degree of determination proceeds inwards--relationships among components of the system become increasingly diffused. A broad typology of such relationships is indicated by the categories of consensus, accommodation, integrative conflict, and disintegrative conflict. In this sense a disintegrative relationship in the system would, by feedback, produce systemic change at best and system destruction at worst. Integrative conflict, such as that already mentioned among the technocratic elite over the issue of market versus plan, would produce most of the meaningful systemic change without threatening actual systemic transformation of a revolutionary nature. Again, the systems model and the empirical picture of the German Democratic Republic indicate a strong bias for consensual and accommodative relationships on most domestic, foreign, and linkage issues. The single most significant issue in the determination of East German policy on the German problem--a problem of relevance at various systemic levels (Figures 7.2, 7.3, 7.5, and 7.6) in Europe--is that of legitimacy. That concern, it is submitted here in conclusion, provides a clue to the independent variables most explanatory (and ultimately predictive) of the

FIGURE 7.8

An Approach to Policy Outcome

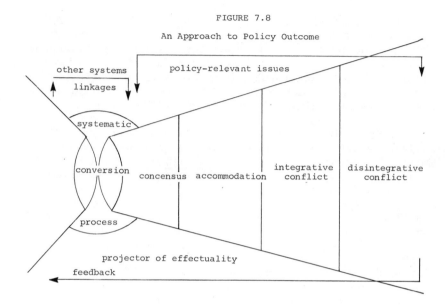

dependent variable cohesiveness, whether at the state, regional, or European level of analysis.

Moreover, as we plot linkage patterns from one level to another, a systemic hierarchy is seen as reinforcing the strength of the legitimacy issue in the determination of East German domestic, foreign, and extra-systemic or international relations.[12] Although the preoccupation with systems in this analysis is open to scholarly and scientific criticism to be sure, its projection of a European realpolitic hopefully provides genuine alternative future paths for policy-makers, as opposed to emotional appeals for a preferred future.

NOTES

1. See James N. Rosenau, "Foreign Policy As an Issue Area," in his Scientific Study of Foreign Policy (New York: The Free Press, 1971), pp. 401-40. Rosenau opts for a simple dichotomy of domestic/foreign issue areas, considering issues that fall into an overlap area as "exceptional," thus providing little assistance in the explanation of policies in states that are influenced on most issues by other systems. This is particularly the case in the GDR, as the state itself is a foreign policy issue.

2. See William A. Welsh, "The Usefulness of the Apter, Easton, and Spiro Models in the Study of Communist Systems in Eastern Europe," Newsletter on Comparative Studies of Communism 5, no. 4 (August 1972), pp. 3-20, for a valuable critique of strengths and weaknesses of the systems approach.

3. See the several essays in Klaus Knorr and Sidney Verba, eds., The International System: Theoretical Essays (Princeton, N.J.: Princeton University Press, 1961), in particular the essay on levels by J. David Singer, "The Levels of Analysis Problem in International Relations," pp. 77-92.

4. See the discussion on "levels of discourse" in Fred N. Kerlinger, Foundations of Behavioral Research: Educational and Psychological Inquiry (New York: Holt, Rinehart and Winston, 1964), pp. 67-80.

5. The "Russian doll" analogy to systemic levels was introduced in a compelling argument for the study of Europe as a single subsystem in an introductory paper by Jean Siotis at the panel on "East and West Europe as a Single Sub-System," International Studies Association annual meeting, Dallas, March 3-5, 1972.

6. For a complete discussion of the linkage problem between levels of analysis, see James N. Rosenau, ed., Linkage Politics: Essays on the Convergence of National and International Systems (New York: The Free Press, 1969). Due to the problem of an explicit dichotomy between domestic and foreign areas in the Rosenau framework, however, the application of his linkage politics to many of the systems of Eastern Europe seems quite strained. See, in particular, R.V. Burks, "The Communist Polities of Eastern Europe," pp. 275-303, which posits a conclusion in contradiction to almost all research on the integrative process in Eastern Europe: "If in order to survive over the longer run the regimes, or some of them, evolve away from Marxism-Leninism, then we will no longer be able to speak of a special set of linkages. There may remain profound institutional similarities, such as state ownership of the means of production, or one-party governments, but these similarities will not be interrelated from state to state by special institutional ties. Eastern Europe will in that case have returned to normal

linkages" (p. 303). Evidence to the contrary may be found by using the approach of "linkage groups" as defined in Karl W. Deutsch, "External Influences on the Internal Behavior of States," in R. Barry Farrell, ed., Approaches to Comparative and International Politics (Evanston, Ill.: Northwestern University Press, 1966), pp. 5-26.

7. Special mention must be made here of the entire field of comparative policy analysis in the American states as found in the writings of Thomas R. Dye, Richard I. Hofferbert, and Ira Sharkansky, among others. In particular the "funnel of causality" utilized here is based upon the original conceptualization by Angus Campbell et al., in their The American Voter (New York: John Wiley, 1960).

8. See Peter Christian Ludz, The Changing Party Elite in East Germany (Cambridge, Mass.: The MIT Press, 1972).

9. See the recent review of Ludz by Thomas A. Baylis, "Political Change in East Germany," Problems of Communism 21, no. 6 (November-December 1972), pp. 72-75.

10. For an excellent discussion of the relationship of the economic debate and the issue of legitimacy, see Thomas A. Baylis, "Inquest of Legitimacy," Problems of Communism 21, no. 2 (March-April 1972), pp. 46-55.

11. See Peter C. Ludz, "Continuity and Change Since Ulbricht," Problems of Communism 21, no. 2 (March-April 1972), pp. 56-67.

12. Witness the conclusion by Arthur M. Hanhardt, Jr., The German Democratic Republic (Baltimore: The Johns Hopkins Press, 1968): "There is no one among the hopefuls who has the qualities of leadership and authority to move the German Democratic Republic far from its present place in the formation of the communist party state system" (p. 113). For a new and interesting discussion of this process of continuity due to a systemic hierarchy, see Steven L. Spiegel, Dominance and Diversity, The International Hierarchy (Boston: Little, Brown, 1972).

8

EUROPEAN REALPOLITIC II:
BONN'S OSTPOLITIK
Louis J. Mensonides

The future of Europe will depend in various respects on the course and policies pursued by West Germany. This has also been true in the last two decades. In a speech delivered in Stockholm on December 12, 1971, Chancellor Willy Brandt declared:

> No nation, however deep it may have fallen, can and wants to live without pride forever. The boundless cruelty of the Hitler regimes seemed to have made the European judgment of the Germans irreversible. It has not been easy to keep alive faith in a decent Germany. However, it is not only the individual who can think things over and mend his ways. A nation, too, can overcome an evil past and re-define its place in history. . . .
> We in Germany, and in Europe, had to struggle and suffer our way through the bitter aftermath of the war and the Cold War, until a new Germany was able to participate actively in organizing peace--a Germany that has found its image in the Federal Republic as a State based on a liberal system obeying the rule of law.
> Chancellor Adenauer was able to accomplish the first important part, namely, to build up understanding and trustful co-operation with the countries of the West. Ours was the task of tackling the equally important second part; that is, reconciliation with our neighbors in the East and all-European co-operation leading beyond and overriding the East-West conflict.
> In Oslo I spoke about what, from my point of view and experience, European peace policy should be in our day and age. That we need absolute renunciation of force; a reduction and, if possible, also control of armaments. And in spite of all continuing differences and conflicts a

network of practical co-operation spanning all Europe:
economic, technical and scientific, as well as cultural.
And also more tolerance, more readiness to hear and
weigh the other party's arguments.[1]

This "reconciliation with our neighbors in the East," frequently
called the Ostpolitik, a new approach toward Eastern Europe, has
become one of the main features of West German foreign policy, and
therefore one of the "new realities" of Europe. Brandt has said,
"It is in the nature of things that even those countries in Comecon--
the Soviet-East European economic bloc--will normalize their relations with the European Community as well as with Japan and probably
also with the United States."[2]

Some of the realities have not changed over the years as seen
in the present context. And, as such, Chancellor Brandt is constantly
trying to keep his Ostpolitik closely balanced by his "Westpolitik"
as evidenced by a statement in April 1972:

In the Federal Republic of Germany there is not a single
question of any importance that could be treated outside
the context of American-European relations. This applies
to international currency and trade affairs as well as to
security policy and above all to efforts to decrease tensions between East and West.[3]

It is the object of this chapter to examine several aspects of
the Ostpolitik and its evolution into the second phase once the
existing Social Democratic Party (SPD) and the Free Democratic
Party (FDP) coalition has received a mandate from the West German
electorate. An attempt will be made to examine some of the reasons
for the progress made in the reconciliation policies, what continuation will be dependent on, and finally what the goals of the Ostpolitik
may lead to.

THE POSTWAR ERA

Ever since World War II the United States has pursued a
foreign policy toward Western Europe that on the whole must be
rated a success. The containment formula was to give Europe the
opportunity to recover from the war and become the cornerstone of
U.S. policy.[4] The remarkable economic progress, coupled with the
region's relative political stability, now forms the background for
the initiatives of Europe--and particularly West Germany--toward
the East.

The approach to the East is therefore the result of a long period of West European consolidation as well as an outgrowth of a reevaluation of the geopolitical realities of Europe. As these realities have evolved, so too has the Ostpolitik as one aspect of them-- initially failing, then going through a frustrating phase in 1960-68, followed by the first Brandt period of 1968-73.[5] Up to this point the Ostpolitik must be regarded as an outgrowth of the relationships of Europe rather than a policy superimposed to change Europe's relationships; this differentiation is the key to understanding the apparently successful efforts of the present German government, with the result that Brandt's Ostpolitik is regarded as one possible vehicle for a general détente in Europe, the others being the SALT talks, the Berlin agreements, the Helsinki meetings in preparation for a general European security conference, and the Nixon-Brezhnev Moscow agreements. There is an interdependence in all of these, for it is not mere coincidence that progress has been made in all of these areas of potential conflict.

A number of specific developments in the 1950s and 1960s stand out. Technologically both superpowers, the United States and the Soviet Union, had developed nuclear parity by the end of the 1960s while at the same time realizing the increasing economic and political costs involved in upgrading and producing even more sophisiticated defensive and offensive weapon systems.[6] This led to several declarations by both sides requesting arms limitations and reductions, which a major Warsaw Pact statement coming at the meeting in Prague on January 25-26, 1972.[7]

A second development has been the growing strength, influence, and prestige of China. Whether this has led to the development of a tripolar situation as opposed to bipolarity or even multipolarity is debatable.[8] Nor is it agreed what the precise consequences have been for the Soviet Union, and subsequently for Europe.[9] All agree that some realignment is taking place, and that is a noticeable variable in United States-USSR-European relationships.

A third fact is the changing face of the East European satellite countries. All are becoming stronger economically, with East Germany boasting in 1972 that it ranked tenth in the world economically.[10] Many are also demanding more political latitude, calling for national sovereignty.[11] All in all these changes posed a threat to the Soviet Union's immediate security system in Eastern Europe. Forceful action and response was demonstrated by the USSR in 1968, and was defined more specifically by the Brezhnev Doctrine; a reinterpretation of the West German question and threat was already in progress.[12]

Fourth, the Common Market was a reality, even for Moscow. The enlargement to ten (later nine) members was not received enthusiastically, and an increase in the integration tempo even less. Efforts to provide Western Europe with an alternative needed to be made, possibly even driving a wedge between Europe and the United States as well.[13] Furthermore, the Soviet Union was faced with food shortages, consumer demands, technology needs, and security problems (Middle East). These hastened a willingness to come to a settlement in Europe.

For West Germany this period consisted mainly in consolidating its position within the EEC and the Atlantic alliance and gaining economic and political mobility. Nevertheless, in the early 1960s Gerhardt Schroeder, foreign minister of the Erhard government, had begun the policy of "kleine schritte" (little steps) with the backing of the FDP and the SPD. These policies resulted in a trade mission to Poland and a solemn German promise to renounce the use of force. Even Konrad Adenauer visited Moscow in 1955 and established diplomatic relations with the USSR, in apparent disregard of the Hallstein Doctrine. Thus even though the official policy of West Germany was that of the cold war, it still acted pragmatically in its relations with Eastern Europe and the Soviets. It has even been stated that Adenauer kept Hans Kroll, the controversial ambassador, in Moscow in the hope that his special goodwill with Soviet Premier Khrushchev might lead to serious East-West talks.[14]

Throughout the early 1960s, however, German attempts to reconcile relations with neighbors, especially Czechoslovakia and Poland, were met with charges of revanchism and militarism. The Eastern bloc also demanded concessions impossible at the time, such as German renunciation of nuclear weapons; recognition of the Oder-Neisse line; nonvalidity of the Munich agreement; recognition of East Germany; and abandonment of Bonn's claim to be the representative of all Germans.[15]

Bonn's Ostpolitik was initiated in a careful outline by West German Chancellor Ludwig Erhard in 1966. Instead of the old policies of Konrad Adenauer, the new policy reflected the changing situation and a new appraisal of the political relationships of Europe. Rather than a frontal assault, this early Ostpolitik was designed to capitalize upon the circumstances and conditions that seemed to make possible a new German role in Europe. Bonn hoped to exploit its American alliance, its economic strength, the defiance of some members of the Soviet bloc, Soviet internal economic problems, the Arab (that is, Soviet) defeat in the Middle East, the increasing polycentrism of world Communism, and presumably the threat of China. All of these were estimated to be effective weapons to promote the ultimate German aim, namely, the creation of conditions conducive to German reunification without violence. Bonn thus attempted to become a counterweight to Soviet influence by offering economic inducements and technical aid while agreeing to the territorial status quo. At the same time Bonn hoped to reorient the satellite states to a more conciliatory stance that might be to their advantage. The 1968 Prague invasion put an effective end to all of these efforts and assumptions.

At the time it was widely assumed that Czechoslovakia was going to recognize Bonn (as did Romania in 1967) in exchange for an extension of economic credits. A week prior to the intervention, a West German official had announced that Bonn was willing to declare the Munich Pact of 1938 "void from the outset," thus eliminating the major obstacle to improved relations. Czechoslovakia also let it be known that it would soon apply for credits from the World Bank. In many capitals these two events were seen as indicating a successful West German penetration of East Europe.[16] The invasion of Czechoslovakia in August 1968 demonstrated that the Soviets were well aware of the threat posed by German economic penetration, and thus responded in a manner that shook the political capitals of the world. Thus ended the political life of phase one of the Ostpolitik.

This initial Ostpolitik had concentrated on direct economic, diplomatic, and cultural ties with the countries of East Europe. The Soviet leaders had rejected this direct approach in the summer of 1968, but were divided as to the proper combative measures. The Kremlin had correctly perceived these inroads as directly affecting Soviet hegemony in Eastern Europe, and responded with warnings, threats, compromise, and finally military occupation.

As a result of the Brezhnev Doctrine the old Ostpolitik was dead, evolving in its place the controversial new Ostpolitik of Brandt. Instead of building a wall, the Soviet leaders had decided to exploit Bonn's economic strength while attempting to prevent West German economic inputs from overflowing into the political and diplomatic sphere. The Brezhnev Doctrine was thus a seal that attempted to immunize the countries of East Europe from the political, ideological, and military penetration of the West, while allowing limited cultural and economic contacts. Thus Brandt's new Ostpolitik was a compromise between West German awareness that Moscow would accept no political change and Moscow's acceptance of the increasing power of the West German state.[17]

Following the Czech invasion and the signing of a treaty for the "temporary" garrisoning of Soviet troops, Moscow attempted to calm the West and "normalize" East-West relations. Willy Brandt and Soviet Foreign Minister Andrei Gromyko met in New York in October 1968 and agreed to drop the rhetoric of invasion and seek common interests. Further Soviet interest was demonstrated when Soviet Ambassador Tsarapkin returned to Bonn in January 1969 and expressed his government's willingness to initiate political negotiations and possible increases in cooperation.[18] The Warsaw Pact's Political Consultative Committee met in Budapest in March and issued a call for a European security conference. There was a notable lack of anti-German pronouncements such as "militarism," which had usually flavored the committee's announcements. Also conducive to a favorable atmosphere was the decision of the SPD party congress in April 1969 to adopt a party program pledging full cooperation with

Pankow at all levels short of full recognition, thus leading the way to the eventual "state-like" recognition for East Germany. This decision, adopted by a vote of 344-10, was clearly a turning point for German-Soviet relations.[19]

April 1969 turned into what could be described as the beginning of a Soviet diplomatic offensive. At the fiftieth anniversary of Commintern, the Russians instructed the delegates not to do anything that might endanger the chances of Brandt's SPD in the upcoming fall elections.[20] Brandt also contributed by making a favorable speech based on Soviet Ambassador Tsarapkin's assurances that recognition of East Germany was a subject of a conference rather than a pre-condition. On Tsarapkin's suggestion, envoy Rudolf Heizler was sent to Moscow; he reported that Moscow was interested in negotiations, and talks concerning commercial air routes were soon started.[21] These warming trends continued throughout May 1969 and were highlighted by Gomulka's (Poland) speech of May 17, in which he spoke of the decline of the German threat and opened the possibility of accommodation with Bonn. Brandt replied on May 19, referring to the Gomulka speech as "remarkable," and proposed the negotiation of agreements renouncing the use of force.[22]

Thus with tentative agreements for future meetings, the SPD-FDP coalition had to face a referendum on its proposed policies, the West German elections in fall 1969. While the Ostpolitik was enjoying an unprecedented acceptance abroad, it would have to face its first and most significant test before the West German electorate.

All three major political parties agreed on the basic tenets of West European policy and held similar views on the Western alliance policy. But agreement on the East was lacking and became the main emphasis of the election. The SPD focused its campaign to the East, thus gaining the alliance of the Free Democrats (FDP) who have favored recognition of East Germany. The SPD platform forced the Christian Democratic Union (CDU) to have a moderate Eastern policy, which at the same time could cause the loss of CDU's right wing. The National Democratic Party further complicated the CDU's position by adopting an ultra-nationalistic platform; thus the CDU, desiring not to be passed on the right, adopted a national conservative platform. The CDU also hoped that it could undermine the SPD by stressing the "Western aspects," such as the alliance, but the end result of this position was to leave the SPD alone in the area of foreign policy to the East.

The CDU also clung to its traditional policies in that it continued to claim that East Germany was an artificial state, a Soviet puppet, and that the East German Communist party (SED) did not have deep-rooted sovereignty but depended on Soviet influence for its existence. The SPD on the other hand felt that the SED and East Germany were, for the present, there to stay. The SPD also recognized that East Germany was the fifth industrial power in Europe, positively viable and somewhat autonomous from the Kremlin. Thus the election was really a national referendum on the question of the cold war. The electorate could choose the CDU and keep things the same, or it could give the SPD a chance with its new Ostpolitik. The election results proved a mandate for the SPD to pursue a more flexible policy toward the East. Thus German public opinion seemed to have changed from a postwar concern with unification to a more realistic goal of attempting a détente, with lessening of tensions thus promoting some sort of eventual German union.[23]

After their mandate, Willy Brandt (SPD) and Walter Scheel (FCP), the leaders of the respective parties, launched a new compromise Ostpolitik with the hope of achieving a new rapport in East-West relations.

DEVELOPMENTS IN 1969

Most of the key points of the second phase of the Ostpolitik program were outlined by Chancellor Brandt in a speech to the Bundestag, the lower house of the German legislature, on October 28, 1969. Brandt spoke of a desire to enter a European peace order, "designed to undo the treacheries of the Hitler regime." He felt that the new regime must "prevent further alienation of the two parts of the German nation . . . arrive at a modus vivendi . . . and proceed to cooperation." While stating that recognition of East Germany was out of the question, his government would continue its attempts, initiated in 1966, to negotiate with the East German regime concerning agreements renouncing additional trade and Berlin. Brandt also spoke of increased cooperation in the United Nations and a desire to increase trade with "all states in the world." Also stressed was the West German determination to contribute to the defense of Europe and to continue its membership in NATO.[24]

The program outlined was basically a West German acceptance of the status quo in Europe and reflected a desire for mutual security guarantees with the East. This so called "peace" program was aimed at "accepting the realities of Central Europe" and increasing rapport with the USSR, especially with Hungary, Poland, Czechoslovakia, Bulgaria, and East Germany. In pursuance of this policy Brandt also agreed to revoke the Hallstein Doctrine, which had declared the formation of the German Democratic Republic (GDR) an unfriendly act.

The position of the Brandt-Scheel coalition in 1969 was precarious at best, with a majority of only 12 seats in the 497-member Bundestag. In spite of this situation the governing parties announced that they would sign a treaty acknowledging the existence of "two states of the German nation" without foreclosing eventual unification.[25]

Some accommodation with the GDR was uppermost in Brandt's mind. But he proceeded on a number of assumptions, not the least of which was that the road to East Berlin as well as to Warsaw led through Moscow. He also realized that he had more flexibility and room to maneuver than either the previous German government or the Western alliance powers had. The initiative should be taken by the Germans themselves and not be left to others. Other assumptions were that European security could not be dealt with until the German question was settled effectively. And since the Warsaw Pact had called for a European security conference, the time to act on the German problem was of first priority.

Time was a basic factor for the chancellor. Not only was his political life and that of his SPD party and his coalition at stake but the GDR was gaining economic strength and advantage and there was an increasing clamor for U.S. troop withdrawal from various directions. If the coalition was to bargain from a position of strength, time was of the essence.

And, finally, any accommodation would surely help the status of West Berlin, the most sensitive issue of all. Obviously the West Germans could offer the East concessions in return. As already mentioned, there was the technical and economic aid West Germany had to offer. Renunciation of territorial claims and border recognition was another meaningful concession, as was a renunciation of force. Soviet fear would play into Brandt's hands in that having a favorable government in Bonn willing to make concessions is better than a hostile one. The 1972 West German elections substantiated this point. And Brandt recognized that the USSR could and would exert pressure on the GDR, something that has indeed been acknowledged by both the USSR and East Berlin.[26]

The immediate aim of the new policy in 1969 was to seek a "provisional settlement of indefinite duration, to govern relations, until the division of Germany is eroded by time." Brandt estimated that a détente and unity in Europe could decrease the importance of borders in 20 to 30 years. Thus a new rapport would help prevent the door from closing on the possibility of future German reunification. The vehicle for a "provisional German peace treaty" is a renunciation-of-force pact with Moscow and each Warsaw Pact country. Brandt stated, "Since the German people in its entirety cannot hope for a peace treaty in the foreseeable future, the renunciation of force can furnish the basis for settling with the various countries of East Europe, individual political questions now capable of solution."

In view of Brandt's proposals, on December 3 and 4, 1969, seven Soviet bloc members met to decide a joint policy toward Bonn. Four separate policy lines were immediately evident at this meeting. Poland demanded the right to enter negotiations. Romania also was in favor of the proposed talks, as it had had diplomatic ties with Bonn since 1967. Czechoslovakia, Bulgaria, and Hungary were more cautious and supported the noncommittal view of Moscow; only East Germany opposed dealing with the new Bonn government.[27]

The East German government replied on December 18, 1969, with a long list of demands that seemed to put the entire Brandt-Scheel effort in jeopardy.[28]

Despite this hardline approach by East Berlin, the Brandt government would vigorously pursue (see below) the "functional division of labor" approach in negotiating, as outlined by the Warsaw Pact group in the Moscow declaration following the December 3 and 4 meetings.[29]

THE OSTPOLITIK: 1969-72

There are four major aspects to the Ostpolitik between 1969 and 1972: Bonn's relationwhip with East Berlin, the Bonn-Moscow negotiations, the Bonn-Warsaw treaty, and the Berlin agreements which involved the occupation powers but became a key factor in the policies of both Bonn and East Berlin. Although the full implications of the Berlin agreements go beyond the scope of this chapter, some attention to them is warranted because of the interrelationship mentioned. While the SPD-FDP coalition had won the September 1969 election, it had a very marginal base of 12 seats (later reduced to zero) and the Brandt-Scheel team decided to wage a vigorous Ostpolitik with a quick payoff. A Bonn-Moscow accord became the first step in the negotiations with the Warsaw Pact states. Its priority seemed logical; success here would open the way for further treaties with other Warsaw Pact members. A nonaggression pact became the key for all future negotiations and was to test the seriousness of Moscow's intentions.

From previous statements by Warsaw Pact states there were seven preconditions or demands that Bonn would have to meet if it wanted an easing of tensions: (1) recognition of the Oder-Neisse line and acceptance of all other central European borders, (2) legal status for East Germany, (3) renunciation of the 1938 Munich agreement, (4) renunciation of the Hallstein doctrine, (5) nonpossession of nuclear weapons, (6) support for disarmament, and (7) independent status for West Berlin.[30]

In several speeches between September and December, Brandt indicated his government's willingness to meet most of these demands. This led to simultaneous negotiations with Moscow and Warsaw, although the Moscow agenda took priority. Such bilateral negotiations were endorsed by the Warsaw Pact's Moscow declaration of December 5, 1969.[31]

Succeeding statements by the Warsaw Pact member states made it clear that a "division of labor" or a "functionalism" in negotiations with Bonn had been established at the Moscow meetings: The USSR would set the tone in nonaggression discussions with Bonn and would handle the West Berlin problem with the Western occupation powers.[32]

And so on August 12, 1970, the Soviet-West German treaty was signed, pledging: (1) the right of German self-determination; (2) expansion of economic and technical cooperation; (3) recognition of the "actual situation existing in the region" as the basis of normalizing relations with other states; (4) renunciation of force and peaceful settlement of disputes; (5) respect for territorial integrity of all European states, renunciation of territorial claims, and recognition of existing borders including the Oder-Neisse line and the frontier between the GDR and West Germany; and (6) continuation of the allied rights and responsibilities for Berlin and Germany (in a note issued in conjunction with the treaty).

Moscow immediately interpreted the treaty as Bonn's acceptance of the status quo of a very permanent nature.[33] Bonn, on the other hand, felt the treaty would facilitate the process of normalization with other Warsaw Pact states, provide the basis for a Berlin settlement to which Moscow was committed, reduce Moscow's rights of intervention, and provide acceptance of the status quo in Berlin--a quid pro quo. Furthermore, no reparations were to be paid; West Berlin's economic ties with West Germany also remained unchallenged, and additional economic opportunities were now possible with the East European states.

Obviously there were many reservations as well.[34] The most important of these, as stated in the Bundestag debate, were:

1. The treaty had indeed confirmed the status quo in Europe, in Moscow's favor,

2. Berlin's solution was dependent on Moscow's good graces and the initiative was lost to the West,

3. There was a tacit endorsement of the Brezhnev Doctrine, a disregard for historical and contemporary public sentiment in the East European countries,

4. It might well lead to estrangement of Bonn from its allies and at least cause ambiguity and suspicion of Bonn's credibility in its Westpolitik,

5. Bonn was helping Moscow to consolidate its power over the satellite states, thus enhancing Soviet power and prestige.

What is clear is that the treaty greatly influenced the course of events between Bonn and Warsaw, as well as Bonn's relations with East Berlin. First, the Bonn-Warsaw developments.

The Moscow-Bonn Treaty had set the tone; nevertheless, the Poles had their own worries about being caught between Germany on one side and the Soviet Union on the other. In the twentieth century alone, Poland had experienced 39 border changes; it also had been occupied for some 700 years in its history, and subjected to all forms of aggression. Especially on the "lost territories" questions as well as the German minorities problem, much negotiation was necessary, with Poland refusing to accept any compromise formula. Only when the Bonn-Moscow Treaty was signed did Warsaw begin to give some ground.* On November 12, 1970, agreement was reached and the Moscow formula largely accepted, with additional clauses for reparations, emigration, and diplomatic recognition. All in all, the de facto Oder-Neisse line concession by Bonn stands out as the single most important achievement for Poland.

The Bonn-Moscow Treaty made East Germany the main loser on August 12, 1970, particularly by minimizing the East Berlin demands placed on Bonn and by acknowledging Moscow's final responsibility for Germany and Berlin, a direct slap at East Germany's sovereign status.

However, all through the winter and spring of 1970 the Bonn-East Berlin talks had been extremely difficult since the East Germans tried to outmaneuver the Bonn negotiators and repeatedly made impossible demands. They made recognition a precondition, to be followed by negotiations, whereas the Poles had reversed the priorities. The polemics lasted until late March 1970, when Willy Brandt and Willi Stoph met in Erfurt in East Germany as heads of their respective governments. It was a most significant date in German relations and in the Ostpolitik.

Stoph restated the original seven demands during the Erfurt meeting. Brandt replied that he could never consider the GDR a "foreign country." He said he saw two German states in one German nation; proposed to collaborate in a "neighborly fashion"; and in turn offered a list of tentative steps of cooperation, such as establishing working-level secretariats in each other's capitals, easing human relationships, and stopping discrimination against each other. A stalemate followed. In May Ulbricht visited Moscow, after which Stoph kept his appointment with Brandt in Kassel, West Germany, on May 21. It seems Moscow did not want to jeopardize its negotiations with Bonn, nor did Warsaw. Economic agreements with other East European states also were signed during the period, pointing to increasing isolation for East Germany in its relations with Bonn.[35] Several anti-East German outbursts in Kassel did

---

*The points at issue had been whether there would be a conflict between the Potsdam agreements of 1945 and these subsequent Bonn-Warsaw agreements. Also at issue was whether Polish German minorities were strictly an internal Polish matter or a point for negotiation. After conclusion of the treaty, some 92,000 Polish Germans emigrated.

nothing to improve relations but deepened the freeze lasting well into 1972.

At Kassel, Bonn's plans for coexistence were stated in the so-called 20 points.[36] They again restated Bonn's main objectives: respect for each other's territories, independence, borders, membership in international organizations, exchange of diplomats, renunciation of the use of force, easing of travel, and visitation rights. All were rejected out of hand by Stoph; the gulf had widened and no break was to come until 1972 after Ulbricht had left, the Berlin agreements had been signed by the Big Four, and the Brandt-Scheel coalition needed a boost to retain power in the November 1972 West German elections.

The fourth aspect of the Ostpolitik was the Berlin situation, although primarily the responsibility of the Big Four. And so in any consideration of détente one must consider the question of Berlin, as this is perhaps the most volatile area in Europe. In order to have a real détente, an agreement was needed concerning the status of Berlin. Thus a discussion of the Big Four Berlin talks must be included as a significant aspect of the West German Ostpolitik. The allies proposed such talks in 1969, but were surprised when the Russians replied affirmatively in July.

On March 26, 1970, ambassadors from Britain, France, the USSR, and the United States met in the former Control Council building in the American sector. The initial goals of the parties were as follows: The USSR wished to reduce Berlin to a "special status," in other words, to cut its ties with West Germany and limit West German political activity in the city. The allies wished to keep West Berlin firmly tied to West Germany, gain free access to the city, and gain Soviet acknowledgement of the four-power responsibility for the city. As to the seriousness of the Russians, this was the first meeting concerning the status of Berlin in eleven years. The official communique stated that views had been exchanged and the next meeting was scheduled for April 28. The very presence of the Soviets at such a meeting demonstrated that they were interested in a détente. They may not have been willing to grant concessions at this stage, but they were willing to discuss the situation. The United States also favored the talks and expressed hope for "modest but perceptible steps" toward a solution for Berlin. Washington was skeptical of the Russian desire to reach agreement on Berlin, and thus cautioned Bonn to move with care.

While Bonn was basking in the limelight, the United States was being constantly consulted in regard to the Western position. The behind-the-scenes role the United States played was underscored on October 20, 1970, when Gromyko met with President Nixon in an attempt to clear up the Soviet position on Berlin. He also indicated to Nixon that the USSR was no longer insisting that Bonn remove its government offices from Berlin.[37]

The consultation eased the strains on the Western alliance and Bonn realized that it could only attain its goals by negotiating from a position of strength. Thus while the United States advised caution in dealing with Moscow, it was in favor of the negotiations. When relations did become a bit strained in December 1970, Scheel announced that he and Brandt would visit the United States and Britain in 1971.[38]

As the Big Four talks progressed, a deadlock developed in February 1971. To add further problems, Ulbricht continued to delay traffic to Berlin in an attempt to sabotage the possibility of a Berlin agreement. In March the allies called for an end to the deadlock and for progress toward a settlement.[39] While the Berlin talks were deadlocked, the Ostpolitik remained in a state of limbo. The German-Soviet treaty had been signed, as had the Bonn-Warsaw treaty, but both lacked ratification due to the failure of the Big Four to reach a Berlin agreement.

Suddenly toward the beginning of May the Soviets began to make conciliatory moves. On May 3, 1971, Walter Ulbricht was replaced by the more moderate Erick Honecker. On May 14, the Soviet leadership indicated that the USSR was interested in discussing with NATO leaders troop withdrawals from Europe. On May 20 President Nixon announced a major breakthrough in the SALT talks.[40] On June 7 the Berlin talks began to show true progress, and on June 15 East German party boss Honecker hailed the Big Four talks and wished them success. He also stated that East Germany would no longer obstruct traffic to West Berlin, and that he was willing to accept something less than full recognition from Bonn.[41] On June 16 Brezhnev announced that Moscow was prepared to seek a "successful completion" of the Berlin talks.[42]

Almost overnight the Soviets had made a real détente in Europe seem possible; they even dropped their demand that troop reduction negotiations take place in the context of a European security conference.[43]

Real progress continued in the Berlin talks, and by August 1971 the Big Four ambassadors had virtually finished a draft of the agreement. The U.S. ambassador described the meeting of August 19 as "a very good meeting . . . we are making real progress." As a measure of the Soviets' intent, it is interesting to note that they had been willing to meet for 50 hours in the last 9 days, and that some sessions lasted up to 14 hours.[44] Then on August 23 the Big Four agreed on a draft of the Berlin agreements after 16 months and 23 days of negotiation. This tentative accord states that traffic will be "unimpeded" to West Berlin and the Soviet Union acknowledges the four-power responsibility for Berlin, thus cancelling a 1955 pact in which the USSR transferred control of access to East Germany. Agreements to speed shipping were also signed, such as the elimination of East German customs by the use

of mutually agreeable seals, and the collection of tolls annually.
The routes should no longer be subject to harassment as East
Germany will mainly check papers and a small sample of shipped
cargo. West Berliners will be permitted increased travel privileges,
but they will not be permitted to travel under West German passports.
The treaty also speaks of reducing West German political activity
in the city, but the 20,000 Bonn government employees will be permitted to remain and the Soviets will gain a 20- to 30-man consulate
in the city. There is no foreseeable razing of the Berlin Wall, but
these accords represent significant gains for the allies and West
Berliners.[45]

The Soviet concessions have been interpreted as a willingness
to make concessions in exchange for a European security conference
and a reduction of tension in Europe. Then troop reductions could
be considered along with a SALT agreement.[46] These concessions
on Berlin and the SALT talks have led some diplomats to believe
that a diplomatic assault would soon begin--a new "peace offensive"
accompanied by token acts of sincerity. Moscow's security conference would legitimize East German sovereignty, legitimize all
borders, and give the Soviets massive coverage in the Western news
media. The Soviets hoped that by creating a mood of détente they
could eliminate Europe as a threat, minimize U.S. influence, erode
NATO, and cause the United States difficulty in justifying its NATO
strength. Not only would such moves operate to Soviet advantage
but they would also detract from President Nixon's China trip and
minimize any future U.S.-China agreements.[47] The subsequent 1972
Moscow summit meeting tended to reinforce the above speculations
and brought this segment of the East-West diplomatic offensive to a
climax. The late 1972 Helsinki meetings and ongoing European
security conference have ushered in a new phase in East-West
diplomacy, and are bound to shed more light on Soviet intentions,
East European flexibility, Western European solidarity, and U.S.
policy toward Europe.

CONCLUSIONS

It seems clear that the timing of the various developments
that together constitute the Ostpolitik of West Germany are interdependent and are linked to various non-European developments as
well as to changes in the big power configurations.

The evolution of Western Europe itself, particularly the continuing integration of the EEC, has reached a critical stage in that
the political unity question will have to be dealt with. USSR intentions are to slow down and if possible to prevent this type of integration, by offering various "concessions" that will be very

appealing to Germany in particular. Although Chancellor Brandt occupies the center stage position in Western Europe at this time, the roles played by French and British statesmen are going to become increasingly significant to guarantee West European unity. Britain's entrance to the EEC is therefore all the more significant and essential. It has been argued that Western Europe even now is not a significant united voice in international affairs. Nevertheless, the Ostpolitik may well lead to greater policy coordination internally and externally by the EEC in particular and Western Europe in general. A disunited Western Europe is not going to be very influential in international affairs.

No doubt it is to some extent true that German questions can best be solved by the Germans themselves. But this is only half true in that Moscow is calling the tune for the GDR in large measure. For West Germany it is not altogether that simple. Whoever is chancellor of West Germany must walk a tight rope, and many paradoxes will surface in this respect. A détente in Europe is desirable, but at what price? The German peoples have much in common, but will the two systems find it possible to compromise? Germans may be able to solve German questions, but will they ultimately be allowed to seek their own solutions? A more loosely organized Western Europe is in Moscow's interest, but is a non-aligned Germany in anyone's interest?

Furthermore, even with the new Berlin agreements and the relaxation of border crossings, West Berlin is still and will remain for the foreseeable future the West's most sensitive nerve spot and consequently its most vulnerable. The Berlin Wall is not going to come down for many years, and true "normalization" is therefore a long way off.

And although Chancellor Brandt's policies have been popular with his own people, the real immediate gains seem to have come for the GDR which will now begin to enjoy legitimacy and gain Western diplomatic recognition as well as accelerated economic advantage in the West. The Soviet Union in turn benefits from this accomplishment for obvious reasons. For West Germany, the Ostpolitik up to 1973 therefore presents only interim solutions; whether the ultimate unification will ever become a reality is highly in doubt. It is therefore ironic that what both sides seem to call a success is considered a success for precisely opposite reasons: West Germany considers it progress toward greater unity and harmony, while the East consider it a ratification and legalization of the existing de facto separation. It could therefore lead to entirely new sets of frictions and strains. It was no accident that Chancellor Brandt did not go to East Berlin in December 1972 to sign the agreements in that an outburst of East German popular approval for Brandt would have greatly annoyed and irritated the GDR government and emphasized the previously mentioned polarization of objectives.

Still, it can be safely concluded that West Germany will play an increasingly dynamic role in the non-German East European states including the Soviet Union. There will be a greater toleration of mutually respected interests, and the margin for tolerating error will be wider here than between the two German states.

Another way to express the ideological division between the two sides is to say that each side expects modification, change, and transformation from the other while considering real convergence undesirable and even dangerous. The opposing positions can be expected to be emphasized in the European security conference discussions and communiqués.

UNRESOLVED ISSUES AND QUESTIONS

Obviously there remain many unanswered questions, particularly since for Bonn the Ostpolitik is only the beginning in its definition of what real "normalization" constitutes. However, some issues will become increasingly important. Some of these are discussed below.

Chancellor Adenauer was able to place Bonn's Westpolitik above party politics; it no longer was a political issue. Will this remain the case? Will Chancellor Brandt be able to do the same with Bonn's Ostpolitik, or will it become a potentially explosive domestic issue that can be exploited internally and externally? It may even be questioned whether the West German state has sufficient political maturity to handle both issues simultaneously with success.

It would be impossible to pinpoint the areas of controversy and danger. But there are definitely areas of incompatibility in Bonn's Ostpolitik in that the USSR and satellite states such as the GDR do not agree on all issues. Can Bonn exploit the disagreements discreetly? And what about the disagreements between Bonn's Ostpolitik and its Westpolitik? Will this lead to ambiguity for West German officials and friction within the EEC and the Atlantic alliance itself? Consultations among the Western powers will be essential here, but such meetings may underscore the differences as much as resolve them.

A third area of concern will have to be the status of the United States in a Europe caught up in détente politics. The United States will not be able to leave Europe, but what role it can and will be expected to play is not very well defined. With an increase in economic competition and a decline in NATO's military importance especially as seen from a European point of view, the United States may well be in for difficult years despite its existing and carefully nurtured ties with Europe. Whether Western integration, including the United States (as in NATO), is compatible with Eastern détente is not altogether clear or obvious.

Fourth, there have been statements to the effect that détente leads to shifts in forces within the blocs, and that this carries major implications and opportunities for bloc members as well as uncertainties. Some view the Prague spring as one illustration of this phenomenon which had serious consequences. Is Europe going to have more of such events now that détente fever sweeps the continent? Or is Moscow using the European security conference as a weapon and warning against just this possibility?

Finally, there is the relationship of economic growth and development to political stability and moderation--a very important connection to be carefully kept sight of by any Bonn government, particularly in its foreign policy aims, for it must know how to match these with Europe's political and economic realities.

NOTES

1. Willy Brandt, "A Nation Can Overcome an Evil Past," in Central Europe Journal 20, no. 3 (March 1972), p. 113.

2. Willy Brandt, "Germany's Westpolitik," in Foreign Affairs 50, no. 3 (April 1972), pp. 425-26.

3. Ibid., p. 416, as well as numerous other public speeches and statements by Chancellor Brandt and other West German government officials.

4. For the authoritative statement on the doctrine of containment, see George F. Kennan, "The Sources of Soviet Conduct," in Foreign Affairs 25, no. 4 (July 1947), pp. 566-82. A more recent reappraisal of containment is given in an "Interview with George F. Kennan," Foreign Policy, no. 7 (Summer 1972), pp. 5-21, and in George F. Kennan, "After the Cold War: American Foreign Policy in the 1970's," Foreign Affairs 51, no. 1 (October 1972), pp. 211-27.

5. A detailed account of the Ostpolitik is found in several scholarly journals and books. One of the most thorough and authoritative is the work by Lawrence L. Whetten, Germany's Ostpolitik: Relations Between the Federal Republic and the Warsaw Pact Countries (London: Oxford University Press, 1971).

6. Francois Duchère, "SALT, The Ostpolitik and the Post Cold War Conflict," The World Today 26, no. 12 (December 1970), p. 502.

7. See "Declaration on Peace, Security and Cooperation in Europe," in U.N. General Assembly Official Records, 27th session.

8. There is no agreement among scholars and analysts on this point. For a detailed discussion of all the models, see Joseph L. Nogee, "International Politics in a Tripolar World," paper presented at the Southern Political Science Convention, Atlanta, November 2-4, 1972.

9. Many argue that China has become a threat to the USSR; see Richard Lowenthal, "Russia-China: Controlled Conflict," Foreign Affairs 49, no. 3 (April 1971). Others argue that China is not a superpower, is not a threat, and cannot intimidate the USSR, and that the conflict is highly overstated; see John K. Fairbank, "The New China," Foreign Affairs 51, no. 1 (October 1972), pp. 31-43.

10. Statement by Eric Honecker in interview, see New York Times, November 26, 1972.

11. Whetten, op. cit., pp. 35, 37-45.

12. Ibid., p. 35. See also R. Bayrnes, "Russia in East Europe: Hegemony Without Security," Foreign Affairs 49, no. 4 (July 1971), pp. 582-697.

13. Recent general studies of Soviet foreign policy include Thomas W. Wolfe, Soviet Power and Europe, 1945-1970 (Baltimore and London: Johns Hopkins Press, 1970); Vernon V. Aspaturian, Process and Power in Soviet Foreign Policy (Boston: Little, Brown, 1971). A collection of pertinent readings is found in Erik P. Hoffmann and Fredric J. Fleron, Jr., eds., The Conduct of Soviet Foreign Policy (Chicago: Aldine-Atherton, 1971).

14. T. Roberts, "Is Germany's Ostpolitik Dangerous? A Diplomatic Balance Sheet," Encounter 36, no. 5 (May 1971), p. 65.

15. Ibid., p. 66; Whetten, op. cit., p. 115.

16. André Pierre, "Implications of the Western Response to the Soviet Intervention in Czechoslovakia," Atlantic Community Quarterly 11, no. 1 (September 1969(, p. 62.

17. Vernon Aspaturian, "Soviet Aims in Eastern Europe," Current History 59, no. 350 (October 1970), p. 211.

18. Lawrence Whetten, "The Role of East Germany in West German-Soviet Relations," The World Today 25, no. 1 (December 1969), p. 507.

19. Ibid., p. 509.

20. Ibid.

21. Ibid.

22. Ibid.

23. Ibid., p. 507.

24. New York Times, December 1, 1969. See also Willy Brandt, "West Germany: Policies for the Future," Vital Speeches, December 1969, p. 105.

25. New York Times, October 8, 1969, p. 46.

26. New York Times, November 26, 1972.

27. New York Times, January 16, 1970, p. 3.

28. Whetten, Germany's Ostpolitik, op. cit., p. 123.

29. Pravda, December 5, 1969; New York Times, December 6, 1969.

30. For a more complete discussion of all these points, see the excellent treatment given in Whetten, Germany's Ostpolitik, op. cit.

31. Pravda, December 6, 1969.

32. See Whetten, Germany's Ostpolitik, op. cit., pp. 120-26.

33. Tass report of August 12, 1970.

34. For a full and detailed discussion of all the pros and cons of the Moscow-Bonn Treaty, see the Bundestag Bulletin of September 22, 1970.

35. Bundestag Bulletin, May 26, 1970.

36. Europa Archives, 25th year, 1970, pp. 332-33.

37. "Gromyko Meets Nixon, " New York Times, October 20, 1970, p. 1.

38. New York Times, January 10, 1971, p. 10.

39. B. Weller, "U.S. Bids Soviet Resolve Issues of Berlin Access," New York Times, March 2, 1971, p. 17.

40. New York Times, June 20, 1971, p. 4.

41. David Binder, "East German Chief Hints at Softer Stand," New York Times, June 16, 1971, p. 3.

42. New York Times, June 20, 1971, p. 4.

43. Ibid.

44. New York Times, August 19, 1971, p. 10.

45. David Binder, "Accords on Berlin," New York Times, August 24, 1971, pp. 1, 14.

46. B. Gwertzman, "Easing of Tensions on Berlin," New York Times, August 24, 1971, p. 15.

47. "Soviet Objectives: European Security Parley," New York Times, August 28, 1971, p. 3.

9

A NEOCLASSICAL VIEW
OF POSTWAR EUROPE
Gordon Tullock

As a good methodologist, David Hume believed in basing his theories on the minimum possible assumption set. When developing his theory of the balance of power,[1] he implicitly used only three basic assumptions. The first was that in the long run nations act as if they would like to aggrandize themselves, that is, to expand. It is not assumed that they will attempt to expand at each and every moment, only that the possibility of attempts to expand in the future is positive. The second was that nations wish to remain in existence, that is, they are interested in defending themselves. The third was that nations have some elementary ability to foresee the likely future consequences of present actions. From these three assumptions-- which ignore, as I shall, the internal decision-making processes of nations--it is possible to deduce the balance of power.

Since nations are attempting to aggrandize, as well as to defend themselves, all will tend both to take occasional advantage of opportunities for aggression and to anticipate similar activity on the part of other nations. Having elementary foresight, they will be opposed to permitting any other nation to get into a position where it would have the power to destroy them. Thus, the expansion of the power of any given nation automatically sets in motion a process of developing a coalition against it.[2]

POSTWAR DEVELOPMENTS

Hume was, of course, dead in 1814, but he would not have been surprised in the slightest that the first bit of action at the Congress of Vienna--which was nominally called to arrange the terms of peace between England, Russia, and Austria-Hungary on the one hand and their enemy, France, on the other--was the signing of a secret treaty of alliance between France, England, and Austria-Hungary against Russia. Nor would he have been surprised that the English and French sent forces to support Poland against their former ally, Russia, at the end of World War I. (There were, of course, reasons other than the balance of power involved in this particular incident.) What would have surprised him was the extremely slow and hesitating way in which similar developments occurred after World War II. At a time when the United States was actually fighting a most bloody war with a Russian puppet, the Americans were still dismantling plants in Germany and shipping them to Russia and preventing the Germans (and the Japanese) from rearming. To this day, it would be easier to explain British and French policy in Germany as aimed at restricting development of the German military forces than as promoting an alliance with the Germans against the Russians.

Indeed, it can even be argued that the existence of an East German area under military occupation by 21 Russian divisions is largely the result of French foreign policy in the years right after World War II, rather than a success of Russian policy. The Russians made a number of proposals for national elections and establishment of a national government; these proposals were always vetoed by the French.*

The failure to quickly and immediately develop a powerful alliance against the Russians in Europe, and the continued failure of the European countries to use their immense resources to develop military strength, is the most astonishing feature of the postwar period. The Japanese case is another example of the same phenomenon. The purpose of this chapter, however, is to argue that it may be deduced from the same assumptions that Hume used, if they are applied to the rather unusual situation that existed at the end of World War II.

Before turning to what I believe is the correct explanation of the phenomenon, I should like to briefly discuss an alternative explanation that I cannot rule out at the moment because I cannot think of a statistical test that would completely eliminate it. Historians of Greece have normally blamed the failure of Athens to fully recover after the fall of the first Athenian empire, that is, the extremely feeble nature of the second Athenian empire, largely upon

---

*Both Russian and American policy at this stage were particularly confused. It was clear that the Russians could not conceivably win any kind of democratic election in Germany. Even if they allocated to themselves all the people elected from their zone, they would still be outvoted. Nevertheless the Russians did propose such elections and the United States objected to them, for the ostensible reason that the Communists might win.

a primitive version of the welfare state. The Athenian government developed the habit of making direct payments to the voters. The voters tended to favor such payments, and as a consequence there was not enough money to maintain military forces at the strength necessary for an imperial role.

I do not know whether this explanation is correct with respect to Athens, but it is possible that the somewhat similar explanation of the behavior of the European countries after World War II, which I will outline below, is correct.

Prince Bismarck's invention of the modern welfare state has been gradually growing in most democracies and some despotisms in modern times. For a variety of reasons, Hitler was a great proponent of this development, and the general policy normally referred to as social security grew to a higher level under him than in any other country in history. Growth was general throughout Europe and was accelerated during both the great depression and World War II. The present basic welfare scheme in France, for example, was actually enacted by the Vichy government.

At the end of World War II, all the countries in Western Europe had on their books legislation providing for very massive transfers of funds within their populations. It may be that these transfers played the same role as the direct payments to the Athenian voter. Surely in the early days of the development of NATO, European countries frequently alleged that they could not increase their military resources because their expenditures on social welfare were very heavy and could not be cut, and taxes were already so high that they could not be raised. It may be, then, that the basic reason Western Europe has not rearmed has been that the individual voter prefers a direct benefit received from the state right now to the purchase of insurance for the future by way of armaments. If so, this would explain the weakness of Western forces along much the same lines historians have used to explain the failure of the second Athenian empire.

As previously noted, I cannot think of a simple way of demonstrating that this hypothesis is untrue, but I am somewhat skeptical. First, in the early days of NATO, the most powerful non-Communist armies in Europe were the Turkish, Swedish, Swiss, and Spanish. If the welfare state hypothesis were correct, one would anticipate that the smallest armies would be held by those countries with the largest welfare state, and this listing of the largest armies does not seem to fit that hypothesis. Still, this is clearly not conclusive.

THE HUMEAN APPROACH

Having presented an alternative hypothesis, I should now like to turn to what might be called the Humean approach. At the time of the German surrender, there were five countries with major military forces: Germany, Russia, England, the United States, and Japan. The Western allies--instead of regarding the Japanese and German armies as defenses against Russia, as England and Austria-Hungary had thought of the French army after the Napoleonic wars--promptly and immediately dismantled both the German and Japanese forces. England, the United States, and Russia began demobilization, but in quite different ways.

To all intents and purposes, England ceased to be a major military power with the demobilization of its World War II forces. There would be a very partial recovery in British military strength as a result of the Korean War, but basically England ceased to be a major world power in late 1945. The reasons why England took this step will be discussed later, but at the moment it should be noted that for England, in any event, this behavior during and after World War II showed an absence of desire to annex territory. This would not have terribly surprised Hume, who did not anticipate that all countries would at all times be engaged in aggression. For his system to work, it is only necessary that there be a positive potential for nations to engage in aggression.

The demobilization of Russia and the United States was much less significant than that of England. In the first place, Russia demobilized in the same sense that France demobilized in 1918--the reserves went back to their civilian life but remained on call. Like Sweden and Switzerland, Russia would now have only part of its army on active duty at any given time, but the remainder could be called into action immediately. The situation would be the same as existed all over the continent of Europe before 1914, and all over Europe except Germany, Austria, and Hungary from World War I to World War II.

It is notable that this demobilization has been largely misunderstood by Western intelligence. One of the standard criticisms of the pre-World War I French army was that it considered only troops actually on active duty in its intelligence rosters. The German army, as it approached the Battle of the Marne, was underestimated by half because French intelligence did not count reserve divisions. Although the French have been heavily criticized for this, the same mistake has been made since World War II with respect to the Russian forces. Even such quick, efficient mobilization of the reserve as occurred during the invasion of Czechoslovakia does not seem to have led to any revision of these estimates. (The reserves were not used to fight; they simply replaced the units that invaded Czechoslovakia.)

On the other hand, as time went by and the Russians continued to find themselves confronted with a military vacuum on their western frontier, they did let the fighting potential of their army run down gradually. There was, after all, no point in having a mobilizable army ten times as large as could be mobilized on your west. There has also been a revival of the tendency (so pronounced between World War I and World War II) to gradually move toward a professional army, presumably on the grounds that this is politically more trustworthy than a conscript army. As a result, it is still generally true that what the Russians need to reach the English Channel are shoes, but it would not be as easy now as it would have been in 1948. The Russians also began a basic technological change in their armed forces structure, but this can best be explained by making a deviation through the American military arrangements.

The United States also demobilized, but at the end of the demobilization in, let us say, 1948, the conventional forces it held were in manpower much larger than in 1940. However, it is not at all obvious that they were greater in combat capacity. During this period, the tendency of the American armed forces, already pronounced before and during World War II, to develop immense rear echelon facilities was accentuated. Discounting for the technological improvement in weapons between 1940 and 1947, it is quite possible that U.S. forces in 1940 were more significant in combat capacity than the much larger numerical forces in 1947-48.

But all of this was relatively unimportant; the really significant development in American forces was a drastic technological change, a switch from dependence upon what we may call conventional methods to a military force whose basic combat capacity was nuclear. In a way, we can say that since 1947-48 the American military force has been basically a nuclear delivery system, a small auxiliary force capable of engaging in small-scale conventional warfare, and a monster staff and rear echelon activity that appears to exist to a large extent simply for the purpose of giving jobs to its employees. Beginning in 1947-48 the United States became, as it is today, almost completely dependent upon its nuclear force for significant military activity. Minor wars could be fought with conventional forces, but there was and is nothing capable of dealing with, for example, a Russian invasion of Western Europe.* But in any event, the policy of relying on nuclear weapons was enunciated by the Truman administration and given firm cementing as the basic U.S. military posture in the famous B-36 bomber hearings just before the outbreak of the Korean War.

The Russians immediately began steps to make the same technological change in their military force. They had the good fortune to be fully advised as to the technical methods of making the atom bomb by way of a fairly elaborate espionage structure they had

---

*As a sort of illustration of U.S. helplessness in this area, the U.S. reserve pattern for Western Europe involves placing in Europe the equipment for just two divisions, whose personnel can then be airlifted to Europe in the event of a Russian attack.

built up during World War II, and were able to use a good many captured German scientists for further work. Indeed, they actually used German industry for this purpose. During the period when the Russians were most vigorous in denouncing the Western powers for not eliminating all segments of war industry in West Germany, they were manufacturing the porous barriers for their gaseous diffusion plant in East Germany because apparently they could not make them themselves. However, for the first 20 years the Russians were well behind the United States in this area, and hence were always aware of their distinct military inferiority. One of Khrushchev's criticisms of Stalin was that he risked war with the United States at a time when Russia was completely helpless against an American nuclear attack. In fact, Stalin understood Truman better than Khrushchev did.

The United States for obvious reasons did not want Russia to conquer Western Europe. The great U.S. superiority in nuclear weapons meant that Russia could not safely make use of its equally great superiority in conventional power on the ground in Europe. Stalin, in any event, was a very cautious person. Nevertheless, it certainly would not have been wise to let the defense of Western Europe depend entirely on a guess as to the nonaggressive nature of the Russians, and no one did. Along its entire border, Russia confronted the potential of war with the United States if Russia pushed ahead and, granted the technological circumstances, it was a war Russia would certainly lose. Russia's choice not to fight under the circumstances is perfectly intelligible.

American policy in this period was somewhat unusual for the world as a whole, but not unusual for America. The United States has been very aggressive within what is now called its continental bounds, but not outside them. The United States is surrounded, and has been for a long time, by much weaker countries and could easily have annexed any of them at almost any time after 1850. Indeed, it seems likely that the failure of the effort to annex Canada in 1812 did not reflect the inherent strength of the American and British positions along the Canadian border so much as the extraordinary ineptitude with which the Americans conducted the war.

Why the United States has followed this line of strictly selective aggression, with the aggression terminating at the Pacific coast, is not clear. But it is clear that this has been the case. A war with Spain led to the independence of the areas the United States took over, with the modest exceptions of Puerto Rico, which at least is completely self-governing, and the island of Guam. Efforts by Grant to organize annexations of Cuba were unsuccessful, and a proposal to annex a large part of northern Mexico actually failed ratification in the U.S. Senate after it had been accepted by the Mexicans.

Whatever the motive behind this policy, the fact remains that the United States apparently does not want to annex land just now, and certainly did not wish to annex any part of Europe.* The European powers found themselves in a peculiar historical situation. They were allied with one very powerful nation and feared attack from another less powerful nation. On the other hand, they did not fear attack from their protector at all. Nor did they fear that their protector would sell them out. Traditionally, relations between allies have been uneasy and distrustful. This was the unique case in which the major ally could be trusted. Under the circumstances, the lesser powers had no substantial motive to spend their resources on arms.[3]

Consider England, which in this case decided to disarm, whereas France and others decided not to create military forces. British military forces could add only infinitesimally to the defense of England against Russia, granted that the United States was providing the bulk of that defense. On the other hand, England would have had to pay the full cost of any military structure it built. Under the circumstances, England was probably quite wise to let arms fall sharply, and to use its arms mainly in areas where it was obvious the United States would not come to Britain's defense--that is, in the scattered remnants of the British empire.

France apparently made about the same decision. Indeed, France's principal military efforts in the twenty years after World War II were entirely directed against minor opponents where American assistance was neither likely nor wanted. (At the very end France did make a mild effort to obtain American aid for its Vietnamese venture. But during most of this time, and to a considerable extent even at the end, France's principal objective was to prevent American intervention. Indeed the fall of Dien Bien Phu was to a considerable extent the result of France's refusal to permit American pilots to fly combat missions over that beleaguered outpost.)

---

*I do not think, however, that other countries in the world should take the view that the United States is permanently and totally nonaggressive. And various interferences in other countries were a part of American foreign policy. Schumpeter, in his remarkably clairvoyant prediction of the shape of the postwar world in 1942, defined American foreign policy as "ethical imperialism," or the effort to impose upon other people the U.S. idea of what was right and good. There was, in fact, added on to this as a sort of minor-key activity, various efforts by individual Americans to make profits from the dominant role of the United States in the rest of the world. The sum total of these profits was surely a small part of the resources the United States put into foreign policy, but recently a number of individuals have alleged that this was the main motive of the policy. Even they, however, will concede that the United States has annexed no real estate.

But if there was no reason why England and France should arm for defense against Russia, there was at least some reason why they should prevent Germany from arming. A strengthening of the German military forces would, once again, have only a marginal effect on defense against Russia. But it could easily lead to a situation in which the English or French would have to increase their military forces unless they wished to see the Germans developing a markedly more powerful army. Their decision to push hard against any real development of the German army, to insist that it be integrated into a higher NATO command, and above all to see that Germany did not get nuclear weapons is therefore quite intelligent.

This does, however, raise the issue of why American policy did not favor the armament of West Germany. The armament of West Germany would surely have been followed rather rapidly by an increase in forces in both France and England; hence, the development of a significant military force in Europe would follow. It is true that the three countries concerned might not have been willing to cooperate permanently in peace time, but they surely would have cooperated in the event of war with Russia. Therefore, why the United States did not force a rearmament of Germany is something of an open question. In my opinion, the answer turns largely on the simple diplomatic ineptitude the United States had consistently exhibited since 1800.

The situation changed somewhat with the outbreak of the Korean War. In this war, the United States demonstrated that it was not exactly eager to use its nuclear power, even when presented with a situation where the mere threat of the use of nuclear power would have voided a very bloody war. (The war in fact ended when Truman was replaced by Eisenhower, and Eisenhower threatened nuclear war.)

Nevertheless, most Europeans seem to have felt that the United States would use nuclear weapons in Europe, but the British decided to take out insurance. The British Labour government began a major program to develop an English nuclear weapon. Originally the weapon appears to have had essentially a catalytic objective, that is, it was intended that if the Russians began an invasion of England, they would find themselves subject to nuclear attack. Preferably the attack would occur under circumstances in which the Russians could not tell whether it came from the United States; hence Russia would tend to reply to the United States and bring the Americans into the conflict.

With time, however, England developed a genuine and not totally contemptible nuclear force of its own. It now seems to be aimed at strictly terrorist objectives. Its apparent targets are the principal Russian cities, and the intent is not the military objective of damaging the Russian military system but the aim of inflicting very high costs on the Russians in the event of war. Of course, it is not obvious that, in the event of a two-nation war between Russia and England, the English would choose to inflict these very high costs because they would have to surrender unconditionally immediately thereafter. It is likely that the Russians would then execute, probably painfully, all the people concerned with the weapons.

The French decision to acquire an even more modest nuclear establishment is somewhat harder to explain. It may have been simply a part of De Gaulle's usual "grandeur." On the other hand, certainly it is true that development of at least the possibility of retaliating against the Russians has some value to the French if they are beginning to doubt the security of the American commitment to Europe.

Thus the situation at the beginning of the 1960s would not have surprised David Hume. I do not think he would have been surprised by developments in the 1960s and early 1970s either, but he would have had to base his relative lack of astonishment on his general skepticism about human abilities rather than on the balance of power. During this period, the United States permitted its relative military power to run down very sharply. Indeed, the United States has entered into a treaty with Russia under which the Russians are to convert their present sizable advantage in intercontinental ballistic missiles into a much larger one in the name of disarmament. Granted the United States' long history of odd foreign policy, this is not particularly surprising; indeed, we might say the period from 1945 to roughly 1963-64 is the surprising period.

What is surprising, however, is that U.S. allies in Europe have not attempted to supplement the gap. Indeed, if anything, they too are reducing the size of their military forces. It may be that they feel there is nothing they can do, and hence there is no point in wasting money on maintaining military forces now that the United States no longer presses them to do so. More likely, however, here again democracy is eating into the rationality of foreign policy. In this case in particular, a contributing factor may be the terrible nature of nuclear weapons and most people's consequent desire not to give them careful thought. There is a widely held view that the United States will not start a nuclear war and that the Russians will not invade Western Europe, because the United States would start a nuclear war if they did.

It used to be said that in nuclear problems it paid to give your opponent the impression that you were insane. In a way, American foreign policy today depends on giving the Russians the view that Americans are deeply muddled. No one seems to know what the United States would do in the event that Russia invaded Western Europe, or even what it should do. The Russians therefore face a very risky situation, and this may be adequate deterrence. On the other hand it may not, and with time the American position may be clarified.

In any event, the future for the Western powers is obviously not promising, but one can see many scenarios in which they would survive. Chance and technological change are important in foreign policy, and many possible developments in the next ten years could save the West. Meanwhile, the Finlandization of Western Europe continues in parallel with the Polandization of Finland. All of this would not deeply surprise David Hume, but I cannot think that it would make him happy.

NOTES

1. David Hume, "Of the Balance of Power," in Essays: Moral, Political and Literary (Oxford: Oxford University Press, 1963), pp. 339-48. (The original publication date of Essays was 1741-42.)

2. This theme is more thoroughly developed in my forthcoming book, The Social Dilemma (Chicago: University of Chicago Press).

3. Mancur Olson and Richard Zeckhauser, "Collective Goods, Comparative Advantage, and Alliance Efficiency," in Roland McKean, ed., Issues in Defense Economics (New York: Columbia University Press, 1967), pp. 25-63.

10

We must remember the only time in the history of the
world that we have had any extended periods of peace
is when there has been balance of power. It is when
one nation becomes infinitely more powerful in relation
to its potential competitor that the danger of war arises.
So I believe in a world in which the United States is
powerful. I think it will be a safer world and a better
world if we have a strong, healthy United States, Europe,
Soviet Union, China, Japan, each balancing the other, not
playing one off against the other, an even balance.

Richard M. Nixon

With this remarkable statement President Nixon joined the
time-honored debate among international relationists about the
desirability and stability of balance of power systems. Granted
certain historical inaccuracies--balance of power systems easily
have seen their fair share of war and suffering, while unipolar
hegemonic systems have produced many a "generation of peace"--
and granted the familiar conceptual pitfalls to which balance of power
thinking is subject,[1] still the statement is couched in terms to which
international relationists can respond. With our reasonably well-
developed literature and dialogue on balance of power models,[2] we
should be in a good position to assess Nixon's vision of the emerging
global system. This is not to say that scholars can provide definitive
judgments; we know too much about our ignorance to be so foolhardy.
But we can speculate carefully, in a manner disciplined by the

*The author wishes to thank E. Thomas Rowe for a careful
critical reading of this chapter.

historical knowledge and analytical tools that have developed over the past few decade in the field of international relations.

Clearly the pentagonal system Nixon describes has not yet emerged. Bipolarity may have given way to multipolarity in certain spheres of life (economic and technological, for example), but in what Stanley Hoffmann calls "high politics" (military-strategic-political) the United States and the Soviet Union still dominate. Japan and Western Europe depend for their ultimate security upon the United States, and China is too hampered by economic and techno-logical underdevelopment to yet claim great power status on a global (as opposed to regional) scale. So for the next few years an "even balance" in the nineteenth century sense (which seems to be the basis for Nixon's neo-Metternichean vision) cannot materialize, simply because of huge power inequalities among the five major actors.

But what about a longer time span, say ten or twelve years? Suppose the world system continues to develop along its present course, with its tendency to equalize power among the "Big Five." What kind of a world will it be in a decade or so? We can pose the question more carefully. Assuming that in 1984 (ten or twelve years from now) the international system is composed of five major actors of more or less equal power and that balance of power policies are the prevailing mode of interaction:

● How stable and peaceful will this system be?
● What kind of behavior will it induce and demand from its constituent members?
● How will Europe fare in such a system?

DIMENSIONS OF POWER

Before proceeding, however, it is necessary to scrutinize this basic assumption of rough equality among the five great powers of 1984. Simply put, it is not a realistic assumption.[3] Tables 10.1 and 10.2 offer indicators of two dimensions of "power" (GNP and military expenditures) for 1970 and 1984. Note that power parity is achievable only with the most generous estimates of economic growth and reallo-cation to defense considerations in Japan and China--as well as marked decreases in U.S. economic growth and Soviet defense expenditures. For China to average an annual 10 percent growth in GNP between 1970 and 1984 is nearly inconceivable; it is almost as difficult to imagine Japan simultaneously building a major military force and sustaining its economic growth boom. Both feats would require extraordinary efforts. This calls attention to a second and more hidden assumption, that the disruptive impact of new entrants into the

TABLE 10.1

GNP and Defense Expenditures, 1970

	GNP (billions of dollars)	Defense Expenditures as Percent of GNP	Defense Budget (billions of dollars)
United States	977	8	78
Western Europe	660	3.7	24
USSR	497	10	50
Japan	197	0.8	2
China	120	8.3	10

Source: U.S. Arms Control and Disarmament Agency, Bureau of Economic Affairs, World Military Affairs 1971 (Washington, D.C., 1972), pp. 10-12.

TABLE 10.2

"Generous" Estimates of GNP and Defense Expenditures, 1984

	Assumed Average Annual GNP Growth Rates	Estimated GNP (billions of dollars)	Estimated Defense Expenditures as Percent of GNP	Estimated Defense Budget (billions of dollars)
United States	3	1,480	5	74
Western Europe	5	1,300	5	65
USSR	7	1,280	5	64
Japan	10	750	10	75
China	10	455	15	68

Source: U.S. Arms Control and Disarmament Agency, Bureau of Economic Affairs, World Military Affairs 1971 (Washington, D.C., 1972), pp. 10-12.

central international system will not be sufficient to destroy it. For the global system of 1984 to be composed of five actors whose power is more or less equal, three of them will have to move swiftly up the international power hierarchy in order to catch up with the two super-powers. Such rapid mobility is a destabilizing force. Established great powers cannot help but view with trepidation the onrush of new competitors whose capabilites are increasing but whose intentions are not yet clear.

For instance, consider a Soviet Union flanked on the west by an increasingly assertive Western Europe and on the east by Japan and China striving full tilt toward great power status. The temptations for at best obstructive tactics and at worst preemptive war may well prove irresistible. That is, one or both of the superpowers may act to pre-vent the emergence of a fully multipolar system. Hence, the process of creating a multipolar system may sow the seeds of its own destruc-tion. For our purposes, however, we shall simply assume that a multipolar system exists in 1984, without inquiring into the dynamic by which it came about. It is worth noting, though, that were this assumption to be relaxed by more thoroughly considering the destabi-lizing impact of rapid power mobility, this chapter's rather pessimis-tic conclusions would be reinforced.

PROSPECTS FOR STABILITY

How stable and peaceful would a multipolar balance of power system be in 1984? In attempting to deal with this problem it seems wise first to stipulate the conditions necessary for peace and stability in multipolar systems and then to estimate the extent to which they are likely to obtain a decade from now.

Some scholars have argued that multipolarity itself enhances the probability of peaceful interaction among states; that is, the structure of the system, composed of five or more actors of equal power, creates the conditions necessary for peace and long-run stability.[4] Others, less mathematically and more historically inclined, stress the need for additional conditions; a multipolar structure has to be fleshed in with the requisite values, habits, skills, and mechan-isms to keep the system healthy; if these are insufficient, then multi-polarity is just as prone as other distributions of power to war and breakdown.[5] The issue is drawn in this way: Is multipolarity a sufficient condition for peace and stability, or are other factors necessary?

Comparative analysis is well suited for dealing with this kind of issue, which involves assessing the relative impact of separate variables. We can compare multipolar systems that have had dif-ferent outcomes to see if additional variables seem to have had an impact. Put differently, we can hold multipolarity constant and allow our dependent variable (peace and stability) to vary; we can then search for possible independent variables (such as values of moderation) that seem to be associated with changes in the dependent variable. Space does not allow a full-fledged comparative analysis, but a brief exercise might prove illustrative.

Nineteenth century Europe experienced a succession of international systems--1815-48, 1848-71, 1871-90, 1890-1914--all of which might be viewed as multipolar balance of power arrangements.[6] The first was the famous Concert of Europe system of Metternich, which produced a remarkable period of peace and predictability after the upheavals of the French Revolution and Napoleonic imperialism. The last was the post-Bismarckian system of imperialism and arms races, which collapsed into systemwide violence with the onset of World War I. Both systems had similar distributions of power among five major actors and both operated within essentially the same arena, but they produced radically different outcomes. What accounts for this difference?

Students of the early Concert of Europe period are quick to point out the consensus on values and goals, as well as a common language and operational code, that existed among the major actors of the system. This is the legitimacy Kissinger emphasizes as being present in the Metternichean era and absent in more conflict-ridden times such as the cold war period.[7] By the time of Bismarck's political demise in 1890 this legitimacy had eroded severely. The spread of "isms"--nationalism prime among them--undermined the intellectual and emotional commonalities that lent cooperation and self-restraint to interstate relations in the earlier period. Whatever common values existed in the post-Bismarckian system were negative in content, and diplomacy was marked more by a growing fear of war among the major powers than a positive sense of shared goals and trust.[8]

Indeed, attitudes toward war can be viewed as a separate variable that helps to explain differences between the two systems. Limited force and intervention (into the affairs of nonmajor actors) were considered legitimate means for enforcing Concert decisions and preserving the system against "revolutionary" disturbances. But as the century drew to a close, war as a discrete instrument of policy grew increasingly unusable. This fear of war had perverse consequences. All Europe became preoccupied with and prepared for what came to be generally regarded as the "inevitable" outbreak of violence. As a manifestation of this search for security, alliance partners grew increasing committed to each other. Indeed, for the first time military alliances were confirmed well before the outbreak of war, in sharp contrast to earlier practice whereby actors withheld their alliance decisions until war was declared.[9] On this score, the post-Bismarckian system is akin to the twentieth century pattern where alliance-making activity precedes the onset of war, in contrast to the nineteenth century pattern where the sequence was reversed.[10]

The pattern of alliance can be considered a third variable that distinguishes the Concert system from its post-Bismarckian descendant. The former entailed flexible, short-lived, and limited alliances; the latter was characterized by rigid, near-permanent alliance commitments. Working conference and flexible alliances among the great powers (who were ready to use limited force if necessary) comprised the "balancing mechanism" of the Concert system. Rigid alliance blocs and arms races provided the means for power balancing in the latter period.

Mention of arms races brings to our attention an additional variable, technological change, which helps to explain differences between the two systems. The latter half of the nineteenth century was marked by enormous advances in the application of scientific knowledge to practical purposes, and the military sphere of life was by no means neglected by the spread of new techniques. Technological change can be viewed, following Richard Rosecrance, as one among a number of "disturbances" that must be regulated by a system if it is to remain stable.[11] Clearly technology imposed an unmanageable burden upon the already weak regulatory mechanisms of the post-Bismarckian system; indeed, in a perverse way, the growing panoply of military techniques contributed to the rigidity of the balancing machinery.

Finally, we can call attention to the different "safety-valves" in the two systems. Especially in its early years, the period 1815-48 saw a return to the eighteenth century practice of territorial compensation as part of its balancing mechanism. Change and conflict among the powers were adjusted through the exchange of strategic territories, within and outside of Europe. But by the end of the century this outlet had been exhausted. The early part of the post-Bismarckian era was a time of extraordinary expansion into the non-European world, but by 1900 opportunities for compensation through colonization and imperialism had become scarce. In Rosecrance's terms, the system's "environment" no longer contained enough variety to absorb the many disturbances threatening its stability.

This comparative exercise is meant to be suggestive, not exhaustive. (Other factors, such as diplomatic skills, could have been examined, and other systems should have been tested for a more complete treatment.) The point is simply that multipolarity is not sufficient for peace and stability. Additional conditions are necessary. Our cursory comparison has suggested that the list of these conditions might include:

- A high degree of legitimacy accorded the system by its constituent members,
- A "folklore of war" that treats violence rationally and prudently,
- A flexible pattern of alliance,
- Rates of technological change that can be managed by the system's regulatory mechanisms,

- Adjustment through compensation and exchange, among the regulatory mechanisms.

To what extent are these conditions likely to prevail in 1984?

Legitimacy

Even under the optimistic assumption that the "age of ideology" is on the wane and will have run its course by the end of the decade, there is little hope for the kind or degree of consensus among the great powers that existed in the days of Metternich. The spirit of détente we are witnessing today may deepen, but its potential for building a positive consensus is limited. Détente is energized by a negative goal--avoidance of great power confrontations--that is difficult to translate into a vision of the desirable state of the international system or, even more, into a collective sense of purpose. The consensus during the Concert of Europe's heyday can be exaggerated,[12] but there is no gainsaying the common code of self-restraint which went beyond mere "pragmatic" considerations of avoiding violent confrontation and satisfying short-term interests. Diplomats could adjust their differences in a system of conferences because they agreed that the system itself was worth preserving. Détente, however, is based on something considerably less than commitment to the status quo; mere desire to reduce tension lacks the attractive force to wed the powers to the system.

The best that can be hoped for is a tenuous marriage of convenience that eventually develops into something approaching a love affair. But such arrangements are notoriously fragile. They thrive in periods of peace and prosperity, but they lack the durability to survive hard times. If we assume sustained economic growth and technological development among all the great powers, there is a chance that détente can harden into an enduring commitment to the system. On the other hand, if we assume (more realistically) cycles of prosperity-recession, expansion-contraction, free trade-protection-- as well as conditions of uneven growth--then détente has a less promising future. The chances of building legitimacy are further reduced if we inject assumptions of intermittent political disputes, misunderstandings, and perhaps most important, uncertainties about military security.[13]

If détente offers an improbable basis for legitimacy in 1984, is there an alternative foundation for mutuality? One school of thought emphasizes the logic of the contemporary industrial-technological era, which impels all the powerful states in essentially the same direction--mass consumer production, bureaucratization, and a welfare-statism that would eventually dilute whatever ideological divergences might remain.[14] The underlying assumption is that an international system composed of essentially identical regimes will enjoy the common interests and common outlook requisite for a sense of legitimacy. But this line of reasoning is fraught with debatable propositions.

First, there is considerable evidence that industrialization produces variety, not convergence, in the nature of regimes. Phenomena as different as Nazism and Communism, apartheid and populism, have boiled out of the industrial crucible. Totalitarianism itself is (was) a twentieth century phenomenon, made possible by modern technology.

Second, even if we assume that industrialization eventually does create a kind of convergence (perhaps in the "maturing," "solidification," or "post-industrial" stages of development), there is still difficulty with the notion that a system of identical regimes will necessarily be a system of commonalities. It is easy to imagine a worst-case situation in which all the major actors are competing for the same scarce resources by virtue of their homogeneity.

A best-case situation would involve a system of high interdependencies in which the chances for the emergence of legitimacy for the system would be increased, given roughly similar development among the constituent powers. But interdependence presumes specialization, which entails a departure from identicality and involves the danger of uneven development. If we assume high interdependence, will the system of 1984 be analogous to the EEC (where development has been relatively even among the actors) or to the East African Common Market (where specialization and uneven development have undermined commitment to the system)?[15] My guess would be the latter, but if the former model does materialize it will be the result of policies adopted by the United States, and to a lesser extent by the Soviet Union, which deliberately assist economic and military development among the lesser powers, China in particular. Put differently, it would be an international system into which mechanisms have been designed to benefit developing actors at the expense of already developed superpowers.[16] Such a "welfare" system would accept the burden of high interdependence, but it would hardly be a "balance of power" system (one that would "increase capabilities but negotiate rather than fight; fight rather than pass up an opportunity to increase capabilities").[17]

All in all, then, my judgment is that a multipolar system in 1984 will not enjoy a reserve of legitimacy commensurate with the demands that can be expected to draw on it.

Attitudes Toward War

This factor offers a good deal more hope for a stable 1984 than legitimacy. There exists now, and can be expected to exist at least for the next decade, a rational, prudent attitude toward war that goes beyond mere "balance of terror" considerations. Perhaps a brief comparison with the post-Bismarckian system will illuminate this line of reasoning.

The period prior to World War I was marked by ambivalent attitudes toward war. As mentioned earlier, political elites among the great powers responded to growing awareness of the perils of modern war by protective closure (arms build-ups, secret alliances, and contingency plans entailing greater military participation in the policy-making process). Little attention was given to procedures for limiting war if it were to break out. On the other hand, among the masses there was little awareness of these developments or their implications. "La Belle Epoque" (1900-14), with its growing materialism, cynicism, and jingoism, succumbed to an almost pathological urge to "get it over with" in one short burst of war and glory.[18] With little experience by which to judge the horrors of modern warfare, mass opinion bridled not governments' ability to prepare for war but their freedom to meneuver diplomatically.

The contemporary era is quite different in these respects. Soviet-American relations have evolved as part of a long learning process. Concepts such as "stable mutual deterrence" have taken hold as deeply considered strategies for balancing the security interests of the individual powers with the stability interests of the collective system. Moreover, considerable attention is devoted to war limitation and prevention, arms control, and force reduction-- although unfortunately resources expended in this direction come nowhere close to matching allocations for weapons research. The consensus-through-collusion developed by the Big Two for averting nuclear disaster and limiting wars will likely serve as the foundation for the strategic code of behavior in the emerging multipolar system. Obviously there are unknowns (such as Japanese attitudes if Japan were to "go nuclear"), but if the present situation is an indication, ruling elites among the Big Five are likely to assume a prudent posture.

Similar comments can be made about mass attitudes in 1984. Contemporary opinion in the United States, Europe, and the Soviet Union gives little evidence of mass pressures toward bellicosity or warlike atavism; indeed, public opinion has applauded détente diplomacy. It is commonplace to remark on mass rejection of war and the instruments of warfare among the Japanese masses. And there is little evidence of significant warlike attitudes among the Chinese masses (although of course we know next to nothing about opinion in China). For the next ten years we can expect these deep currents of opinion to flow, given their source in memories of World War II and the horrors of nuclear explosions. But memories fade, and we cannot necessarily expect this factor to remain potent many more years beyond 1984, since a new generation with no direct experience with global war will be coming to maturity.

Flexible Pattern of Alliance

For the international system to enter an era of flexible alliances, the United States must first dismantle the far-flung network
of military commitments it extended during the cold war era of rigid
alliances. Put differently, in order to create working conditions for
a balancing mechanism that operates through shifting alliances
among the Big Five, the United States must first withdraw its nuclear
umbrella from Japan and Western Europe. Otherwise, three of the
five actors will continue to be linked by security considerations of
the highest order, and flexibility in the classical balance of power
sense would be unattainable.

Such a step on the part of the United States would entail enormous costs, not only for itself but for the international system as a
whole. First, in order to fill the void left by U.S. decommitment,
Japan and Western Europe would come under almost irresistible
pressures to develop their own nuclear weaponry; indeed, an "even
balance" among the Five would entail such nuclear proliferation.
Second, Western Europe would have to assume enormous decision-
making and defense burdens at a time when its political institutions
were fragile and underdeveloped, increasing the likelihood of a
failure of unity or will. These costs will have to be fully calculated
by any future U.S. administration as the Nixon Doctrine moves toward
its logical conclusion.[19] My guess is that the United States will continue to prefer high alliance costs (assuming others' defense burdens)
with moderate certainty to lower immediate costs with low certainty
about systemic stability and the behavior of former allies. That is,
it will continue to extend its nuclear umbrella to Japan and Western
Europe.

If this estimate is accurate, then the multipolar system of 1984
will not boast the alliance flexibility of the classical European systems. On the other hand, it need not succumb to the rigidity of the
pre-World War I system, particularly if the Sino-Soviet dispute
remains alive, for in that case both China and Russia will continue
to cast about for ad hoc alignments with elements in the "Western"
alliance. This phenomenon entails a secondary effect that also
impels the system toward alliance flexibility: The element of the
"Western" alliance that aligns with the Soviet Union or China (in a
manner short of full alliance commitment) strengthens its bargaining
position vis-à-vis its alliance partners. This mechanism will help
to assure that there will be no reversion to the cold war system of
tight, hierarchical alliance blocs. In short, the alliance pattern of a
multipolar 1984 will be considerably more flexible than in the cold
war era, but there is a ceiling that will likely prevent the system
from attaining the full-fledged flexibility of the classical balance of
power systems.

Technological Change

The likelihood of slowing the pace of technological change within the next ten years is remote. Scientific knowledge has been growing exponentially for centuries, and while exponential curves tend eventually to flatten out, there is no indication of deceleration in the contemporary era.

In the field of military technology, even if SALT II and its future incarnations were to succeed in controlling research in missile delivery and nuclear weaponry, the bag of just-around-the-corner tricks is staggering in its implications. Lasers, military satellites and space stations, nuclear-powered aircraft, chemical and biological warfare, weather control, genetic control, thought control--these are some of the most obvious candidates for technological application within the next decade or so. Consider the disturbing effects of a "breakthrough" in antisubmarine warfare if it were to occur earlier than expected, that is, before land-based missiles become obsolete toward the end of the 1970s.[20] The "stable mutual deterrence" upon which the present system depends would be seriously undermined. Consider, further, the destabilizing impact of not two but five centers of advanced military research and development, a situation we would expect to find if a true balance of power system were to evolve. Disturbances from technology do derive not solely from the "objective" consequences of new techniques and devices; the "uncertainty factor" is an equal partner in the process by which rapid change corrodes the trust and predictability underlying a stable international system. Uncertainty is likely to increase as bipolarity shades into multipolarity.

Compensation

Clearly, territorial compensation along the lines followed by the eighteenth and nineteenth century European systems is no longer possible to any significant degree. What were once "free areas" are now "filled up" by nationalism and politicized populations. But many other possibilities exist. Compensation is a kind of exchange relationship--determined no less by the values (or preferences) of the contracting partners than by the availability of resources in the system's environment. Strategic territory may have been valued in the nineteenth century, but today actors attach more value to technological advancement, and in 1984 they may prefer mass prosperity to both.

East-West relations today seem to be entering a pattern by which "trade and technology" and "recognition" are used as compensation by the NATO powers to induce a reduction of tension on the part of the Soviet bloc countries. That is, by accepting the status quo in Eastern Europe and recognizing the Soviet Union as a coequal nuclear power, NATO and the United States have been able to extract various concessions (such as Berlin and Vietnam) that serve to relax cold war stresses. Agreements to open up trade and transfer technology (for example, computers) have been part of such "package deals." Similar comments can be made about recent China-U.S. relations.

The point is simply that the adjustment mechanism of a balance of power system need not depend on the classical devices. Tangible resources other than territory or spheres of influence can be transferred, and intangible resources such as recognition and prestige are equally likely to enter the exchange nexus. New values and resources lend fluidity to international relations. Stanley Hoffmann has likened the emerging international scene to a complex set of games played on multiple chessboards, with each game affecting the course of the others.[21] If the present trend continues, the multipolar system of 1984 will embody a lively network of exchange relationships, by which (for instance, to use some Lasswellian values) wealth or knowledge or safety or status can be exchanged for, converted into, and/or compensated by military and political power, and vice versa. It would be a highly flexible network, perhaps sufficient to compensate for a lack of flexibility in alliance relationships.

The major danger in such a system is decision-making overload. It would be a complex world indeed that undertakes explicitly to feed data from many spheres of life into the balancing calculus. The rules of conversion from one "game" to another would be complicated, unclear, and unstable. A standard criticism of classical balance of power systems notes the difficulty of calculating qualitative and quantitative changes in military power. These difficulties are compounded immeasurably by injecting additional elements of power into the choice-making machinery. If the multipolar world of 1984 were to take on the calculating, manipulative stance of balance of power politics, uncertainty bred by technological change would be exacerbated by uncertainty rooted in perplexing rules of the game.

Conclusions on Stability

If I have seized upon the right variables and if I have assessed their future correctly, then a multipolar 1984 will be less stable and more prone to violent disruption than the contemporary system. This condition will derive neither from aggressive intent (or foolishness) on the part of one or more actors nor from intractable disputes among the powers--although such factors could easily contribute to instability. Rather, the root cause of insecurity and disequilibrium in such a system will be uncertainty. Uncertainty from technological change, uncertainty about one's allies, and uncertainty spawned by a complex system of multiple actors, multiple arenas, and multiple sets of rules--these factors will impose immense burdens on decision-makers. Furthermore, in the absence of an agreed concept of legitimacy, "reasonable" solutions to these problems will be difficult if not impossible to manage.[22] The system today is already highly complex; it is likely to become much more so over the next decade. The chances are remote that all the actors in the system can consistently muster the skill and will requisite for dealing with such complexity. How will the rest of the system respond to one or more actors whose internal resources appear deficient? The answer is unclear, which adds to the burden of uncertainty.

It seems clear, however, that if actors respond by invoking the classical balance of power rules--which prescribe exploiting the weaknesses of other actors--the system of 1984 will be more unstable than if a set of rules with more emphasis on self-restraint and interdependence were applied. Put differently, "multipolar" and "balance of power" are not synonymous concepts. The first term implies a particular distribution of power, the second a set of rules that can be applied in multipolar situations;[23] the first designates certain structural attributes of a system, the second a normative component. In behavioral terms, the multipolar system of 1984 will be complex, unstable, and uncertain, no matter what the political culture with which it is infused. But these difficulties would be compounded immeasurably if the tactics and attitudes of "balance of power" politics were to prevail.

BEHAVIOR OF MAJOR ACTORS

Assuming that multipolarity and balance of power arrangements prevail in 1984, what are the internal attributes necessary for the major actors? What are the domestic requirements of states in balance of power systems?

Quite obviously, a decision-making capacity of high order is necessary. This entails a foreign policy apparatus that is both skillful and flexible. Hoffmann specifies further the decision-making instrument requisite for balance of power poltics: a small professional elite that is (1) "coherent enough to provide the flexibility, negotiating skills, discretion and imagination essential to that type of strategy, [and] continuous enough to prevent sudden reversals not required by shifts in the outside world, and to nurture traditions" and (2) insulated from the currents of domestic politics.[24]

Another requirement is unity. A broad consensus about the general features of an actor's foreign policy must exist, not only to prevent internal paralysis but to assure the other members of the external system a measure of predictability and continuity. An actor rent by fundamental conflict over foreign policy--at the elite or mass levels, or both--will lack the flexibility and will necessary for the game of balance politics. Moreover, its allies and adversaries will be unable to act on the basis of its "national interest" because it is unable to define it.

Lastly, an actor must be autonomous if it is to operate effectively in a balance of power system. Balance of power prescriptions issue from the notion of strategic interdependence, where the actions of one state affect the decisions of another so pure autonomy is neither possible nor desirable. But on the other hand, the decisions of one actor cannot be directly controlled by another. Were an actor to lose its freedom of action in some crucial sphere of international intercourse, it can be said to have been eliminated as an "essential actor" in the system.[25] Classical balance of power theories placed prime emphasis on a state's ability to exert strategic military force; an inability to call on military power rendered it susceptible to superior power. Today in the age of mass politics there is an additional opening for leverage from the outside: Public opinion can be manipulated by external decision-makers through propaganda, example, linkage groups, and so forth. The "mass politics" factor is likely to become more important as the welfare state concept takes firmer hold during the next decade. Whether or not this will entail increased external penetration is problematical, but the potential is there.

With these comments in mind and assuming the accuracy of the analysis in the preceding section, I would rank the following international systems in order of increasing need for skill, flexibility, unity, and autonomy among their constituent actors:

1. Bipolar cold war system,
2. Classical European balance of power system,
3. Multipolar system of 1984 emphasizing interdependence and cooperation,
4. Multipolar system of 1984 emphasizing balance of power.

Multipolarity imposes a greater decision-making burden on actors than bipolarity, and a multipolar system informed by balance of power precepts makes even greater demands than one in which some other code of operation gains currency. I am skeptical about the ability of any actor to meet the requirements of a stable balance of power system in 1984, but the task at hand asks for an assessmer of Europe and its potential for success a decade from now.

PROSPECTS FOR EUROPE

How will Europe fare in a multipolar 1984? If international relations becomes primarily a matter of power balancing and shifting alliances, will Europe develop the internal resources and attributes requisite for successfully playing the game? Let us look first at Western Europe.

Western Europe

A Balance of power system in 1984 would be disastrous for Western Europe. Multipolarity itself will strain emerging political structures to the limit, but if power balancing and checking relationships become the watchword, then either a failure of will or a breakdown of whatever unity exists will enjoy a high probability.

Simply put, a balance of power system would compel each major actor to "go it alone"--and Western Europe obviously does not have the political wherewithall to take on such a burden now and cannot be expected to have it within a decade. The statesmen of the EEC need all their imaginative and diplomatic resources for the task of absorbing new members and building stronger political structures to accommodate the imperatives of economic integration. To immerse them in a climate of realpolitic would complicate and burden their tasks enormously. Likewise, the European leaders of NATO are already faced with a coming decade of subtle and difficult problems ("modernizing" their strategic concepts, meeting U.S. demands for greater contributions to defense, dealing with Soviet diplomatic and naval initiatives, reversing disintegration). Balance of power requirements would likely break down the creaky NATO machinery. To be sure, new challenges can induce favorable integrative responses in Western Europe. But there is always a threshold beyond which the weight of new tasks simply overloads decision-making networks. My judgment is that balance of power politics in a multipolar 1984 would take Western Europe well beyond that threshold.

In more specific terms, Western Europe is unlikely to develop sufficiently the four internal attributes we previously identified as prerequisites for entry into the game of power politics. Skill is a commodity whose future supply is very difficult to predict. No doubt Western Europe will continue to be blessed with its De Gaulles and its Brandts, who can provide vision and leadership and even build about themselves that small, professional elite Hoffmann feels is necessary for balance of power maneuvering. But such a supply of skills lacks continuity; to rely on the emergence of great men is to place faith in forces that are intermittent at best. Institutionalized

structures for recruitment and training of a diplomatic cadre are
necessary for consistency and predictability. The separate nations
of Europe have their individual apparatuses, of course, but no
Western European institution presently exists that performs the
function of turning out high-quality foreign policy decision-makers.
To develop such institutions requires not only time (probably more
than a decade in the best of circumstances) to elicit the necessary
élan, but also the delicate process of balancing the many national
points of view. This is not to say that managing this task is impossible, but unless it receives high priority (unlikely) it is improbable.[26]

Lack of flexibility is another deficiency likely to hound Western
European decision-makers. True, the populations of Western Europe
probably impose fewer constraints upon the foreign policy behavior
of their governments than, say, their counterpart in the United States.
But the real bind, of course, will exist not between the separate
populations and their governments but between the separate governments and whatever higher structures of unity emerge. Almost two
decades of intermittent economic integration have seen the development of decision-making structures that still leave substantial
discretion in the hands of individual member states. One decade of
more politicized integration--concerned more with what Hoffmann
calls "high politics"--is unlikely to see an erosion of national
autonomy to anywhere near the extent required. If the spillover from
economic integration to political integration proceeds gradually and
only under special "depoliticized" conditions,[27] the chances are
slim that a rapid transfer of decision-making authority can take
place in the high-pressure circumstances of competition for big
stakes. No matter how favorable the external environment, West
European unity--if it develops at all--will evolve gradually and in a
manner that treats ginerly the separate interests of its constituent
states. This speaks disfavorably about its capacity to act as a
maneuverable power in a multipolar world a decade from now.

Unity and autonomy are closely related and can be considered
together. A simple model suggests the dilemma in which Western
Europe is likely to find itself in the next decade: The more the world
comes to resemble a balance of power system, the more Western
Europe will be forced into a situation of tradeoff between unity and
autonomy. That is, the more realpolitic becomes the mode of interaction, the more Western Europe will come under pressure to
increase its autonomy (especially militarily), but measures to
increase autonomy will entail considerable debate and internal conflict, which correspondingly reduce unity. External pressures will
reinforce this process. The Soviet Union, as Western Europe's
most immediate great power neighbor, under the best of circumstances will allow the development of either unity or autonomy, but
not both together, for fear of being flanked by a strong Europe on
the west and a strong China (and Japan) on the east. Were Western

Europe to become powerful enough as a unit to threaten Soviet security, the Soviets would act either to drive a wedge in European unity or to reduce Europe's capacity for independent military action.

To illustrate this speculative model, consider the following scenario of events in Western Europe. As the United States increasingly takes on the role of a balance of power actor, its nuclear guarantee to NATO becomes less credible. Elites and opinion-makers in Western Europe begin to prepare their publics for the eventuality that a massive program of strategic weapons development must be inaugurated. Counterelites and contrary opinion-makers enter the fray, citing the enormous psychological and financial burdens incumbent upon big-time military status. Mass sentiment is aroused, divided within or--a more serious danger for political integration--between nations. At the same time, the Soviets demonstrate their displeasure by threatening to retarget missiles, hinting at interventions in East Europe, reminding Berlin of its vulnerability, holding out attractive unilateral offers to individual West European states, influencing public opinion through propaganda and Communist parties, and so forth. This is done in a manner calculated to foster dissension and to avoid the heavy-handedness that would reunify opinion in the West.

"Objectively," a West European strategic security force may not be necessary, but a balance of power system increases the probability that it will be seriously contemplated, which in turn increases the probability that divisive forces inside and outside Europe will be set in motion.

The relationship between unity and autonomy in balance of power situations can be considered more fully by examining some of the models presented by Alastair Buchan.[28] Two of his models of Western Europe's future entail heavy dependence upon and interaction with the United States. In what he calls Atlanticized Europe, the United States dominates almost every sphere of life; politically, economically, and militarily it is the senior partner. Both unity and autonomy are low, and in no sense can we speak of Western Europe as playing the role of an independent actor. A more interesting model is Partnership Europe, in which strong federal institutions are constructed (unity is high) but for which cooperative arrangements on an "equal" basis with the United States are a permanent feature (autonomy is low, although higher than in the former model). Buchan predicts two major problems inherent in this model. First, internal unity would be severely strained by issues relating to autonomy (American military presence in Europe, nuclear sharing, whether or not to work toward greater independence from the United States). Second, the Soviet Union would regard Partnership Europe as a direct threat and would act to reverse Europe's growing unity or to eliminate the partner relationship, with emphasis on the former course:

> [The Soviet Union] would no doubt prefer to continue her
> "limited adversary" relationship with a conservative
> United States, providing the latter was content not to
> stir up trouble in Eastern Europe, than to deal with a
> new, unpredictable power in Western Europe, subject to
> growing pains and likely to be a disturbing factor on her
> Western frontier.[29]

In other words, because U.S. presence in Western Europe affords a
modicum of predictability and control, the Soviet Union would prefer
a situation of low autonomy (U.S. dominance) and low unity to one of
low autonomy and high unity. It would prefer an Atlanticized Europe
to a Partnership Europe.

Two additional models posit cases in which unity is low but
autonomy high. In a Europe des Etats the separate West European
states are held together only by certain common attitudes and goals,
the most important of which is the desire to play an independent role
in global politics. No strong institutions and only minimal efforts to
coordinate action are pursued, however. The Soviet Union would
prefer this model to either of the previous two, because the special
relationship with the United States will have been eliminated, and
even more because of the opportunity for maneuver and bilateral
alignments provided by a Western Europe whose solidarity is ques-
tionable. Buchan claims that a major drawback of this model for the
Soviet Union would be a threat to its position among its satellites,
since presumably a major common goal for Europe des Etats would
be "European reconcilation" through closer links with the eastern
half of the continent.[30] (But this need not be a necessary goal of
Europe des Etats; "bridge-building to the east" is simply a Gaullist
variation on the theme.)

A more extreme version of this model is Fragmented Europe,
in which the separate national interests of Western Europe gain full
expression and all efforts to act as a common unit are forsaken.
Hence unity is very low while autonomy remains high (in the sense
that for Western Europe as a whole, no external powers exert
inordinate influence). Such a configuration is nearly ideal for Soviet
interests, since it would facilitate Russian freedom of diplomatic
maneuver in the West without requiring concessions in the East.
Only two situations are preferable from the Soviet standpoint: (1)
where West European unity is high, autonomy is low, and where the
Soviet Union is the dominating power--what we might call the
Finlandized model; and (2) where both unity and autonomy are low
and the Soviet Union dominates--what we might call the Sovietized
model.

One last model remains to be considered. This depicts a situation in which high unity is combined with high autonomy in Western
Europe. This is what Buchan calls Independent Federal Europe, an

entity unified by common institutions and energized by a desire to carve out a position of independence from the United States and the Soviet Union. A nuclear-armed Europe (especially one in which West Germany is the keystone) would be welcomed by neither superpower. Such an eventuality would represent a major failure for Soviet policy; Russia's basic aim since World War II has been to prevent a massive power build-up on its western flank. The United States as well would view nervously the emergence of a major nuclear power, especially one so well situated for threatening Soviet security interests (and in turn, global stability) as Western Europe. Hence, even if entente were otherwise nonexistent, the two superpowers would likely agree at least on the undesirability of Independent Federal Europe.

Table 10.3 ranks these seven models in order of preference for the Soviet Union and the United States. Note that their preference schedules are not mirror images of each other. In particular, the aggregate "preference score" of Independent Federal Europe is less than any of the other alternatives. Superpower collusion against a newcomer so hazardously sited as Western Europe would enjoy a strong probability.

TABLE 10.3

Soviet and American Preferences Among Alternative Models
of the West European Future

Model	Unity	Autonomy	Dominated By
Soviet preferences			
Sovietized Europe	low	low	USSR
Finlandized Europe	high	low	USSR
Fragmented Europe	low	high	
Europe des Etats	low	high	
Atlantic Europe	low	low	United States
Partnership Europe	high	low	United States
Independent Federal Europe	high	high	
American preferences			
Partnership Europe	high	low	United States
Atlantic Europe	low	low	United States
Independent Federal Europe	high	high	
Europe des Etats	low	high	
Fragmented Europe	low	high	
Finlandized Europe	high	low	USSR
Sovietized Europe	low	low	USSR

Independent Federal Europe is the one model that fits full-square into a balance of power system, since it alone presumes both unity and autonomy. However, for both internal and external reasons, it is the model (other than an outright Soviet takeover) least likely to emerge. Not only would a world in which balance of power considerations held sway be unstable and unpredictable but it would increase the chances that a European power bloc will never materialize.

Eastern Europe

Seen as a region that lies between Western Europe and the Soviet Union, Eastern Europe's future will be determined largely by the relationships that develop between them. These external forces exerted upon Eastern Europe can be encapsulated in two contradictory propositions that make for a kind of interaction which perhaps can be best described as "dynamic ambiguity." The first proposition describes a direct relationship between military-political developments in Western Europe and Soviet perceptions of its security needs: The more Western Europe becomes and acts like a great power, the more the Soviet Union will regard Eastern Europe as a buffer; or, the less unified and autonomous Western Europe is (especially militarily), the less the Soviets will feel obliged for military-security reasons to stifle movements toward East-West rapprochement in Europe. The second proposition posits an inverse relationship between the Soviet Union's perceptions of military and ideological threats to its position in Eastern Europe from the West: The less the perceived military threat, the greater the danger of ideological "infection" from Western Europe, and hence the greater the chances of losing control of events on the Soviet western flank.

These propositions represent the horns of a dilemma. To the extent the horns remain firm and sharply defined, indeterminacy and tension are the inevitable results. Hope for Eastern Europe--more contact with the West, more freedom of maneuver, secure relations with both West Germany and the Soviet Union--lies in blurring the elements of each proposition, twisting the horns, so to speak, so that the dilemma is no longer perceived by the Soviets. In other words, it is in Eastern Europe's interest to play down the "balance of power," for the propositions would be most sharply relevant in a world in which balance of power calculations held sway. In other words, the more balance of power conditions prevail, the more the dilemma will obtain. This can be seen by considering each proposition separately.

In a world that emphasizes power-checking relationships, the Soviet Union will continue to regard Eastern Europe as a shield against a resurgent attack from the West. This conservative, defensive concept of security--which fits well with realpolitic notions--has been a trademark of Soviet foreign policy since World War II. Soviet tactics may change to suit new circumstances, but the basic strategy has remained consistent: to gain recognition of the status quo in the East and to retard a military-political build-up in the West.[31] A system in which balance of power precepts gain currency will merely reinforce this policy. First, it will "legitimize" hard-nosed Soviet tactics in Eastern Europe as a posture fully commensurate with the expected realities of power politics. Second, it will further encourage the Soviet Union to define its interests in terms by which all kinds of power--economic, technological, political--are translated into potential military power; a special characteristic of "balancing" is that ultimately all relevant resources come to be converted to a military common denominator in the power calculus. Hence, a vibrant Western Europe in contact with its Eastern counterpart is likely to be perceived as threatening.

Under such circumstances, if East-West economic and cultural integration were to continue apace, the Soviet Union would feel secure only if Europe were neutralized militarily and dominated politically by Moscow. This Finlandization would of course eliminate Europe as a major independent actor. "Bridge-building" between East and West requires a normative atmosphere in which economic and cultural developments are decoupled from military considerations.

To turn now to the second horn of the dilemma, in which the Soviets perceive a tradeoff between military and ideological threats to the status quo in Eastern Europe,[32] similar comments apply. In a balance of power world, the "reliability" of the satellite regimes in Eastern Europe will have enhanced importance to the Soviet sense of security. The greater the military threat to them--especially from West Germany--the more they will adhere to their Soviet protector, and hence the smaller the chances of an internal "softening up" from the lure of Western ideas and prosperity. But as the military threat wanes, it will be more difficult for the Soviet Union to justify prophylactic measures against the West and there will be a greater perceived probability of ill-health within the Eastern bodies politic. Even if the West adopts the Europe des Etats or the Fragmented Europe model--not to speak of the more integrated versions--of the future, this danger would exist in Soviet eyes. The answer from the East European point of view is to change the Soviet Union's perceptions so that its interpretation of "security" accords more with theirs:

> [The Soviet Union] follows the principle of as much unity
> in the East as possible and as much collaboration with the
> West as necessary. Moscow's allies, on the other hand
> (except for East Berlin), want to reverse this order of
> priorities--as much unity as necessary and as much
> collaboration with other Europeans as possible.[33]

This shift of Soviet perspectives is unlikely in international systems that put a premium on fine calculations of power gains and losses. It is more conceivable in a world whose code of action is less preoccupied with the military-security implications of international interaction and more given to isolating from the balancing matrix such collaborative efforts as economic integration and cultural exchange.

If this analysis is close to the mark, then it is clearly in Europe's interest to downplay the "balance of power"; to hush talk of playing the powers against each other; to discourage the neo-Metternichs and latter-day Bismarcks; to avoid calculation of an "even balance" and the mental set to which it gives rise--in short, to scotch the emergence of an international political culture that lays prime emphasis on competition for power. The world system is likely to continue its transition toward a multipolar structure in the next decade. This structure will be fleshed in with a congeries of interrelated attitudes, motives, perceptions, values, and beliefs about international politics--a political culture, however ill-defined. If this political culture were to coalesce around the classical balance of power notions of realpolitic and shifting military alignments, then both the Eastern and Western components of Europe will lead a precarious existence at best. If, on the other hand, European statesmen can encourage the acceptance of values stressing the cooperative and interdependent side of international realities, they will have enhanced Europe's chances for playing an active role in the emerging system.

NOTES

1. Ernst Haas, "The Balance of Power: Prescription, Concept or Propaganda?" World Politics 5, no. 4 (July 1953), pp. 446-77.

2. Hans Morgenthau, Politics Among Nations, 5th ed. (New York: Alfred A. Knopf, 1973); Inis Claude, Power and International Relations (New York: Random House, 1962); Quincy Wright, A Study of War (Chicago: University of Chicago Press, 1942); Richard Rosecrance, Action and Reaction in World Politics (Boston: Little, Brown, 1963); Morton Kaplan, System and Process in International Politics (New York: John Wiley, 1964); Harold Lasswell, World Politics and Personal Insecurity (New York: McGraw-Hill, 1935).

3. I am indebted to E. Thomas Rowe for pointing this out to me.

4. Or, more properly put, multipolar systems have a greater probability of peace and stability than other structures, especially the bipolar varieties. See, for instance, Karl W. Deutsch and J. David Singer, "Multipolar Power Systems and International Stability," World Politics 16, no. 3 (April 1964), pp. 390-406.

5. Claude, op. cit.; K.J. Holsti, International Politics: A Framework for Analysis (Englewood Cliffs, N.J.: Prentice-Hall, 1967); Stanley Hoffmann, A State of War (New York: Praeger, 1966).

6. The particular periodization presented here is based on my reading of Gordon A. Craig, Europe Since 1815 (New York: Holt, Rinehart, and Winston, 1966); R.R. Palmer, A History of the Modern World (New York: Alfred A. Knopf, 1960); Carsten Holbraad, The Concert of Europe (London: Longman, 1970); M.S. Anderson, The Ascendancy of Europe 1815-1914 (London: Longman, 1972); and Rosecrance, op. cit.

7. Henry Kissinger, A World Restored (Boston: Houghton-Mifflin, 1957), and American Foreign Policy: Three Essays (New York: W.W. Norton, 1969).

8. Craig, op. cit.

9. Ibid.

10. J. David Singer and Melvin Small, "Alliance Aggregation and the Onset of War: 1815-1945," in Singer, ed., Quantitative International Politics (New York: The Free Press, 1968).

11. Rosecrance, op. cit.

12. See Holbraad, op. cit., for an account of the diverse interpretations of "Concert" that existed in Britain and Germany.

13. Much of the critical literature on balance of power systems stresses the difficulties of identifying and calculating power shifts. See, for instance, Lasswell, op. cit., and Claude, op. cit.

14. For a statement of this position--and an argument rejecting it--see Zbigniew Brzezinski and Samuel P. Huntington, Political Power: USA/USSR (New York: Viking, 1963).

15. J.S. Nye, "Patterns and Catalysts in Regional Integration," International Organization 19, no. 4 (Autumn 1965).

16. John Galtung, "Europe: Bipolar, Bicentric or Cooperative," Journal of Peace Research, no. 1 (1972), pp. 1-26.

17. These are the first two of Kaplan's well-known set of rules for behavior in "balance of power" systems. See Kaplan, op. cit.

18. Herman Kahn and R. Bruce-Briggs, Things to Come: Thinking About the Seventies and Eighties (New York: Macmillan, 1972).

19. Walter F. Hahn, "The Nixon Doctrine: Design and Dilemmas," Orbis 16, no. 2 (Summer 1972), pp. 361-76.

20. Herbert Scoville, Jr., "Beyond SALT One," Foreign Affairs 50, no. 3 (April 1972), pp. 488-500.

21. Stanley Hoffmann, "Weighing The Balance of Power," Foreign Affairs 50, no. 4 (July 1972), pp. 618-43.

22. Kissinger, American Foreign Policy, op. cit.

23. For one version of the rules of balance of power systems, see Kaplan, op. cit.

24. Stanley Hoffmann, "Will the Balance Balance at Home?" Foreign Policy, Summer 1972.

25. The term is Kaplan's. See Kaplan, op. cit.

26. Hoffmann, "Will the Balance Balance at Home," op. cit., estimates that it will be difficult for the United States to develop the requisite cohesive, continuous foreign policy elite. If this is true, consider the difficulties facing an actor not yet unified.

27. See the writings of Ernst Haas, for example, Beyond the Nation-State (Stanford, Calif.: Stanford University Press, 1964), on the special conditions necessary for economic integration to "spill over" into political integration.

28. Alastair Buchan, Europe's Futures, Europe's Choices (New York: Penguin Books, 1969).

29. Ibid., p. 119.

30. Ibid., p. 59.

31. Thomas W. Wolfe, Soviet Power and Europe: 1945-1970 (Baltimore: Johns Hopkins University Press, 1970); Josef Korbel, Détente in Europe: Real or Imaginary? (Princeton, N.J.: Princeton University Press, 1972); Zbigniew Brzezinski, "How the Cold War Was Played," Foreign Affairs 51, no. 1 (October 1972), pp. 181-209.

32. Peter Bender, East Europe in Search of Security (Baltimore: Johns Hopkins University Press, 1972), contains a concise discussion of the factors at work producing this relationship: "The more the fear of war dwindles in the course of time, the greater become fears of ideological 'softening up' and economic dependence" (p. 137).

33. Ibid., p. 141.

LOUIS J. MENSONIDES is Associate Professor of Political
Science at Virginia Polytechnic Institute and State University, where
he has taught since 1964. Dr. Mensonides received a B. A. degree
from Calvin College and an M. A. and Ph.D. in diplomacy and inter-
national politics and economics from the University of Kentucky.
He is the author of U. S. Foreign Policy Toward Germany: The
Eisenhower-Dulles Period and editor of two forthcoming volumes,
American Foreign Policy and the New Europe: Eastern and Western
Views and Detente and the European Security Conference.

JAMES A. KUHLMAN is Associate Professor in the Department
of Government and International Studies, University of South Carolina,
Columbia, where he has taught since 1969. He is director of graduate
studies in the Program of Comparative Politics and International
Studies and is currently serving as Vice-President of the International Studies Association South.
Dr. Kuhlman is editor of two forthcoming volumes, The Foreign
Policies of Eastern Europe: Domestic and International Determinants
and Regional Integration: Theory and Research on Eastern Europe.
He is coeditor (with Richard P. Farkas) of a forthcoming volume on
the development of the social sciences in the socialist community.
Dr. Kuhlman received his B.S., M.A. and Ph.D. degrees in
political science from Northwestern University, and a M. A. degree
in international affairs while with the Institute for Sino-Soviet
Studies, School of Public and International Affairs, George Washington University.

WALTER L. BARROWS is Assistant Professor of Political
Science, Virginia Polytechnic Institute and State University, on
leave with Boston University's Army Education Center in Europe
during 1973-75. Dr. Barrows specializes in international politics
and African areas studies.

ROBERT H. DONALDSON is Associate Professor of Political
Science at Vanderbilt University, on leave during 1973-74 as a
Consultant to the Bureau of Intelligence and Research at the State
Department, under the auspices of a Council on Foreign Relations
Fellowship. His teaching and research centers in the areas of
Soviet and American foreign policies and comparative communist

political systems. His book on Soviet Policy toward India: Ideology and Strategy, was published by Harvard University Press, 1974.

CHARLES W. KEGLEY is Associate Professor of Government and International Studies at the University of South Carolina. He is co-author with William S. Coplin of A Multi-Method Introduction to International Politics (Markham, 1971) and has contributed articles to numerous scholarly journals.

DENNIS C. PIRAGES is Assistant Professor of Political Science at the University of California, San Diego. He is author of Modernization and Political Tension Management (Praeger, 1972) and co-author with Paul Ehrlich of ARK II: Social Response to Environmental Imperatives (Viking Press, 1974).

JACK D. SALMON is Assistant Professor of Political Science, Virginia Polytechnic Institute and State University since 1969. Dr. Salmon's specialty is U.S. national security and military policy and Far East area studies. Salmon's research and publication has been on Japanese political developments, the cultural revolution of the People's Republic of China, U.S. economic and military aid programs, and U.S. national security policy.

RICHARD F. STAAR is Associate Director of the Hoover Institution on War, Revolution, and Peace at Stanford University. Dr. Staar has specialized in the government, politics and international relations of the communist-ruled states. His most recent publications are as editor of World Communism: A Handbook, 1918-1965 (Stanford University Press, 1973) and author of The Communist Regimes in Eastern Europe (Stanford University Press, 1971).

CHARLES LEWIS TAYLOR is Associate Professor of Political Science, Virginia Polytechnic Institute and State University. He is the author of the World Handbook of Political and Social Indicators: Second Edition (Yale, 1972), Aggregate Data Analysis (Mouton, 1968), Learning with Computers (Sage, 1974) and articles in cross-national data analysis.

GORDON TULLOCK is Professor in Economics and Associate Director of the Center for the Study of Public Choice, Virginia Polytechnic Institute and State University. He was a Foreign Service Officer from 1947 to 1956. The most recent of his numerous scholarly works have been The Logic of the Law (Basic Books, 1971) and Private Wants, Public Means (Basic Books, 1970).

WILLIAM A. WELSH is Professor of Political Science at the University of Iowa. Dr. Welsh specializes in government and politics of the Soviet Union and Eastern Europe. Professor Welsh is co-author of Comparative Communist Political Leadership (McKay, 1973); his most recent book is Studying Politics (Praeger, 1973).

RELATED TITLES
Published by
Praeger Special Studies

EAST EUROPEAN PERSPECTIVES ON
EUROPEAN SECURITY AND COOPERATION
edited by Robert R. King and
Robert W. Dean

EAST GERMAN CIVIL-MILITARY RELATIONS:
The Impact of Technology, 1949-72
Dale R. Herspring

THE POLITICS OF MODERNIZATION IN
EASTERN EUROPE: Testing the Soviet Model
edited by Charles Gati

SINO-AMERICAN DETENTE AND ITS
POLICY IMPLICATIONS
edited by Gene T. Hsiao